More praise for
Liberalism as a Way of Life

"In his amiable and conversational style, Alexandre Lefebvre offers the most persuasive defense of what liberalism stands for in the modern world. Through an ingenious rereading of John Rawls, Lefebvre makes it clear that liberalism isn't neutral, as some of its advocates pretend, but is premised on a robust conception of the good life. This book is nothing short of thrilling."

—SAMUEL MOYN, author of *Liberalism against Itself*

"With wit and insight, this marvelous book tells you what it's like to be a liberal, and how to be a good liberal. It's written by a cheerful but highly reflective liberal, for liberals of all stripes—including the grumpy, the overconfident, and the wavering. But it can also be read with profit and enjoyment by nonliberals, antiliberals, and even by the harbingers of liberalism's doom."

—CHANDRAN KUKATHAS, author of *The Liberal Archipelago*

"It's hard to express just how much I loved this book. With great humanity and plenty of humor, Lefebvre shows how liberal values and practices can help each of us live with generosity, integrity, and joy. Beautifully written and genuinely original—this is liberalism as you've never seen it before. I cannot recommend it highly enough."

—DANIEL CHANDLER, author of *Free and Equal*

"With force and subtlety, this groundbreaking book shows how everyday life inspires politics and values, and how these values are shared through popular culture. Indeed, one of the strengths of the book and what makes it so entertaining and instructive is the way Alexandre Lefebvre demonstrates how popular TV shows—not just highbrow ones—disseminate progressive ideas that have become quintessential to liberalism as a way of life and to the desire to defend it."

—SANDRA LAUGIER, Panthéon-Sorbonne University

LIBERALISM AS A WAY OF LIFE

Liberalism
as a Way of Life

ALEXANDRE LEFEBVRE

PRINCETON UNIVERSITY PRESS

PRINCETON & OXFORD

Published by Princeton University Press
41 William Street, Princeton, New Jersey 08540
99 Banbury Road, Oxford OX2 6JX

press.princeton.edu

Library of Congress Cataloging-in-Publication Data

Names: Lefebvre, Alexandre, 1979– author.
Title: Liberalism as a way of life / Alexandre Lefebvre.
Description: Princeton, New Jersey : Princeton University Press, [2024] |
    Includes bibliographical references and index.
Identifiers: LCCN 2023044727 (print) | LCCN 2023044728 (ebook) |
    ISBN 9780691203744 (hardback : acid-free paper) |
    ISBN 9780691255538 (ebook)
Subjects: LCSH: Liberalism—Moral and ethical aspects. | BISAC:
    PHILOSOPHY / Political | POLITICAL SCIENCE / Political
    Ideologies / Conservatism & Liberalism
Classification: LCC JC571 .L3745 2024 (print) | LCC JC571 (ebook) |
    DDC 172—dc23/eng/20240124
LC record available at https://lccn.loc.gov/2023044727
LC ebook record available at https://lccn.loc.gov/2023044728

British Library Cataloging-in-Publication Data is available

Editorial: Rob Tempio and Chloe Coy
Production Editorial: Karen Carter
Jacket/Cover Design: Karl Spurzem
Production: Erin Suydam
Publicity: Carmen Jimenez and James Schneider

Jacket image: Orbon Alija / iStock

This book has been composed in Arno

Printed in Canada

10 9 8 7 6 5 4 3 2 1

To, for, and about Beatrice, young liberal

Optimist: "This is the best of all possible worlds."
Pessimist: "Yes, I know."

—JOHN RAWLS, HANDWRITTEN JOKE
ON THE TITLE PAGE OF HIS PERSONAL
COPY OF *A THEORY OF JUSTICE*

CONTENTS

LIBERALISM AS A WAY OF LIFE

Introduction

WHERE DO YOU GET YOUR VALUES FROM?

I'LL NEVER FORGET my first Christmas in Australia. I moved to Sydney in 2010 with my wife and our newborn daughter, but for the first several years we took regular trips back to Canada to spend the holidays with family. In 2016, though, we stayed put. On Christmas Day we did the usual things—a long breakfast and the opening of gifts—and then planned to head down to our local beach for a welcome novelty: Christmas in full summer. We slapped on sunscreen, grabbed our boogie boards and thongs (an Aussie word I still can't get used to; it means flip-flops), and off we went.

I am not a religious man, and even so I still wasn't prepared for what greeted us. The beach and surrounding area were packed with thousands and thousands of partyers. It was beer, bikinis, Santa hats, and tattooed flesh as far as the eye could see. As I said, I'm not religious, nor I should add prudish, but the thought that came to mind was that this must have been how people from the Middle Ages imagined the fun parts of hell. As if from the brush of Hieronymus Bosch, it was a picture of antisolemnity.

In the spirit of "when in Rome" we stayed and enjoyed ourselves. Everyone was in a great mood, there was plenty of good food and even more bad singing (drunken carols and all), and if you paddled out in the ocean about twenty meters, you could survey the spectacle from a quiet distance. We returned home later that afternoon wondering how our folks back in Vancouver would spend their assuredly cold, drizzly day.

The next morning there was a price to pay. Christmas Day had been literally as well as figuratively trashy. Revelers had left behind sixteen tons of garbage. There was so much that the *New York Times* even reported on it a few days later (go ahead and google "coogee christmas nyt"). As you might expect in our digital age, word quickly got around, and my wife, daughter, and I returned to the scene of the crime to help the community cleanup. Makeshift dump piles were arranged, consisting mostly of food containers, plastic bags, bottles and cans, and also lost or abandoned footwear, clothing, and the aforementioned Santa hats. The mood was a mix of conviviality among the volunteers (most of whom had celebrated on the beach the day before) and low-key grumbling about who was responsible for the mess. A week later, everything was clean and tidy as if it nothing had happened. But ask any local and they'll remember Christmas 2016, if only because its lasting outcome was an alcohol ban at the beach.

Why begin with this story? Those few days had the truth of caricature, with the good, bad, and ugly of my world on exaggerated display: its friendliness, playful irreverence, antisnobbishness, tolerance, and can-do pragmatism, along with its irresponsibility, wastefulness, and potential moral and spiritual emptiness. And it led me to wonder, What kind of society acts like this?

My question may sound judgmental, as if I am issuing a condemnation. "Who acts like this? Barbarous Aussies, that's who!"

That is not my intention. For starters, stick a lovely beach and gorgeous weather in any major Western city in the Northern Hemisphere, and I doubt Christmas Day would play out much differently. More to the point, my question is sincere. Christmas Day 2016 confused me and raised two related issues.

First, I was curious about the values and behaviors on display. Maybe the mishmash I listed above—friendliness and irresponsibility, tolerance and emptiness, pragmatism and wastefulness, freedom and regulation—wasn't a mishmash at all. Maybe it was a coherent package of how people, myself included, navigate the world, however distorted and exaggerated on this occasion. Second, I wanted to know where that package came from. Values and behaviors do not fall from the sky. They are formed and sustained within historical traditions, institutional frameworks, and systems of meaning. The big question raised by Christmas Day 2016 was thus, Where did we, where did I, get those values and behaviors from?

The question of where we get our values from is at the heart of my book. What is remarkable is how ill-equipped many of us are to answer it. A hundred or even as recently as fifty years ago, no one would have struggled. Back then, you could have asked most anyone in the world, rich or poor, Western or non-Western, where they get their core values from, and they would have been able to give a clear and direct answer. Most would have pointed to a religion or spiritual tradition; others to an ideology, such as communism; and a handful of eccentrics might have named a philosophy or philosopher.

The situation is different nowadays, mainly due to the decline of religious belief and practice. To consider only the most populous Anglophone liberal democracies, recent surveys of the United States, United Kingdom, Canada, Australia, and New Zealand show that 30, 53, 32, 40, and 49 percent, respectively, of citizens in those countries claim no religion. In fact, people who tick the "no religion" box on the census are the fastest-growing population of religious affiliation, or in this case, nonaffiliation.

This book is written primarily, though not exclusively, for those of us without religious affiliation. If that is you—and let's be frank, as this is a book on ethics and political philosophy published by a university press, the odds are high—I ask you to ponder a question. Put the book down for a moment, dear reader, and ask yourself, "Where do I get my values from?" I am not just talking about your highest-order principles about right and wrong but also your sense of what is good, normal, and worthwhile in life, and if I can put it this way, your general vibe too. What could you point to as the source for that?

I am willing to bet that you had no good answer, or at least nothing immediately ready to hand. I say so with confidence because whenever I've pestered my students, friends, and colleagues with this question, they are almost always stumped. Their impulse is to say one of three things: "from my experience," "from friends and family," or "from human nature." But to that, and only endearing myself further, I reply that these are not suitable answers. Personal experience, friends and family, and human nature are situated and formed within wider social, political, and cultural contexts. So I ask again, "What society-or-civilization-sized thing can you point to as the source of your values? I'm talking about the kind of thing that were you Christian, you'd just say, 'Ah, the Bible,' or 'Oh, my church.'"

At this point the conversation tends to peter out. I worry that my interlocutor thinks I'm implying that something is wrong with them, as if they lacked a moral or spiritual compass. The opposite is closer to the truth. It is fascinating how people who seem, as far as I can tell, happy and put together, and do not feel adrift or unfulfilled, fail to recognize, or even think to ask, from what tradition they learned how to become themselves.

You do not have to be Socrates, who declared philosophy to be the pursuit of self-knowledge, to see this as a problem. It is good and proper for people partying on a beach not to wonder why they are the way they are. It is something else for these same people, in moments of calm reflection, to be more or less in the dark as to where they get their character and moral sensibility from. It is a problem for self-awareness: you may not appreciate how your moral and emotional life hangs together the way it does. It is a problem for self-development: you may not know how to deepen as well as better enjoy the ideals and commitments you already profess, nor see what resources are available to help you do that. And it is a problem for self-preservation: if you happen to live at a time when the tradition that is the key to you is under attack, you may be ignorant of the personal or even existential stakes of that situation.

I believe that most of my readers should identify *liberalism* as the source of their values: not just of their political opinions, but of who they are through and through. Liberalism, to recall my earlier phrase, is that society-or-civilization-sized thing that may well underlie who you (and I, and we) are in all walks of life, from the family to workplace, from friendship to enmity, from humor to outrage, and everything in between.

Over the next few pages, I will introduce this argument in a patient and careful manner. I will specify what I mean by liberalism, identify its principles and ideals, account for how they shape our sense of self, explain how we might cultivate these commitments, and suggest why that might be a good thing to do. For now, though, let me return to Christmas Day 2016. Suppose a reveler had noticed that I looked a bit dazed. Further suppose, improbably, that they had asked me what was on my mind. Like them, I would have had a couple of drinks. Tipsy and emboldened, I might have said something like,

> Hey, maybe you don't know the source of your morality, but I do; it's liberalism, and it can be a great way to live. The good news is that it's all around us, already in our bones, and we don't have to go looking for some ancient or distant piece of wisdom for how to live well. We just need to double down and take seriously what we already have. The bad news is that it's under attack right now and may well be displaced as the default morality of our time. That sucks for a lot of reasons, but a big one is that should it happen, our source of self can't be taken for granted anymore. It'll suffer the same fate, say, as Christianity in the Western world: a viable option, sure, but just one of many, and no longer the background of our world.

Had I given this speech (nay, sermon), I would have blushed the next morning. Among its many embarrassments is the lack of liberal virtues. There's not much modesty in telling my interlocutor who they are deep down. Nor is there appreciation of pluralism in presuming they don't already subscribe to some other worldview. Worst is the impression of moralism it gives off. Outside forces seem to be the only threat to liberalism, rather than potential limitations in the doctrine itself or a failure of so-called liberal people to live up to its demands. Illiberalism, it would seem, is other people.

Despite all of that, I want to let it stand. Like the day itself, my little speech has the truth of caricature. The suggestion I put to my readers is that liberalism may be at the root of all things us. What we find funny, outrageous, or meaningful; how we comport ourselves in friendship and romance; and the ideals that we set for ourselves as citizens, professionals, neighbors, and family members—maybe all of these things, from seemingly distinctive spheres of life, draw on one and the same source. The goal of this book is to offer an integrated account of a way of living that is prominent and available today. Success in this endeavor depends on the persuasiveness of my depiction of liberalism and whether it clicks with the sense that readers have of themselves. But at the outset, I'll say this. If you struggle to identify a source for your values, yet feel skeptical of the suggestion that liberalism may be it, I have one more question to keep in mind while reading this book: Honestly, what else do you have?

PART I

Our Liberal World

1

The Water We Swim In

IN 2005, NOVELIST AND ESSAYIST David Foster Wallace gave a commencement address at Kenyon College, Ohio. He opened with a vignette that is half joke, half parable: "There are two young fish swimming along and they happen to meet an older fish swimming the other way, who nods at them and says, 'Morning, boys. How's the water?' And the two young fish swim on for a bit, and then eventually one of them looks over at the other and goes, 'What the hell is water?'"[1]

The moral of the story is that the most obvious and important realities can sometimes be the hardest to think and talk about. This metaphor of water is a good place to start our discussion about liberalism. For it strikes me that its defenders today are rather like the two young fish and its critics are like the older fish.

Let me explain. The dictionary definition of *liberalism* is a "social and political philosophy" based on "support for or advocacy of individual rights, civil liberties, and reform tending towards individual freedom, democracy, or social equality."[2] There is much to unpack here. But the first thing to notice is that everything in this definition belongs to the realm of law and politics, broadly understood. When we talk about liberalism, it seems that we're in the land of constitutions, rights, policy, voting, and the like.

People who identify as liberal today think of it along these lines. Academics, journalists, politicians, and officials represent (and when pressed, defend) liberalism by listing the main social and political institutions associated with it, such as individual rights, rule of law, separation of powers, judicial review, free and fair elections, progressive taxation, and open markets. None of this is incorrect. These are the core institutions of liberalism. Yet framed this way, liberalism refers to things *in* the water instead of the water itself. It refers to coral, shells, whales, and kelp, as opposed to the water and its currents.

Critics of liberalism, conservative ones especially, see it differently—closer to the older fish, assuming he loathed the water quality. These critics conceive of liberalism only secondarily in terms of legal and political institutions. Much more significant is liberalism as a worldview and value system—one that in recent decades has consolidated its power everywhere in Western societies. On this account, liberalism has infiltrated not just the usual suspects of news media, pop culture, public school, and universities, but also fundamental aspects of everyday existence, such as sexuality, child-rearing, friendship, and professional life. "Liberalism," says a prominent academic critic, "is thus not merely, as is often portrayed, a narrowly political project of constitutional government and juridical defense of rights. Rather, it seeks to transform all of human life and the world."[3] Or in the coolly delivered diatribe of a sitting US attorney general, "[Liberals] have marshaled all the forces of mass communication, popular culture, the entertainment industry, and academia in an unremitting assault on religion and traditional values."[4] Say what you like about such attacks, but they're about water. Liberal principles, values, and sensibilities have become so pervasive as to be mistaken for common sense or even human nature. To recast the joke, it would read, "Morning, boys," sneers an older fish, "How's the liberalism?" And the two young liberals swim on for a bit, sipping their koi lattes, and eventually one of them looks over at the other and goes, 'What the hell is liberalism?'"

I will engage these critics later. But I should put my cards on the table. I disagree with their condemnation of liberalism as a politically noxious and personally debilitating worldview. But their assessment of the scope of liberalism is correct. Its ideals and sensibilities are indeed omnipresent in the public and background culture of Western democratic societies. And because I agree with their assessment of scope, I cannot adopt the standard definition of liberalism as a primarily legal and political doctrine. The older fish is onto something that, ironically, more deeply and accurately captures how liberalism is lived and experienced by liberals themselves.

My book is about a political topic (namely, liberalism), yet better classified as a work on ethics, living well, and a genre I want to lean into, self-help. This is a crowded marketplace. To say nothing of bestsellers, in my own corner of academic publishing in philosophy, dozens of books have been written in recent years as secular (that is, not faith-based) guides to navigate modern life.[5] I've read many, always with pleasure and profit. I've even contributed to the genre.[6] Granted, at the current rate of production, we'll have inspiration to last several lifetimes. But that's a good thing! The decline of organized religion in Western liberal democracies means an enormous readership looking for plenitude and purpose.

Where does my book sit in relation to this literature? Whatever its merits and faults, it is unique in one respect. It seeks meaning and fulfillment by diving deeper into the mainstream culture we inhabit as opposed to seeking it else-where. To exaggerate for effect, may their authors forgive me, we could say that all the recent "how to live well" books in philosophy are variations on the title of Elizabeth Gilbert's hit, *Eat, Pray, Love: One Woman's Search for Everything across Italy, India, and Indonesia* (2007). On this model, the solution to the unhappi-ness and malaise of contemporary Western societies is to ven-ture elsewhere in search of alternatives. Only this time, instead of leaving New York City for Italy, India, and Indonesia, reme-dies are sought in the distant past (the ancient Greeks or Scot-tish Enlightenment, for example), non-Western places (China or Africa, for instance), philosophies that resist the inauthentic or repressive spirit of modern life (say, existentialism or psycho-analysis), or artifacts and activities seen as reprieves from it (like fine art or travel).

Liberalism as a Way of Life is not like that, which brings us back to the idea of liberalism as the water we swim in, along with my suggestion to dive deeper into it. What do I mean by water? Two things. First, echoing the younger fish, liberal *water* refers to the fundamental legal and political institutions of liberal democratic societies (such as individual rights, separation of powers, progressive taxation, open markets, and judicial review) as well as the public (or political, if you prefer) culture of how citizens and officials comport themselves as members of them. This may sound abstract and remote, but it is not. The institutions and relationships they sustain are the stuff of everyday life. When, for example, we take for granted that goods at the supermarket cost the same for everyone, that's liberalism in action. The same goes for our expectation of fair treatment by government offi-cials no matter who we are. Hence the turbulent situation we find ourselves in today, where public institutions of our democ-racies (for instance, a tax policy that favors the wealthy or justice system that is structurally discriminatory) elicit widespread distrust and anger precisely because they are seen to disregard their liberal principles.

The second thing *water* refers to is what the older fish puts his fin(ger) on: the background culture of Western democratic countries. By *background culture*, I mean something vast: essentially everything that is not the public culture, and that spans civil society (including the workplace, media, social media, and clubs and associations of all kinds) and the private sphere (including personal and romantic relationships, along with the family).

Obviously, modern societies are plural and include all manner of worldviews and ways of living that do not derive from liberalism, are not reducible to liberalism, or alternatively, are actively illiberal (in the sense of opposing liberal tenets). Yet as the older fish and I stress, albeit for opposite reasons, it is a big mistake to overlook or underplay how ubiquitous liberal values and sensibilities are in the background culture of contemporary Western democratic countries. A key claim I make in this book and reinforce with plenty of extended examples is that most popular culture produced in liberal democracies today would be unintelligible to an audience not already steeped in liberal norms, values, and sensibilities. Not all popular culture is united in support of liberalism. Much of it is intended to parody and challenge liberal dogmas. But that only reinforces the fact that liberalism has entrenched itself as the central point of reference.

To preview what I mean, here are a few places where liberalism can be found today: when we pick up a novel by Sally Rooney that dissects the power dynamics of sex and class; when we read a satire by Kevin Kwan about the clashes between individualism and tradition; when we watch comedians like Kumail Nanjiani and Dave Chappelle skewer identity politics; when we binge television shows like *The Office* and *Brooklyn*

Nine-Nine that reimagine the workplace as a setting for self-realization; when we consume such eat-the-rich entertainments as *White Lotus* and *Succession*; when we listen to Beyoncé reclaim her power on *Lemonade*; when we see Disney princesses (from Ariel to Belle, Jasmine, Pocahontas, Mulan, Tiana, Rapunzel, Merida, Elsa and Anna, Moana, and Raya) strive to learn and become who they were meant to be; when we gift *Good Night Stories for Rebel Girls* to a niece or daughter as a modern-day lives of the saints; when we play a video game like *The Last of Us Part II*, the violence of which is matched only by its perspectivism; when we consult human resource codes of conduct about respectful workplace relations; when we visit pornhub.com and the tab for gay pornography is right there on the home page; and even when we tune into reality shows like *The Bachelor* and *The Bachelorette, Love Is Blind, Love on the Spectrum,* and *Indian Matchmaking,* all of which turn romance into a buyer's market. No item on this list is explicitly about liberalism, yet none would be slightly comprehensible without it. Just try, if you are familiar with any one item, to imagine how you would summarize it to someone who did not understand, as opposed to someone who agreed or disagreed with, the principle that everyone is free to lead the kind of life they want so long as it does not interfere with the ability of others to do the same (to name only one signature liberal idea). It would be like sending a code without the cipher on the receiving end. That is why I say that liberalism is the water of our times. Written into our foundational institutions, and underlying so much of the culture we daily live and breathe, liberalism has seeped into our pores so as to profoundly and personally shape who we are.

With this wide scope of liberalism in mind, I can state the thesis of the book: liberalism can be the basis for a personal worldview, way of living, and spiritual orientation. You don't need to be liberal *plus* something else, such as Christian, Buddhist, utilitarian, or hedonist. It is possible, and I contend, rewarding and sufficient, to be liberal through and through. This does not mean that such a person would live their life, and relate to friends and family, in the manner of a citizen interacting with fellow citizens in the public forum. That would be psychologically implausible and ethically stultifying (not to mention socially suicidal). What I propose is that the values and attitudes enshrined in liberal social and political institutions, and everywhere present in the public and background culture of liberal democracies, can and often do inform a much more general sensibility—one supple enough to be realized differently and appropriately in all aspects of life. The good life, for such people, is the liberal life. It is not a model they wish to impose on anyone else. But it is theirs, and for them, more than enough.

This argument is descriptive and normative. It is descriptive in that I claim that a great many people living in Western democracies are already liberals in this robust sense. One ambition for my book is to serve as a mirror for readers and elicit a spark of recognition that, yes, liberalism is the basis of their own way of life. We are liberals all the way down, and consciously or not, hold liberalism as our conception of the good life.

To avoid any misunderstanding, let me state an important qualification. No one in this globalized age is anything "all the way down." There are, for example, no Christians all the way down—no one of Christian faith whose worldview is not entangled with other cultural influences (such as nationalism, democracy, the ethics of capitalism, and liberalism, or going further back, Greek philosophy and various paganisms). There are, moreover, no Christians whose identities, social roles, and personal interests are entirely reducible to their Christianity—as parent or friend, for instance, or a professional or sports fan.

Still, we have no difficulty understanding someone who says, "I'm Christian." Why should the bar be higher for liberals? We are "liberal" to the same degree and depth that they are "Christian." Neither worldview is pure and hermetically sealed off from myriad influences, yet both are the moral and spiritual centers of full and well-rounded personalities. Hence my descriptive aim: to make clear how liberalism already plays this role in the lives of many (and perhaps most) readers of this book.

My argument is also normative in that I propose that liberalism is a *good* way of life. I'm not suggesting that it is better than other ways of life. Any self-respecting liberal would by doctrine and disposition shrink from such a claim. But I have no qualms asserting that a liberal way of life has its own perks and felicities. This is why a key purpose of my book is to demonstrate how a liberal way of life has rewards for those who commit to it, as distinct from its wider effects on our societies, or the advancement of democracy and social justice. Being liberal is an intrinsically fulfilling, generous, and fun way to be.

In identifying liberalism as the water in which we swim, and by adding that a liberal way of life can be good and rewarding, I may sound obnoxiously triumphalist or depressingly complacent. If liberalism is everywhere in our public and background culture, it might be tempting to kick up our feet and suppose we are already living the dream. It would be nice, cynically put, to think that a liberal way of life could be acquired or maybe even realized by switching on Netflix to enjoy the latest algorithmically generated rom-com.

That would be a grave mistake in more ways than one. It would be an error or misapprehension, certainly, but one that leads to all kinds of nasty attitudes that liberals are accused of, such as self-satisfaction and sanctimony. Later in the book, I give this danger a name, *liberaldom*, a term adapted from theologian

Søren Kierkegaard's critique of Christendom, to refer to how easy it is to pat oneself on the back for being (notionally) liberal in a social and political world that is itself (notionally) liberal. The general idea is that a genuinely liberal way of life, along with its felicities, does not come automatically from living or even having been raised in liberal democracy. It takes work and must be cultivated by the individual themselves. That is why, in addition to its descriptive and normative goals, this book has a practical task: to lay out techniques ("spiritual exercises," I call them) that readers can adopt at any time should they wish to deepen and enrich a liberal way of life. All great world religions are replete with such exercises. Prayer, dialogue, song, meditation, and fasting are intended to initiate conversion and sustain conviction. Liberalism needs its own versions. Its doctrine is no less noble, its conception of the good life no less demanding, and the quality of its spiritual life no less beatific.

2

What Is Liberalism?

SO FAR I HAVE BEEN talking about liberalism as if the term were widely understood and could be taken for granted. Unfortunately, that is far from being the case, and the proof of which is that just about every good book or article on liberalism starts the same way: with a declaration on how and why it resists definition. As Exhibit A, consider the first lines of the "Liberalism" entry for the *Stanford Encyclopedia of Philosophy*: "Liberalism is more than one thing. On any close examination, it seems to fracture into a range of related but sometimes competing visions."[1]

As the dominant social and political ideology of the past two hundred years, liberalism contains multitudes. There is the protoliberalism of the early modern period, so-called classical liberalism of the nineteenth century, Cold War liberalism, social democracy, and egalitarianism, and while I believe its membership in the group is tenuous, neoliberalism. There are also distinctive geographic traditions to observe, including US, British, French, German, Italian, and Latin American. The term can even mean completely different things depending on the national context. When a politician is accused in the United States by a right-wing critic of being "liberal," it typically means they're a tax-and-spend do-gooder; in France, on the other hand, the accusation comes from the Left to indict a heartless small-government individualist. Joe Biden and Emmanuel Macron both have cause to avoid the label, but for opposite reasons.

Faced with this complex landscape, philosophers and historians have adopted two different strategies. One is to stipulate a particular idea as the true core of liberalism, and from there, devise a historical narrative to back it up. Liberalism is such a capacious tradition that there are many to choose from. Leading contenders, along with their hero origin story, include individual rights (John Locke), personal freedom (Benjamin Constant and John Stuart Mill), freedom from fear (Michel de Montaigne and Montesquieu), and mutual justification (Immanuel Kant).[2] The advantage of this strategy is that it delivers a clear message: liberalism is defined by X, and from that starting point, Y and Z moral and political principles follow. The downside is that by design, it tells a one-sided story that won't speak to fellow liberals with a different set of assumptions.

Another way forward is to open the floodgates and portray liberalism as the richly contradictory sum of its parts. As the leading scholar of this "contextualist" strategy states, "It is a plastic, changing thing, shaped and reshaped by the thought-practices of individuals and groups; and though it needs to have a roughly identifiable pattern for us to call it consistently by the same name, 'liberalism,' it also presents myriad variations that reflect the questions posed, and the positions adopted, by various liberals."[3] This approach has its pros and cons, which are the inverse of the stipulative approach. It honors plurality and complexity such that liberals of all stripes can recognize themselves in the big picture, even if no single one is the star. But it is not galvanizing. If liberalism means many different and often opposing things, then it is hard to know what to rally around.

We seem to be caught in a dilemma. In the contest between stipulative and contextualist strategies, the choice looks to be between a clear yet partial account of liberalism or an expansive yet rudderless one.

How to proceed? At this point I need to introduce the two authors who have inspired my book. The first is John Rawls (1921–2002), the preeminent political philosopher of the twentieth century. The second is Pierre Hadot (1922–2010), the classicist and philosopher who, more than anyone, revived an appreciation of philosophy as the pursuit of living well. Straightaway, they can help us to get a handle on that deceptively simple question, "What is liberalism?"

Meet John Rawls

Readers with even a passing acquaintance with political philosophy will have heard of Rawls. He spent nearly his entire professional life at Harvard University, and in 1971, published his major work, *A Theory of Justice*. This book was received as a masterpiece, and immediately credited with reshaping moral and political philosophy. Today, the main branches of Anglophone political philosophy—with such names as liberal egalitarianism and political liberalism—are avowedly Rawlsian in orientation, methodology, and terminology.[4] And a small army of commentators has labored for decades to gloss and interpret his writings. As a wit in the field states, today there are only five kinds of doctoral dissertations written in political philosophy. A typical abstract for the second kind reads, "Footnote 458 of *A Theory of Justice* has not been sufficiently explored. Buckle up for 300 pages of exploration!"[5]

My reason for turning to Rawls is not that he is a Very Important Philosopher. That would be a poor justification in general and especially ill-advised in my case. My interpretation of him is unorthodox, so I can hardly claim the authority of the great thinker while reading him against the grain of scholarship that maintains his authority.

I instead appeal to Rawls because he is a superb moralist. I would go so far as to say that he is the moralist we need right now. With this old-fashioned word, I mean he is someone able to discern the existing tendencies of a society, along with the self-conception of its members, and lead it and them in promising new directions.[6] This, you'll remember, is what the metaphor of liberalism as water from the previous chapter is all about. Rawls taps into the deepest yet frequently subconscious sense of who we are as members of a liberal democratic society, and from there, he generates not only a political philosophy for a just social and political order but also an entire moral psychology and existential analytic of what it means to *be* liberal. It is as if he speaks directly to our conscience to say, "OK, if in fact you see your society and yourself in this liberal kind of way, here is what you can do to live up to it." Then he adds (this is the third and final part of *A Theory of Justice*), "Oh, I almost forgot, great joys and benefits come from living this way. Let me show you."

It can be hard to see this side of Rawls. His work can be abstract and often technical. It draws on traditions that seem remote from these kinds of human concerns, such as economic, legal, and rational choice theory. His later philosophy presents special obstacles to learning from him in this way too. For my part, the idea for this book occurred to me only after reading the last paragraph of *A Theory of Justice* over and over. There, after five hundred pages of analysis, Rawls steps back to ask what was at stake in his theory. His answer is extraordinary. "Purity of heart," "grace," "self-command," and even a semidivine perspective on the world (an ability to see it "sub specie aeternitatis") are to be won.[7] We will need to unpack what all of this means, but clearly it is not the standard fare of political philosophy. It is the language of soulcraft.

I am not the first to admire this side of Rawls.[8] My book, however, is not a commentary, and I discuss Rawls only to the extent that he can help liberals to live their best life. That said, I hope to make his thought interesting and relevant even for those who have not (yet!) read him. Rawls is a humane and generous thinker, and perhaps surprisingly in our jaded times, a person who embodied those qualities. I never had the chance to meet him. He died in 2002, the year I began my graduate studies. Still, every account I've read or heard, many by former students who are now leading members of the profession, attests to his genuine kindness. *Decent* is the word that comes up time and again, in the understated sense of unshowy goodness.[9] I hope this book conveys his spirit. Readers who have never read a word of his work may even recognize the best of themselves in it.

Society as a Fair System of Cooperation

I begin with the foundational idea of Rawls's philosophy. A useful way to introduce it is with the publication of *A Theory of Justice*. It was, as I said, an instant classic. What I didn't mention is that despite its daunting complexity, it was also a commercial success. This is a book its own publisher describes as a "600-page work of abstract and uncompromising philosophy," and about which Rawls's close friend joked, "It reads like it was translated from the original German."[10] No one was more surprised by its popularity than Rawls himself. Had he been given a crystal ball in 1971 telling him that his book would sell over four hundred thousand copies in English alone, I suspect that he would have rubbed his eyes, certain he had misread the figure by one or probably two zeros. "I thought," he said in an interview to mark his retirement in 1991, "I would publish *A Theory of Justice* and some friends might read it."[11]

Why was it so successful? In the same interview, Rawls suggested a few reasons. The book had "some merit," he admitted (this, by the way, is Rawls at his most boastful). Mainly, he felt it came out at the right place at the right time: the first systematic philosophical work on justice to be published in decades, and at the moment when the United States was reeling from the Vietnam War and civil rights movement.

The quality and timeliness of *A Theory of Justice* go a long way to explaining its impact and popularity. But perhaps there is an additional reason. At its core, Rawls's great book is inspired by a simple and easily grasped idea. *Society*, he says, *should be conceived of and run as a fair system of cooperation*.[12]

Simple and *easily grasped* are not words that come to mind for anyone who has so much as glanced at *A Theory of Justice*. Yet those adjectives fit if we consider how Rawls arrived at this foundational idea. Crucially, he does not claim it as his own invention. Neither does he derive it from first philosophical principles. He believes instead that citizens of liberal democratic societies by and large *already* see and structure their societies as fair systems of cooperation. That is why this idea is accessible for a wide readership: not merely because his reader "knows" or "understands" what he is talking about, but much more powerfully, because they already affirm it as expressing something essential about themselves and their society. It is like telling a handsome man that he's attractive, or a talented lawyer that she's smart and hardworking. Prone to identify as such, they'll think, "Yep, sounds about right to me." Hence one possible explanation for the popular appeal of *A Theory of Justice*: it reflects the image that most citizens of liberal democracies have (or at least publicly profess) of themselves.[13]

Rawls isn't oblivious to real-world injustices. He knows that no society lives up to this ideal. Nor does he think that citizens of liberal democracies wear rose-colored (or worse, ideologically tinted) glasses. Still, he bases his theory on the assumption that his fellow citizens do in fact recognize that the key purpose of their main public institutions is to ensure that society is seen as and remains a fair system of cooperation. Virtually everyone can be expected to know, on his account, that the purpose of a legal constitution is to establish equal and reciprocal rights, the job of the police is to protect them, and progressive taxation is meant to ensure a level playing field. "Our country," says a philosopher giving voice to this ideal, "is built for everyone."[14]

At a basic level, then, Rawls does not see his work as offering up a fundamentally new idea of what liberal democratic societies should be. Think of him instead as a lepidopterist of moral and political intuitions. He observes and collates the professed moral commitments from the public (or political) culture of a liberal democratic society. Specimens can be found in different places. History is one repository. In the case of the United States, we can look to the Constitution and the values stated in its preamble (including a more perfect union, justice, domestic tranquility and the common defense, general welfare, and the blessings of liberty for ourselves and posterity), Supreme Court decisions that interpret these values, and historic texts that have etched them into national consciousness, such as the Gettysburg Address and Martin Luther King Jr.'s "I Have a Dream" speech. Specimens can also be gathered in less momentous places. In Australia, for example, we have a wonderfully unpretentious phrase that candidates from all political parties use (and abuse) at every campaign stop: to ensure that every citizen has a "fair go" and enjoys genuine equality of opportunity. My point is that Rawls, butterfly collector that he is, gathers these and similar expressions of the public culture of liberal democracies, and from this data, extrapolates a principle—society as a fair system of cooperation—to account for, systematize, and deepen those observed commitments.[15]

I need to be explicit about what Rawls is up to as it is central to my methodology. He does not define liberalism head-on, unlike in the stipulative and contextualist strategies I mentioned at the beginning of the chapter. Rawls takes a different tack: to set out the conception of society that liberalism grows out of. He defines, if you like, the soil (that is, society as a fair system of cooperation) and not the fruit (that is, liberalism itself). To return to the question of what liberalism is, Rawls replies that it is the moral, psychological, and social and political doctrine that grows from the understanding that members of mature liberal democracies have of themselves and their society as a fair system of cooperation. Proceeding this way gets the best of both strategies. On the one hand, it allows us to stipulate a definition of the purpose of society (that is, to be a fair system of cooperation), which provides an account of liberalism with a firm foundation. On the other hand, like good contextualists, we anchor that definition in the self-conception that subjects living in mature liberal democracies can reasonably be presumed to already have. Making liberalism the dependent variable has advantages.[16]

This last point is worth emphasizing. In its simplest form, the thesis of my book is that liberalism has affected all of us deeply and some of us completely in the sense that it is the source of who we are. Yet this claim seems to depend on a dubious assumption: that everyone, whether for or against it, has some working knowledge of what liberalism is. Here I'm reminded of a comedy show, *Billy on the Street*. In a recurrent segment, its host,

Billy Eichner, accosts random passersby in New York City with utterly simple trivia requests—"name three white people!" or "name two of the seven dwarfs!" But when faced with a camera and the demand to answer right away, they freeze. One viral You-Tube clip shows an otherwise perfectly articulate young woman stammer for thirty seconds, before hiding behind her yoga mat and fleeing when unable to "name a woman!"[17] Just imagine what would happen if one were asked to "name a liberal!" or worse, "what's liberalism!?" No one would have a clue.[18] But a question like "what's society good for?" or "what, in principle at any rate, is the point of society?" however odd it sounds when posed point-blank, puts us on solid footing. At least then we can cobble together a response from the official public morality that follows us from cradle to grave. Maybe we'd open with some vague state-ment about the freedom of individuals to live as they choose. After that, we'd add that society needs to guarantee rights, resources, and real opportunities to do so. With the wind at our backs, we might then say a word about how important it is for tolerance and mutual respect to be widely and officially encouraged. Carrying on this way, we will soon have reconstructed an entire moral and political doctrine. Asked the right question, a random passerby might even be capable of a fully adequate description of liberal-ism without otherwise being quite sure what it is.

I will later explore in depth what it means to see society and ourselves in this manner. I will consider how liberalism emerges from this conception of society, and how, of course, liberalism in turn specifies and shapes it. For now, let me say this. Al-though the idea of society as a fair system of cooperation is highly general, it is not empty or devoid of content. Seen from a wide historical perspective, it is downright revolutionary.

First, it means that the social order is not fixed or beyond human judgment but instead designed and maintained for the mutual benefit of all of its members. It can thus be criticized and reformed on that basis. For example, it is unacceptable to state, as would a caste-based society, that certain social inequalities are justified because God-given or natural.

Second, it means that society is not held together by a common good or shared end. Whatever their vast differences, the ancient Greek polis, medieval Christian kingdom, and modern fascist state all work on this model. They understand the purpose of society, and hence social cooperation and coordination, in terms of achieving some shared good or end, whether cultivating certain excellences (ancient Greeks), saving souls and bringing about the kingdom of God (medieval Christians), or securing the good of an exclusive people (modern fascists). A liberal society is not like that. Its only shared end is, so to speak, ironic: to maintain itself as a fair system of cooperation so that members can pursue, within reasonable limits, their own conceptions of the good life.

Third, it means that reciprocity moves to the center of the social bond. Members of such a society tend to see one another and themselves as self-interested *and* other regarding, rational *and* reasonable, and seek their own advantage *and* honor fair terms of cooperation. For better or worse (or rather, for better *and* worse), a society of this kind has a powerful moral psychology built into it.

All of this can be gleaned from the idea of society as a fair system of cooperation. If you suspect that Rawls's method is armchairish, you would be correct. He is not an empirical social scientist and did not interview fellow Bostonians to ask how they conceive of their society. Again, his way of proceeding is to consult major artifacts in the public culture of liberal democracies, and on that basis, reverse engineer an idea he believes that virtually all members of his society can recognize themselves in.

This takes intuition and imagination. If I had to reach for an equivalent, it would be to the storyteller. On receiving the Nobel Prize in 2017, novelist Kazuo Ishiguro said this about his craft: "In the end, stories are about one person saying to another: This is the way it feels to me. Can you understand what I'm saying? Does it also feel this way to you?"[19] Rawls was never going to win the Nobel Prize in literature. His ideas could have gotten him there, but not his prose. Still, the enterprise is similar. He tells a story about who we are, and once he feels confident that his readers will assent to it, proceeds to develop a moral and political philosophy, the entire purpose of which is to lay out in systematic detail what that core idea of society as a fair system of cooperation requires of us, our societies, and our lives.

Two Ideas from Pierre Hadot

At the beginning of this chapter, I said this book is inspired by another author in addition to Rawls. It is high time to introduce Hadot, former chair of history in Hellenistic and Roman thought at the Collège de France, France's most prestigious academic institution. Unlike Rawls, his is not a household name in political philosophy for the good reason that he never wrote on liberalism, democracy, or any political topic. Yet he developed two ideas fundamental for my book.

The main idea that Hadot advanced over his long and distinguished career is that ancient philosophers (Greek, Roman, and early Christian) conceived of philosophy in terms of a commitment to a particular "way of life" (*une manière de vivre* in French). For us moderns, this is an unfamiliar notion of philosophy. At universities, it is taught as one academic discipline among others. More generally, we tend to assume that philosophers are people who ponder big, abstract questions—such as Kant, who asked,

"What can I know?" or Georg Wilhelm Friedrich Hegel, who wondered, "What is the purpose of history?"—and that they answer with formidable theoretical systems. Ancient philosophers were also capable of subtle and systematic speculation. But, says Hadot, they correctly put the horse before the cart: the choice of a way of life was found at the beginning, not the end, of the enterprise of philosophy. Back then, a "philosopher" wasn't someone who developed an original theoretical position. They earned the title if they committed themselves to a certain way of living and seeing the world, as taught by a philosophical school or doctrine (for example, Platonism or Stoicism).[20]

Hadot's second idea follows from the first. Suppose you were a neophyte philosopher in ancient Athens, ready to commit to a way of life. Splendid! What then? Well, each school and doctrine would have a catalog of what Hadot calls "spiritual exercises." These are practices that an individual voluntarily undertakes to bring about a comprehensive change in their way of living. Such exercises can be physical (like dietary or sleeping regimens), discursive (diary writing, for instance, or dialogue with a friend or teacher), or intuitive (meditation, say). The crux of Hadot's interpretation of ancient philosophy is that philosophical discourse is itself a spiritual exercise—one conducted in dialogue and instruction as well as through solitary meditation—to reorient one's way of life and become a living, breathing philosopher.[21]

These two ideas are front and center in my book. The first is announced in the title: liberalism *as a way of life*. The language of a way of life is not standard in academic philosophy. The kind of perspective I advance on liberalism is more typically called a *conception of the good*. Rawls himself gave that latter term its authoritative definition as "an ordered family of final ends and aims which specifies a person's conception of what is of value in human life, or alternatively, of what is regarded as a fully worthwhile life."[22] I'm happy for my argument to be classified under this heading. Still, I worry that this phrase sounds all too cerebral, as if people walk around with a doctrine in their head (liberalism, in my case) fully alert to its values and implications. Hadot's idea of a way of life by no means denies that we hold (at least semi-) coherent notions about what is important and valuable in life. But it also draws attention to the noncognitive and subconscious elements that accompany any sincerely held conception of the good, including perceptions, sentiments, and practices. A liberal way of life is an intellectual, emotional, and embodied package deal.

The second idea of Hadot's that I use, spiritual exercises, comes to the fore in part II of the book. There I will show that several of Rawls's signature concepts—which have arcane-sounding names, such as "the original position," "reflective equilibrium," and "public reason"—can be seen as spiritual exercises. I will interpret those notions as voluntary personal practices that you and I, here and now, can adopt to bring about a transformation of the self.

This is an unorthodox reading of Rawls, and to my knowledge, the first time that liberalism has been connected to spiritual exercises. What is to be gained from it?

Put it this way: many liberals are psychologists of the first rank. Germaine de Staël, Constant, Alexis de Tocqueville, George Eliot, Harriet Taylor, Mill, Sigmund Freud, Henri Bergson, Eleanor Roosevelt, Judith Shklar, Lionel Trilling, Richard Rorty, Stanley Cavell, and Martha Nussbaum are acute diagnosticians of the malaise of modern life.[23] They recognize, first, that tectonic forces such as capitalism, democracy, secularism, meritocracy, individualism, materialism, and nationalism exert distinct psychic pressures, and second, that each of us, down to a person, experiences and navigates those pressures on a daily basis.

To this group of eminent psychologists, I would add Rawls. Understated by comparison, he too takes up his pen against a nasty set of emotions and attitudes that are specially fostered by modern societies. At the top of his list are partiality, cynicism, rage, meaninglessness, and an ugly sense of entitlement. Rawls is well-known for showing how these emotions and attitudes can destabilize liberal democracies.[24] A jaded and furious citizenry will quickly lose faith in itself as anything resembling a fair system of cooperation. But he is equally attuned to how such emotions and attitudes are toxic for individual people as well as their quality of day-to-day life. Moreover, and this is where pairing Rawls with Hadot pays off, I will argue that his spiritual exercises tap into the moral and political tradition in which we swim to help us to become fuller and more contented human beings.

If Rawls is the hero of this book, Hadot is its sidekick. He is my special helper to draw from Rawls what is most essential to help us liberals lead the kind of life we claim to already live. In his seminal essay "Spiritual Exercises" (1974), Hadot explains the approach he brings to classical authors: "When we read the works of ancient philosophers, the perspective we have described should cause us to give increased attention to the existential attitudes underlying the dogmatic edifices we encounter."[25] That is what I hope to do with Rawls: to discern, behind his "dogmatic edifice," a powerful existential attitude—liberalism, conceived in terms of a choice of a certain way of life—and show why it is good and how it can be cultivated today.

Society as a Fair System of Cooperation?!

Much ground has been covered in this chapter. I have introduced my two main authors, used one of them to connect liberalism to the idea of society as a fair system of cooperation, and the other to suggest that the liberal tradition has spiritual exercises to help us deal with the challenges of modern life. To conclude, I need to voice an objection that has likely already occurred to you. It concerns the claim that members of liberal democracies consider their societies to be fair systems of cooperation. The blunt version is, "Are you kidding me? Nobody thinks that! Have you looked at the world lately?!" A subtler approach, with less bark but more bite, might begin with the observation that *A Theory of Justice* is now fifty years old. Our skeptic would then not-so-innocently ask, "So, Alex, how well do *you* think its idea of society as a fair system of cooperation is holding up?"

The answer, of course, is not well. The past ten years alone have seen a worldwide erosion of liberal democratic norms, soaring inequality, and unabated environmental degradation. And if we zoom in closer, the notion that members of liberal democracies all presume their society is a fair system of cooperation might seem laughable. Consider the headlines of a single day, February 21, 2021, which, to twist the knife, is the centenary of Rawls's birth. In the United States, Donald Trump was on every network discrediting the results of the presidential election, daily COVID-19 cases reached 78,000, and Texas suffered a massive yet predictable blackout that hit poor minorities the hardest. In Australia, Facebook blocked all Australian content on its News Feed in retaliation for a proposed small federal tax, and in Sydney, a march was organized to protest the recent deaths of Indigenous Australians in police custody. Whether I take my news from the *New York Times* or *Breitbart, Guardian* or *Daily Mail,* BBC or Reddit, the wheels seem to be coming off the bus. Society as a fair system of cooperation? Good luck with that.

The natural conclusion to draw is that a certain liberal vision of the world has had its day. Although few people outright reject the idea that society *should* be a fair system of cooperation, fewer still seem confident that our actual societies have a real prospect of becoming so. Maybe on quieter days we hope that Rawls's idea shambles on, but even then we sense that it is only as a kind of zombie liberalism: not dead because no one wants to kill it, and not alive because no one can muster the conviction necessary for it.

Several of the coming chapters engage with this objection. But here is my preliminary response. First, there can be no question of a Panglossian (or Pinkerian, for the updated version) rebuttal. Even if we could marshal alternative facts to show that ours is the best of all possible worlds, it would not change the ethical predicament we liberals find ourselves in. Yes, it is clear as day not just that our societies are far from ideal but that each and every one of us, as members of them, is also complicit in keeping them from fully becoming (social, political, economic, cultural, and ecological) fair systems of cooperation. At the same time, and here is the predicament, I will argue that the idea of society as a fair system of cooperation remains integral to how we see ourselves as citizens, and crucially, simply as people going about our daily lives. No matter what trials and tribulations our societies are undergoing at the moment, this idea can't and won't just disappear or be left behind. As a society, we wouldn't know what to do without it. And the real insight I want to work toward is that without it, we wouldn't even know who we are as individual people. It has become constitutive of how we, as subjects of twenty-first-century liberal democracies, understand ourselves and lead our lives. If the goal is to learn how to live as authentic liberals—or to lower the bar, at least not be moralistic phony ones—we need to admit the truth of this objection, all the while not letting go of the idea it seems to put to rest.

3

Liberalism and the Good Life

TO LAUNCH MY INVESTIGATION of how liberalism has shaped us, I begin at the beginning, with the early liberals who created the tradition in the nineteenth century. What is remarkable is that they explicitly conceived of their doctrine in relation to the question of how to live well, and specifically how to do so in light of the many social and political pressures of modern life.

In this chapter, I will not refer to John Rawls, Pierre Hadot, or the idea of society as a fair system of cooperation. That will wait until the next chapter, when I turn to the twentieth and twenty-first centuries. But lest I give the impression that nineteenth-century liberalism is a relic or thing of the past, I want to start this one with a contemporary figure to give it life: Leslie Knope, the hero of the television comedy *Parks and Recreation* (2009–15). To my mind, she is the best—the most vibrant, relevant, relatable, and just generally awesome—representative of the spirit of early liberalism.

Leslie is not the standard face of the tradition. That distinction goes to one of the great, so-called classical liberal thinkers. It is their famous portraits we tend to picture: a windswept John Locke, white-wigged Adam Smith, chiaroscuroed

Immanuel Kant, or muttonchopped John Stuart Mill. But give me a chance to make my case. She belongs to this pantheon as much as any other.

The Greatest Liberal Who Never Lived

Parks and Recreation was initially conceived as a spin-off of another workplace comedy, the US adaptation of *The Office* (2005–13), and its cocreators Greg Daniels and Michael Schur were showrunners of that earlier series. I mention this because the first season of *Parks and Recreation* is in the snarkier vein of its predecessor. Set in the fictional town of Pawnee, Indiana (with the town slogan "First in Friendship, Fourth in Obesity"), the show is about a team of civil servants in the Department of Parks and Recreation. When we first meet Leslie (played by Amy Poehler), she is a thirty-four-year-old midlevel bureaucrat who is trying yet failing to take on the political system from the inside. Smart but not savvy, she is routinely ridiculed and ignored by her colleagues.

Conflict in the workplace is a tried-and-true formula for television. It makes for snappy dialogue and absurd situations. But where *The Office* elevated it to an art form, this formula had unintended consequences for *Parks and Recreation*, specifically for how Leslie was portrayed. In a retrospective on the show, Schur recalled that a test audience member for its early episodes felt that Leslie came across as a "bimbo." That description struck a nerve. It was the opposite of how he had envisaged her as a strong, capable feminist. So the show pivoted. Rather than center on internal conflict within the office team (with Leslie as its butt), going forward its dynamic would be based on external conflict between the outside world and the office team (with Leslie as its leader).[1]

This changed everything. From then on, every season of *Parks and Recreation* revolves around a new threat to the parks, rivers, and playgrounds of Pawnee, whether from state budget cuts, the predations of the private sector, or most often, the stupidity and cynicism of its townsfolk. And every season, Leslie and her team roll up their sleeves to defend the public good with grit and verve. Almost overnight, *Parks and Recreation* went from being a clever yet derivative office sitcom to something else entirely. "What I felt was that the show had an argument to make about team-work and friendship and positivity and being an optimist and believing in the power of public service," said Schur at the ten-year cast reunion. "I don't feel that we left anything on the table. Working on it felt like the most important thing I'll ever do."[2]

Parks and Recreation is indeed admirable and high-minded, but it is first and foremost a comedy. Leslie especially is a mix of the ridiculous and sublime. The show writers give her all the trappings for a US audience to identify her as a capital L Lib-eral. To mention a handful, she (inadvertently) marries two male penguins; is gifted an Obama-style "Knope" (in lieu of "Hope") poster; writes a cookbook titled *The Feminine Mes-quite*; claims that her ideal man would have "the brains of George Clooney inside the body of Joe Biden"; says that were she to have a stripper name, it would be Equality; and hosts an annual celebration, "Galentines' Day," for her female friends. For a slightly longer example, in one episode Leslie serves as a judge in the Miss Pawnee Beauty Pageant. To ensure a genu-inely talented woman wins, she invents her own scorecard with the categories "teeth, interior life, knowledge of herstory, presentation, intelligence, fruitful gestures, lack of ostentation, je ne sais quoi, the Naomi Wolf factor, voice modulation." And in case Leslie's over-the-top liberalism hasn't hit you yet, here is the interview question she poses to the most conventionally pretty contestant: "Alexis de Tocqueville called America the 'great experiment.' What can we do as citizens to improve on that experiment?"[3]

That is the ridiculous. But there is also the sublime. I am serious about Leslie being a singularly compelling representation of the liberal spirit. Explaining why will lead to the topic of this chapter: how liberals in the nineteenth century sought to give a modern answer to the age-old question of how to live well.

If *Parks and Recreation* has a political philosophy, it is about the value of the commons along with the need to keep public land, resources, and institutions free. From that core idea stems three features that make Leslie a model of early liberalism.

The first is an unstinting commitment to the public good. Early liberalism has a bad and misleading reputation in this regard. One term is largely to blame, *classical liberalism*, which refers to a version of liberalism that privileges individual rights, free markets, small government, and moral individualism. Whatever we may think of that package, it is important to recognize it as an anachronism when applied to the nineteenth century. Early liberals didn't walk around referring to themselves as classical. What would that even mean given that they were busy inventing the tradition? The term was instead coined by twentieth-century economists and social theorists who worried about egalitarian and socialist tendencies in the liberalism of their own day.[4] In response, they invented a term—classical liberalism—to designate what they regarded as the true core of liberalism, projected it back onto the eighteenth and nineteenth centuries, and then claimed themselves as its true and rightful heirs.

This is all well and good as a polemical tactic. Yet it is revisionist and historically inaccurate. Precious few early liberals would have understood themselves in the classical doctrine imputed to them. "Liberals always saw themselves as fighting for the common good and continued to see this common good in moral terms," writes Helena Rosenblatt in her superb *The Lost History of Liberalism* (2018). "Today we may think that they were naive, deluded, or disingenuous. But to nineteenth-century liberals, being liberal meant believing in an ethical project."[5] To return to *Parks and Recreation*, many characters dismiss and deride Leslie as naive or deluded. But no one ever suggests that she is disingenuous. When we leave her in the final episode, it is with real moral and political weight that she twice cites Theodore Roosevelt's credo, "Public service is the chance to work hard at work worth doing." Early liberals would heartily endorse that message.

The second feature that marks Leslie as an early liberal is a love of localities. If you've seen *Parks and Recreation*, you know that over and above the many romantic pairings of its characters, the real love story is between Leslie and the town of Pawnee itself. It is a rocky relationship, to be sure. Still, all of her strivings are dedicated to ameliorating *this* place and making *it* special. Seasons 1 and 2, for example, are about transforming a giant pit into a park. Season 3 centers on reviving Pawnee's traditional harvest festival. With each subsequent season following suit, *amor mundi*—care and love of the world—might as well be the show's motto.[6] That brings Leslie into the company of the great early liberals. They too were apprehensive and saddened by the tendency of the modern world to flatten difference, and make everything (including people, regions, towns, culture, opinion, language, food, sport, and art) uniform and sterile. Thus when Leslie is elected to city council in season 4 and ends her acceptance speech with "I love this city," it comes with an implicit promise to protect it from all that threatens sameness and mediocrity. Here as well, nineteenth-century liberals would nod in agreement.

The third feature may be surprising: a suspicion of democracy, if not outright hostility toward it. Right from its plucky theme song, *Parks and Recreation* seems light and upbeat. Yet it has a dark and even misanthropic message: your average citizen in a modern-day democracy is either incompetent or acts in bad faith when it comes to public affairs. Perhaps the show and its writers believe in democracy and "the people" in the abstract, but its contempt for the citizens of Pawnee is boundless (and given that they created those citizens, the contempt is downright Calvinist). From the first episode to the last, *Parks and Recreation* never wavered. The town hall forums it features are equal parts vanity and idiocy; the elected officials it presents are clueless or venal; and the townspeople Leslie fights so hard for are always ready to trade the public good for their own worst impulses. The tension between her and the citizens of Pawnee reaches such a boiling point that when faced with the prospect of being recalled from city council, she lets rip with a speech: "I love Pawnee, but sometimes it sucks. The people can be very mean and ungrateful, and they cling to their fried dough and their big sodas, and they get mad at me when their pants don't fit. I'm sick of it. Pawnee is filled with a bunch of pee-pee heads."[7]

With its talk of pee-pee heads and big sodas, why we should take *Parks and Recreation* seriously? Well, this episode aired in 2013, and Leslie's speech parodies a notorious remark by then-senator Barack Obama from five years earlier. Speaking at a fundraiser in San Francisco, he said that given the failed policies of the Clinton and Bush administrations, it is no wonder that white working-class voters "cling to guns or religion or antipathy to people who aren't like them, or anti-immigrant sentiment, or anti-trade sentiment as a way to explain their frustrations."[8] Those were high-impact words. Besides Hillary Clinton's "basket of deplorables," I can't recall any that incited so much lasting resentment and solidarity with such economy. Later in the book, I will investigate whether *contemporary* liberalism and a *contemporary* liberal way of life is necessarily in tension with democracy. Was Obama's remark just a gaffe or is there something there? It is not an issue to settle quickly or easily. Yet there can be no doubt that *early* liberalism was suspicious of democracy. In fact, as we will see, that was how it got its start: as a doctrine to either contain or train democracy. Like Leslie, early liberals suspected that most citizens most of the time could not be relied on to direct the polis.

Misanthropy

An abiding impression about liberals is that they tend to have a rosy, often Pollyannish view of the world. A prominent conservative once referred to himself as "a liberal who has been mugged by reality."[9] Liberals tend not to take kindly to the suggestion that they are fantasists. But given that most of them believe that people can be reasonable and rational in their dealings with others, and thus have faith in the possibility of human progress, perhaps they can recognize a grain of truth in the slight.[10]

Putting to the side the question of whether present-day liberals can be accused of optimism, no one would dare suggest it of their forerunners. Political theorist Judith Shklar makes this point to great effect in a masterpiece of liberal thought, *Ordinary Vices* (1984). Her book focuses on the early modern thinkers who inspired liberalism, especially two nobles from Bordeaux: Michel de Montaigne (1533–92) and Montesquieu (1689–1755). Shklar's insight about these thinkers is that they are deeply misanthropic. They expect the worst from human beings, and nothing bad we do surprises them.

This is no mere psychological observation. It cuts to the heart of their philosophy, and with it, later developments in liberal thought and practice. Montesquieu is an instructive case. Shklar calls his work "misanthropy's finest hour."[11] Why? Because when confronted with the probability that political rulers will abuse their power and inflict all manner of cruelties to secure their ends, he designed a legal and political system to minimize the damage they could do: "Misanthropy is politically a paradox. Disdain and fear could and did serve as the basis of political decency, legal restraints, and the effort to create limited government that would attenuate the effects of the cruelty of those who rule. Misanthropy can, however, also initiate slaughter. . . . [M]isanthropy is more significant than mere meanness of spirit."[12]

Hatred of the human, Shklar makes clear, can lead to different outcomes. It can lead someone to conclude that we must put our faith in God to save us (as did Saint Augustine). It can also lead to the conviction that it would be best for the human race to let itself die out (as said Hamlet to Ophelia). It can lead another to think the present dispensation of culture is so rotten that it would be best to raze it to the ground and start over (as Friedrich Nietzsche might have felt). But it can lead a politically minded soul in quite another direction. Unlike Augustine, Montesquieu did not place his faith in an outside source. And unlike Hamlet and Nietzsche, his misanthropy was not despairing or destructive. He claims instead that what human beings need are legal and political institutions to protect the weak from the strong. Today we call his solution *constitutionalism*, and its doctrines of the separation of powers and rule of law are foundation stones of our own liberal democracies. Montesquieu's misanthropy did not express itself in hopelessness or violence. He rolled up his sleeves to save humanity from its own worst impulses. He is, in this respect, a little like Leslie.

The Origins of Liberalism

Strictly speaking, Montesquieu is not a liberal. Neither is any-one living and writing prior to the nineteenth century. Historians have been firm on this point in recent years.[13] The fact is that the terms *liberal* and *liberalism* were only recently used in an explicitly political sense: first in Spain in 1810, and then within a decade, across Europe and North America. From this perspective, it is acceptable to call an eighteenth-century figure such as Montesquieu a *proto*liberal, *forerunner* of liberalism, *pioneer*, or even *influencer*. But *liberal*, full stop? That's a step too far.

Are the historians just being pedantic? Not at all. Their guiding premise is eminently sensible: to grasp what makes liberalism special, we need to pay attention to the context that gives rise to it. Only then can we appreciate what causes and concerns motivated early liberals. Pinpointing the origins of liberalism matters. At stake is not just *when* liberalism was created but also *why*.

To explain, let us remain a moment longer with Montesquieu. He developed his political philosophy in relation to an urgent problem of his day: royal absolutism. That problem is why his misanthropy took the form it did, namely, constitutionalism. He designed his ideas of the rule of law and separation of powers to scatter the power of any single person—whether his own fictional antihero Uzbek from *Persian Letters* or a real Louis XIV—who would govern through fear and threat.

Montesquieu is not alone in this endeavor. A similar story could be told about the other major forerunner of liberalism, Locke. Only a few details need amending. He too feared ambitious monarchs—"lions and tygers" such as Charles I as well as his beastly sons Charles II and James II—who would usurp powers that rightly belonged to the people. Moreover, and again like Montesquieu, Locke's misanthropy (or if that is too harsh a word, his healthy skepticism of the great and powerful) had its own celebrated offspring: a conception of political legitimacy as based on the consent of the governed along with natural rights to life, liberty, and possessions.

Not even the most persnickety historian would deny that Montesquieu and Locke are hugely influential for the liberal tradition. On paper, they even furnish most of its main ideas, including the separation of powers, rule of law, consent of the governed, and individual rights. Furthermore, and this is Shklar's argument, they set a mood of misanthropy for those full-fledged liberals who follow in their footsteps. Yet something essential is missing: the development of these ideas and this mood in relation to the single greatest political problem that would animate the nineteenth century. It was up to thinkers who took the name *liberal* to do that.

What was that problem? Ironically, the very thing that brought the world of cruel kings and bold princes crashing down: democracy. Nineteenth-century liberals of all stripes were exercised by the fact that not just political but also social, economic, moral, and cultural power would increasingly be wielded by the common man. Some, like François Guizot and Jacob Burckhardt, flatly opposed this development. Others, like Tocqueville and Mill, hoped to educate and tame it. But nineteenth-century liberals were united in repurposing, among other things, ideas and institutions originally meant to combat royal absolutism—including those I listed in connection with Montesquieu and Locke—to either restrain or guide democracy and the newfound political, social, and moral power of the people. Liberalism was their solution to the problem of democracy. That is why historians are correct to insist that liberalism is not some universal and timeless doctrine that champions freedom in the abstract. To locate its origins in any other

moment in time would miss its crucial feature: a deeply con-
flicted attitude toward democracy.

Early liberalism's ambivalence toward democracy is one of
its most valuable features for us today. Its great authors—and
I will pay special attention to Tocqueville—were extraordinary
observers of modern everyday life. They knew not only that
democracy was about universal suffrage and legal and political
equality but that it also triggered an epochal set of social, moral,
cultural, and psychological transformations. *Individualism*
(meaning the temptation for democratic citizens to withdraw
into private life and cease to care much about public affairs),
materialism (meaning the temptation for democratic citizens to
seek pleasure and fulfillment in small everyday gratifications),
and *conformity* (meaning the temptation for democratic citizens to follow majority opinion without much question or fuss)
are all ushered in by democracy, and have the potential to wreck
our chances for happiness and self-realization. Individualism
paves the way for selfishness, materialism leads to anxiety, and
conformity breeds mediocrity. Those were some of the dangers
early liberals confronted, and a way of life inspired by liberal
ideals was their solution. Being a liberal citizen in the nineteenth century, at least for the thinkers I treat in this book, was
not about trying to squash democracy or push for voter restric-
tions. It was an ethical project of learning to navigate modern
life as best as possible.

And here is the point: I don't know about you, but when I
look at the world today, I don't see the forces of individualism,
materialism, and conformity much abated. The antidemocratism
of early liberalism is thus not something we should want to pe-
riodize as the prejudices of a benighted age. Neither is it something to sanitize by saying that liberalism has today made peace
with democracy and the two are now happily reconciled. Doing

so would not just be historically inaccurate with respect to the nineteenth century but also practically foolish for the twenty-first. We would deny ourselves the resources that the liberal tradition invented to inhabit the democratic world.

Being Liberal: From Plymouth to Pawnee

So far in this chapter, I have worked our way backward: from Leslie as a contemporary embodiment of the spirit of early liberalism to the mood of misanthropy that informs so much of it, and then to the suspicion of democracy that started it all. To complete the picture, I need to take a final step back and examine the word *liberal* itself. That will allow us to see what being a liberal person meant for the founders of liberalism, and how that aspiration can continue to inform a liberal way of life.

Liberalism, we have just learned, is only two hundred years old—a newborn by the standards of intellectual history. *Liberal*, however, is a much older word and idea. It has Latin roots, and the terms *liber*, meaning "free and generous," and *liberalis*, "befitting a freeborn person," have for two thousand years been at the heart of Western discourses about ethics, religion, and citizenship. Each epoch of Western history, in fact, reinvents what it means to be liberal from within its reigning moral framework. In ancient Rome, being free referred to the status of not being a slave and under the domination of another. The noun *liberalitas* also signified an aristocratic attitude essential to the cohesion and smooth operation of society. A free person was generous in thought and deed to their fellow citizens, ready to give their talents, wealth, and even life to the republic or empire. In the Middle Ages, the ideal of liberality was adapted to Christian virtues, especially charity. The word *liberal* appears a dozen times in the King James Bible, usually in connection with how to treat the poor. Later, during the Reformation and then Renaissance, tolerance and broad learning moved to the forefront of liberal virtues. Finally, recalling the Roman ideal, in British North America, being liberal meant contributing to the public good and ensuring the viability of the colonies.

Readers interested in the word history of liberal and liberalism should consult a book I mentioned a few pages ago: Rosenblatt's *The Lost History of Liberalism*. Along with fellow intellectual historians, Rosenblatt identifies liberalism as a nineteenth-century invention. What sets her argument apart, however, is that she situates the creation of liberalism in the nineteenth century against the background of a millennia-long genealogy of the liberal virtues and what it meant to *be* a liberal subject through the ages. We cannot follow her history through its twists and turns, but the upshot is that by the time nineteenth-century liberals took up their pens, "Europeans had been calling liberality a necessary virtue for more than two thousand years. If ever there was a liberal tradition this was it."[14]

The Lost History of Liberalism is an inspiration for my own book. Where Rosenblatt asks what being liberal meant for the nineteenth century, I have tried to do the same for the present day. But if I may voice a minor criticism (and altogether unfair, given that it is a failing of language itself), I find its title misleading considering what the book accomplishes. The problem is the word *liberalism*, which like any ism, freezes its object into a settled doctrine. *The Lost History of Liberalism* makes it seem that we have achieved this thing—that is, a stable and fixed liberalism—for which the author provides antecedents. Yet this belies the wonderful quality of the actual book, which is a flowing account of how myriad thinkers, writers, and statespersons (and journalists, novelists, soldiers, and more) were trying, on the fly and in the lived present, to figure out how to rescue and reinvent the ideal of liberality in relation to problems that no ancient philosopher, medieval theologian, or Renaissance humanist ever dreamed of. How, these nineteenth-century denizens asked, are we to remain free and generous despite all the temptations and coercions that democracy, capitalism, and nationalism put into play? A more representative title for Rosenblatt's book—which admittedly, no publisher would have accepted—would be closer to a picaresque novel or telenovela: *The Continuing Adventures of the Ideal of Liberality in the Face of Unprecedented Setbacks and Opportunities*.[15] A title of that kind, however quixotic, conveys her achievement: to have represented decade by decade and country by country an idea and sensibility working itself out, rather than the assumed and settled doctrine we all too quickly take liberalism to be.

Let me turn to a book that captures the emergent and lived quality of early liberalism: Tocqueville's *Democracy in America*. At once singular and not, this text is ideal for my purposes. On the one hand, Tocqueville's concern that democracy threatens to erode character is utterly typical of his time. Benjamin Constant, Germaine de Staël, and Mill, to name a few contemporary greats, were all astonished and apprehensive about how democratic ideas and tastes were reshaping politics, religion, arts and letters, the family, and professional life. On the other hand, what sets Tocqueville apart is how he investigated this phenomenon. Through a mix of political sociology, ethnography, aesthetic criticism, and moral and political philosophy, he brought *homo democraticus* (or *homo americanus*, if you prefer) to life, and in doing so, showed exactly what attempts to preserve liberality as a political and ethical ideal had to contend with.

The origin of Tocqueville's *Democracy in America* has the status of legend: a young nobleman voyages to the United States and is blown away by what he finds. "A new political science," he then announces, "is needed for a world altogether new."[16] But the reason why he decided to travel to the United States in the first place is rather more pedestrian. He needed to get away from his family. Tocqueville's family, though, wasn't just any. His was one of the eminent houses of France. His great-grandfather Malesherbes led Louis XVI's legal defense and paid with his life. His father was an architect of the Bourbon Restoration. And his mother, who avoided the guillotine only because Maximilien Robespierre met it a day earlier, was traumatized for the rest of her life, rarely venturing from the family estate in Normandy. Safe to say, then, that Alexis did not grow up in a household friendly to the following words: reform, democracy, and liberalization.

This brings us to the pickle he found himself in just after the 1830 July Revolution. France's new ruler, the liberal Louis Philippe, required all of his officials to swear an oath of allegiance to the new regime. What was twenty-five-year-old Alexis to do? Refusing would kill any career ambitions he entertained. Consenting would anger and disappoint his family. He ended up walking a fine line: Tocqueville pledged loyalty to the new liberal regime, yet he also accepted a government commission to travel to the United States to study and report on US prisons with an eye to reforms happening in France. It was a smart move. With a single decision, he publicly affirmed his liberal commitments, saved his career, took some distance from his family, and embarked on a fun and fateful trip.[17]

Tocqueville, along with his friend and fellow aristocrat Gustave de Beaumont, toured North America in 1831 for just under a year with extended stays in New York City, Boston, and other parts of Massachusetts, and visits to the frontier West, the South, and Lower Canada. Thrilled that the French nobility had taken an interest in their newly formed nation, their hosts rolled out the red carpet. Everywhere the young aristocrats went they were treated to soirees and concerts.

But Tocqueville and Beaumont worked hard. They took their prison commission seriously and produced a detailed report.[18] Both men also filled several notebooks with observations of US politics, culture, customs, and mores for their respective book projects. In 1835, Beaumont published his novel *Marie, or Slavery in the United States*, which was part love story and part indictment of race relations. Tocqueville wrote up his reflections in two parts: *Democracy in America, Volume 1* (1835) and *Democracy in America, Volume 2* (1840).

Commentators on *Democracy in America* have long pointed out differences between the two volumes. The most significant is optimism and pessimism, respectively, about the future of democracy.[19] Tocqueville was impressed by many aspects of democracy in the United States, and volume 1 is written in the afterglow of his visit.[20] Volume 2 has five additional years of observation behind it and Tocqueville's gaze trained on Europe. To say that he grew less sanguine is an understatement. Here, in his most misanthropic hour, are his parting thoughts on the kind of person democracy produces:

> I see an innumerable crowd of like and equal men who re-volve on themselves without repose, procuring the small and vulgar pleasures with which they fill their souls. Each of them, withdrawn and apart, is like a stranger to the destiny of all the others: his children and his particular friends form the whole human species for him; as for dwelling with his fellow citizens, he is beside them, but he does not see them; he touches them and does not feel them; he exists only in himself and for himself, and if a family still remains for him, one can at least say that he no longer has a native country.[21]

Invective can be fun to read. Until, that is, you realize it's about you. Tocqueville's message is that more likely than not, we who grow up in democracies are selfish, lonely, cold, restless, distracted, and mediocre.

Here a democrat might stop in a fit of pique to demand the reasons why. Isn't democracy simply about citizens deciding for themselves how they will be governed? Tocqueville wouldn't disagree. Yet his special gift is an ability to see how democracy—and especially its underlying principle of equality—fosters a whole set of attitudes, desires, and expectations in the public and private lives of its subjects.

Consider the passage I just cited. Its words of abuse form three clusters. The first includes the following: "revolve on themselves," "withdrawn and apart," "a stranger to the destiny of all the others," and "he exists only in himself and for himself." These observations pick out what Tocqueville calls *individualism* (a word he even coined). This is a complex and extended topic in *Democracy in America*.[22] The short version begins with the fact that democracy grants everyone equal civil and political rights. That, however, is a mixed blessing. On the plus side, individuals are free to live as they please. The downside is that once people see themselves as free in this manner, they become motivated in large part by self-interest. Faced with any demand on their time or energy—whether it comes from school, work, a friend, lover, country, or God Himself—even the best American will silently wonder, from deep within their democratic lizard brain, "What's in it for me?" Huge consequences follow from this little question. As a rule, democrats pour their desires and ambitions into private life (broadly understood to include the professional and domestic spheres), and withdraw care and concern from public affairs. What Oscar Wilde reputedly said of socialism applies to how democrats feel about civic engagement in general: it takes up too many evenings.

A second cluster of pejoratives in the passage identifies *materialism*—our obsession with "small and vulgar pleasures"— as intrinsic to democracy (and especially democracy entwined with capitalism). On this matter, Tocqueville takes his cue from another great French pessimist, theologian Blaise Pascal, who claimed that human beings are doomed to a spiritual condition of distraction and disquiet (*divertissement* and *inquiétude*).[23] Tocqueville doesn't say whether he agrees that humans are by nature fated to distraction and disquiet. Yet he certainly thinks that the modern world so inflames those mental states that they have become effectively universal and inevitable. Democracy is again the culprit. Equality of opportunity places small comforts and material gratifications within everyone's reach. As with individualism, this is both good and bad. It is nice that nice things are widely available—a dinner out, stylish clothes, and a cool phone and fast car. Still, a life centered on procuring and consuming such goods is miserable. Democrats bounce from endless calculation to acquire more (distraction) to constant anxiety about how it can be lost and who else might be doing better (disquiet). In fact, when Tocqueville first arrived in the United States, its materialism shocked him.[24] Here was a society that seemed to be all middle-class and prosperous like no other, yet restive and sad behind its energy and apparent cheer. By the time he wrote volume 2 of *Democracy in America*, his fears had only deepened. Distraction and disquiet were not uniquely American pathologies but rather psychic correlates of democracy itself.

A final cluster of insults lurks in the first line of the above passage. "An innumerable crowd of like and equal men" names one of Tocqueville's most famous insights: the extraordinary *conformity* of democrats. For his contemporary French readers, this was a surprising claim. With the recent experience of Jacobinism seared into the national memory, democracy was associated with violence and lawlessness, not sameness and mediocrity. Yet that was exactly Tocqueville's argument. Because democrats tend to think that everyone's individual opinion has the same worth, they place great faith in the majority. After all, if the authority of specific individuals is discounted (for example, priests and nobles in Tocqueville's day, or so-called elites in our own), who else can democrats turn to for guidance? "The public," says Tocqueville, "has a singular power among democratic peoples, the very idea of which aristocratic nations could not conceive. . . . In the United States, the majority takes charge of furnishing individuals with a host of ready-made opinions, and it thus relieves them of the obligation to form their own."[25] An entire train of consequences—political, religious, moral, and aesthetic—follows from this line of thought, and Tocqueville develops each one. The most depressing is spiritual: in time democrats will not consult, or even come to learn, their own tastes and preferences but instead take their cue from majority opinion. When twenty years later, Mill cuttingly remarks that "by dint of not following their own nature," his fellow Victorians are left with "no nature to follow," he knowingly reprises Tocqueville's lament.[26] Democracy, say the two greatest nineteenth-century liberals, makes everyone boring and blah.

In sum, individualism, materialism, and conformity are bad features of democracy.[27] They can, on the one hand, lead to new forms of tyranny. A despot (whether an individual ruler or centralized bureaucracy) wants nothing more than subjects who are happily depoliticized, held in thrall by consumerism, and led by majority opinion. In this section, on the other hand, I emphasized a different set of dangers linked to democracy: its effects on character. When Tocqueville thus paints his damning portrait of the democratic soul—that we are cold, restless, mediocre, and all the rest—his criticism is not just that we are self-centered, mean, and uninspiring in our dealings with other people. We will have become people whose desires and self-conception sabotage our prospects for happiness and fulfillment.[28]

The development of liberalism in the nineteenth century was driven by this two-pronged problem, political *and* personal: how to ensure that polities and people remain free and generous in spite of the obstacles democracy throws up. Naturally, early liberals proposed various solutions. For his part, Tocqueville believed he had found a model on the shores of the New World: the New England towns, which will bring us back full circle to Leslie and Pawnee.

The first thing to note about Tocqueville on the New England towns is that he never actually saw them in action. When he traveled to Boston, Tocqueville met with prominent citizens who described in glowing terms the importance and precise operation of the towns. These interlocutors (most notably Jared Sparks, a historian and later president of Harvard University) even provided detailed written notes and personalized essays, many of which were incorporated into *Democracy in America*.[29] Clearly, then, Tocqueville's account is an idealization. From his hosts, he was fed a careful line about an institution central not only to US governance but also to its own national myth given that so many founders—Benjamin Franklin, John Adams, and George Washington—had cut their political teeth in their own local towns. Moreover, on Tocqueville's side, the institution of the town resonated with his own intellectual formation. He had attended a lecture series on local government by the great antidemocratic liberal Guizot in the early 1830s, and was also steeped in arguments by reactionaries (such as Joseph de Maistre) that democracy and sovereignty were mutually exclusive concepts.[30] Indeed, the New England town fascinated Tocqueville because it seemed to offer a decisive counterexample to skeptics (as different as Guizot and de Maistre) who felt that democracy could never be ordered and functional. Popular sovereignty, it turned out, could be responsibly exercised and integrated into the everyday routines of ordinary people.

So what were New England towns? They were communities of approximately two thousand citizens. Autonomy was their defining feature in the sense that citizens locally administered public affairs, largely independent of state and federal governments. That required two things: a great many elected officials along with an active and engaged citizenry. When, for example, funds needed to be raised to build a school or church, or plans for a new road finalized, a meeting was called and the townsfolk would assemble to direct their elected officials. The New England town, in short, operated like a minirepublic or ancient polis. Connected through extensive networks of rights and duties, citizens would deliberate and act together on matters of public concern. Here is how Tocqueville represents a day in the life of a town:

> Life in the township makes itself felt in a way at each instant. . . .
> The inhabitant of New England is *attached* to his township
> because it is strong and independent; he is *interested* in it because he cooperates in directing it; he *loves* it because he has
> nothing to complain of in his lot; he *places* his ambition and
> his future in it; he *mingles* in each of the incidents of township life: in this restricted sphere that is within his reach he
> tries to govern society; he habituates himself to the forms
> without which freedom proceeds only through revolution,
> permeates himself with their spirit, gets a taste for order, understands the harmony of powers, and finally assembles clear

and practical ideas on the nature of his duties as well as the extent of his rights.[31]

Had Tocqueville written a book of self-help for democrats, it would have had a single message: get out of your own head! For the key to happiness in democracy is to escape the egocentrism to which it all too naturally predisposes us. New Englanders, Tocqueville argued, had hit on the right formula. Just look at the verbs in the first half of this passage. Each bears a lesson. By *mingling* in the affairs of the township and becoming *interested* in its governance, the townsperson exits the private sphere and combats individualism. In *placing* their ambition in the town, and chasing personal status in relation to it, the townsperson gains a set of strivings that are not materialist. And in *attaching* themselves to the town, and learning to *love* and care for it, the townsperson acquires a love of locality that resists the leveling and conformist tendencies of democracy.

Reading *Democracy in America*, it is easy to get the impression that Tocqueville thinks himself superior to his American hosts. In a word he lets slip here or an aside there, we can just picture the handsome young aristocrat smiling about some brash display. But by the time we reach the final paragraphs of the book, respect shines through. "We ought not," says Tocqueville, "to strain to make ourselves like our fathers, but strive to attain the kind of greatness and happiness that is proper to us."[32] Greatness and happiness, *grandeur* and *bonheur*—those are big words. But in the United States, or at least pockets of it, Tocqueville felt he had found them in a people who had learned how to become liberal in democracy, and despite the pressures of the age, live generously and freely.

You might object that Tocqueville's account of life in the New England towns is more fiction than fact. For our purposes, it doesn't matter. First, whether historically accurate or not, it represents his ethical ideal of the citizen and person. Second, we have a compelling contemporary representation of it in Leslie. Do I think that the writers of *Parks and Recreation* sat at their table, seminar style, with personal copies of *Democracy in America* to plot the show? No, but that's the point. It is proof of Tocqueville's acumen that he saw, in a vision that is now two hundred years old, exactly where democracy takes us. The townsfolk of Pawnee are messed up in exactly the ways he predicted. More impor-tant, Leslie is a full and complete human being in just the way he thought necessary in democracy. It is as if she hopped into a time machine parked in Plymouth, Massachusetts, circa 1810 to travel to Pawnee, Indiana, circa 2010. The only difference, and it is significant for her own pursuit of happiness, is that only Leslie and her closest friends act like liberals from the past. They alone fight individualism by throwing themselves into public affairs; they alone resist materialism by giving prior-ity to love and friendship; and they alone strive to preserve Pawnee as the special place it is and not just some town off I-65. They alone are liberal in a democratic world.

Let me put it more forcefully. What if, instead of leaping for-ward in time from Plymouth to Pawnee, Leslie was beamed backward, from Pawnee to Plymouth? In volume 1 of *Democ-racy in America*, she would have found a home (assuming she were white, male, and propertied, that is). In that earlier vol-ume, Tocqueville believed that the modern world could, if it tried, produce Leslie. It would need to swim upstream against the currents of the age, but with luck and dedication, it could be done. The New England town proved that.

In volume 2, he lost faith. To his mind, those deadly currents had only strengthened their pull over democratic hearts and minds. If Leslie were to exist in the second volume's pages, it would be by miracle, not design. The Tocqueville of volume 2, then, would have shrugged off criticisms that his account of the towns from five years earlier was optimistic and unrealistic. What would have sounded much more implausible to him was that such places could endure, in nearly that same form, for two hundred years, and continue to make committed citizens and integrated human beings like Leslie.

This is where Tocqueville lands at the end of *Democracy in America*. Yet something about Leslie would have been illegible to him. Like his fellow early liberals—and as we will see in the next chapter, twentieth- and twenty-first-century liberals as well—Tocqueville makes an assumption that this book disputes. He thinks that everyone is liberal (or illiberal) on top of being something else, such as Christian, aristocratic, atheist, or romantic. Leslie is none of those things. She is liberal all the way down, and illustrates what a completely liberal person looks and acts like. This is not to fault Tocqueville. Two hundred years ago, liberal values and sensibilities had not yet saturated the background culture of Western democracies. But once they do, it is a game changer.[33] The rest of this book investigates what it means to be liberal in these altered circumstances. We can still, of course, be either optimistic or pessimistic about whether a liberal way of life can be realized today. We can also dispute whether it is desirable in the first place. But with two hundred years of liberal history behind us, the terrain of discussion is far different from what Tocqueville mapped out.

4

What Liberals Don't Get
about Liberalism

IN THE PREVIOUS CHAPTER, I looked at how nineteenth-century liberals recovered an ideal of liberality, understood as a free and generous way of living, in the face of new challenges posed by the modern world. I now return to the twentieth and twenty-first centuries. To do so, I would like to call on our fish from chapter 1. There were three, if you remember: an older character who complained that liberalism was the water of our times, and two younger fish who were oblivious to the reality they swim in. Their encounter consisted of only a few words. "How's the liberalism?" asked the old grump, with the youngsters swimming on for a bit before wondering, "What the hell is liberalism?"

Suppose, though, that when one of the younger fish returned home, he started to feel annoyed. The old geezer's question had gotten under his skin. What was liberalism after all? It bothered him so much that he decided to study it at college. He applied to all the top schools in political philosophy—Oxford, Princeton, the Australian National University, and many more—to get to the bottom of it. And when he graduated (*scuba* cum laude, naturally), he hoped for nothing more than to meet the old fish and tell him exactly what liberalism is and how he feels about it.

In this chapter, we will see what our guppy would have learned in his studies: a branch of political philosophy known as political liberalism. It is today not just the leading theory of liberalism but rather the reigning orthodoxy of how to do political philosophy within the Anglophone academy. Its goal is to work out a view of liberalism suitable for a pluralist society—that is, a society characterized by reasonable yet unresolvable disagreements between citizens, particularly over questions of value and the good life. Later sections of my book are indebted to this school of thought and how it conceives of the ideal of the liberal citizen. But I introduce it now for quite other reasons. The truth is that its proponents would take strong exception to my fundamental claim: that liberalism can be regarded as a way of life. In their eyes, such a claim returns us to the problematic brands of liberalism (which they call "comprehensive" and "perfectionist") that their theory is designed to correct.

It is important to state up front that I accept the teachings and accompanying strictures of political liberalism. The young fish and I have no quarrel. We agree that liberal democratic states include members with different and incompatible worldviews. Because of that fact, we also agree that liberal democratic states must not favor certain conceptions of the good life over others.

So far so good. Where we part company is with respect to an assumption that political liberals make at the outset of their theory. They claim—as a premise or axiom, not as an evidenced or demonstrated conclusion—that everyone living in liberal democracies has a conception of the good life that can be specified independently of liberal values and ideas. They take for granted, in other words, that everyone is liberal (or illiberal in the sense of opposing liberal tenets) *plus* something else, whether that be Christian, Buddhist, Hindu, Jewish, Muslim, utilitarian, virtue ethicist, Confucian, Daoist, Kantian, Marxist, Rastafarian, Zoroastrian, nationalist, naturalist, ecofeminist, hedonist, or whatever other doctrine or combination thereof can be imagined. People living in liberal democracies are thus said to be made up of two components that are usually and hopefully integrated with one other. *On the one hand*, you are a citizen of liberal democracy, with its attendant liberal political values and practices; *on the other hand*, you espouse a comprehensive doctrine that while likely affected by liberal values, can be independently identified and described.

I dispute this assumption. Today there is a large class of people who, if asked, would not be able to nominate a conception of the good life that would stand outside liberal values and attitudes. They are liberals, period. At this stage, of course, my claim remains no more than merely a claim, just as undemonstrated as the assertion by political liberals that everyone is made up of two components. Starting in the next chapter, I will make good on my promise to show in empirical detail how liberalism is and can be a way of life. For readers uninterested in the current state of academic political philosophy, go ahead and skip ahead to chapter 5. What you'll miss, however, is a critique of how today's leading political theory is unable to appreciate the fact that its own subject matter has become a widespread ethical (and moral, cultural, aesthetic, and spiritual) option for how people live. Returning to our bright young fish, it will become apparent that he would still have no idea how to respond to the sneering question of his elder. Despite his studies—or ironically, thanks to his studies—he cannot see what it targets: a set of ideals, values, attitudes, practices, relationships, and institutions that have become the water, the only water, in which so many of us swim.

Why does this matter? The inability of political liberals to respond to critics is fun and games when we're talking about hypothetical fish. It is less amusing when we remind ourselves that liberal institutions and values are threatened worldwide. One motivation for my book stems from a sense that liberals could do a much better job of promoting the creed. First, the global conversation about the current crisis of liberalism tends to fixate on the opponents of liberalism, and how horrible populists, nativists, and authoritarians are. Only rarely are the strengths and virtues of liberalism talked up. And when liberalism is positively defended, the reasons given are typically legal or political in nature. Politicians and journalists insist on the indispensability of such institutions as division of powers, rule of law, and individual rights. Certainly, that kind of defense is crucial. But by presenting liberalism as a way of life, I am drawing attention to a whole other set of reasons—call it "spiritual" or "existential," no matter how jittery such terms make liberals—for why liberals should care deeply about what happens to their doctrine. Political liberalism, for all of its admirable insights, makes it difficult to see liberalism in this light.

The Shaky Cathedral

When you have an inconvenient truth, it is best to state it up front and get it out of the way. Mine is that none other than John Rawls, the hero of this book, founded political liberalism, the branch of political philosophy that I contest in this chapter. But if admission is the first step, explanation is the next. In this section, we will see why Rawls felt it necessary to reformulate his theory of justice along these lines. Doing so will introduce the main claims of political liberalism and set up my critique.

We begin with the publication of Rawls's *A Theory of Justice* in 1971. As I said in chapter 2, it was hailed as a masterpiece. Readers admired its ideas and insights as well as its sophisticated technical apparatus. One early reviewer likened it to a Gothic cathedral in its simultaneous simplicity of plan and complexity of detail.[1] Of course, it attracted a great deal of commentary and critical engagement. By one count, an astonishing 2,512 books and articles were published on Rawls in the 1970s, many written by the foremost philosophers, economists, jurists, and political scientists of the day.[2] Ever a modest and generous scholar, he paid close attention and published several replies. Yet one problem especially claimed his time and attention—so much so, in fact, that he felt it necessary to substantially reformulate his theory of justice to accommodate it. Brick by brick, he dismantled the argument he had so carefully constructed, and over the course of a decade, rebuilt it into a new form. Cathedral 2.0 was published in 1993 and titled *Political Liberalism*.[3]

What was wrong with *A Theory of Justice*? The term Rawls used to criticize his earlier work is significant. He did not say it was "wrong," "false," "incorrect," "inconsistent," or any of the standard pejoratives philosophers reach for. He said it was "unrealistic."[4] Specifically, it gave an unrealistic account of how social and political stability could be secured for a society based on his principles of justice.

Let's take a step back. Through the ages, political philosophers have asked what makes people uphold the laws and principles of their society. Obviously, it wouldn't be functional for a police officer (or legionnaire, or whomever) to stand on every street corner to ensure compliance. Most citizens most of the time need to do that on their own. The question, though, is how and why. How does it come to pass that members of a society, no matter their social class or position, support its laws and

principles such that the society in question will reliably reproduce itself from one generation to the next?

Three answers have been given. The oldest and most enduring is that a society is stable when united on some shared conception of the good. A philosopher like Aristotle, theologian
like Saint Augustine, and social reformer like Jeremy Bentham
do not agree on much. But they are of a mind in thinking that a
stable and harmonious social order is achieved when citizens
cooperate to pursue a shared end—whether that be a particular
vision of human flourishing, the kingdom of God, or the greatest happiness for the greatest number. "Communities," said
Aristotle launching a thousand ships, "should have one thing
that is common and the same for all members, whether they
share in it equally or unequally."[5]

The second answer is close to the police officer scenario just
above, yet subtly and importantly different. Its most forceful
(and scandalous) presentation was given by Thomas Hobbes,
who argued that a society need not be united by any shared
purpose. Only a powerful ruler is needed to ensure individuals
pursue their own self-interest within reasonable limits. On
Hobbes's view, the main job of the sovereign—his mighty
Leviathan—is not to punish those who don't follow the rules.
The sovereign is there to ensure I am convinced that *my fellow
citizens* can be counted on to follow the rules and thus guarantee a social order where *I* won't be a chump for doing so as well.
More insurance agent than cop, the sovereign stands above
their subjects, and by threat of force, underwrites the trust citizens can rationally have in one another.

Rawls gives excellent reasons to reject both answers to the
problem of social stability. The first is unsuitable for modern
liberal democratic societies. Given that our own societies are
plural, attempts to unite them on a particular conception of the

good would be oppressive and ideological.[6] The second is a non-starter for different reasons. For all of its tough talk, its proposal is unreliable. If laws are upheld solely out of rational self-interest, free-riding and undetected breaches will become rife. On this scheme, moreover, nothing stops people (or more accurately, powerful social classes) from openly rejecting the rules if they can get away with it. "To each according to their (rational) threat advantage," as Rawls paraphrases Hobbes, is not only wicked but also a recipe for all kinds of destabilizing mischief.[7]

Where does that leave us? A third tradition has tried its hand at the riddle of social stability: the social contract theory of John Locke, Jean-Jacques Rousseau, and Immanuel Kant. As in so many things, this is Rawls's inspiration. Here a society is stable when citizens affirm shared principles of justice that maintain their society as an association of free and equal persons. The social bond is not anchored in a particular conception of the good, nor in the pursuit of mutual self-interest guaranteed by threat of force. What best keeps a society together—and what primarily does in fact keep our own liberal democratic societies together, argues Rawls—is a desire on the part of citizens to honor the constitutional principles and fundamental rights of their society and fellows. Rawls calls this desire a *sense of justice*, and defines it as a "strong and normally effective desire to act as the principles of justice require."[8]

This is one of the trickiest—and for my book, most important—parts of Rawls's thought. The question that opened this section was the following: Why do most people most of the time follow the fundamental rules of their society? At a glance and despite evident flaws, the first two answers I surveyed seem to have the upper hand. Both give clear and psychologically compelling reasons for why people voluntarily uphold the rules. In the first, it is to advance a shared good; in the second, it is to secure self-interest. No fuss, no muss. Rawls's answer, by comparison, seems vague. He says we have a "desire" to uphold the fundamental principles of right and justice of our society. "OK," we might think to ourselves, "but what does that really mean? What is a desire for justice actually a desire *for*?" It must, after all, be pretty powerful to maintain social order amid all the everyday temptations—small ones, such as things we can get away with when no one is watching—to deviate from the publicly professed principles of our society.

Rawls's answer is that we desire to be just, and hopefully act justly, because we want to live up to a certain ideal (or self-conception) we have of ourselves as just people and citizens. *That* is what a desire for justice is a desire for. And a society made up of members who see themselves as just will be as stable as any other. More so, even. For a commitment to principles of justice will be anchored in a durable and emotionally resonant source: the self-conception of its members.

This connection between one's own self-conception, principles of justice, and a desire to act on those principles may sound abstract. The hit movie *Bird Box* (2018) can serve as an example of what Rawls has in mind. If you haven't seen this apocalyptic thriller, the plot is easy to summarize. For reasons unexplained, one fine day the world is suddenly possessed by a strange force that causes anyone who looks outside (that is, sets their eyes on things that are not within contained spaces like a house or tent) to irresistibly want to kill themselves. With a setup like that, you can imagine that the characters spend a great deal of time indoors. But there comes a point in the movie when they need to venture out for supplies. A small team of volunteers, with luck, blindfolds, and a GPS, makes it to the supermarket. To their delight, the shelves are fully stocked. Things seem so good, in fact, that the cynic of the group makes the case that they should just stay and not return to the group. "We have everything we need to live. *Everything*," he emphasizes. "There is no statistical, logical, or legal argument for trying to get back there." The hero of the movie flatly refuses. "Here's an argument," she replies, "we're not assholes. And we're not staying."[9]

You may be surprised to learn that there is an academic literature on the term *asshole*.[10] Defined as someone who "transgresses while knowing that he is doing something wrong," it is in close proximity (negatively, that is) to what Rawls calls standards of right and rightful conduct.[11] "*Not* being an asshole," then, is an intelligible ideal of character and conduct—one that can serve to define who we are and want to be. Anything but abstract, it establishes firm limits as to the kind of reasons that will or will not move us. In *Bird Box*, the sorts of statistical, logical, and legal considerations that might sway the cynic cut no ice with its hero. They are incompatible with who she takes herself to be, and are immediately and decisively dismissed. (Vice versa, the cynic would scoff at the idea that virtue is its own reward, especially in an apocalypse.) As Rawls states in more sedate language, "A certain ideal is embedded in the principles of justice, and the fulfillment of desires incompatible with these principles have no value at all."[12] But substitute the phrase "a certain ideal is embedded in the principles of justice" for the rougher "not being an asshole" and we have the makings of the same argument: internalizing an ideal of rightful conduct, making it a part of our self-definition, and striving to live up to it establishes what we regard as valuable (or not), and what we are prepared to do (or not).[13]

Not being an asshole is also a stabilizing ideal. If everyone thinks like the cynic—weighing up statistical, logical, and legal pros and cons on a case-by-case basis—it makes for a volatile situation. Principles of justice don't mean much if you believe other people will abandon them when expedient. If I'm convinced that my fellow survivors wouldn't return from the supermarket, why should I? A different world, however, presents itself if everyone thinks like, and is known to think like, the hero from *Bird Box*. You can then count on others to do what is right in the knowledge that behaving unjustly would betray the sense they have of themselves. That is a strong, though not infallible, guarantee. And if I can count on others to be just, then I too can intelligently commit to that ideal and won't be a sucker for doing so. Instead of the vicious cycle of the cynic, a virtuous one becomes not only possible but probable too.

Rawls never doubted that stability was best secured when members of a society wanted to live up to an ideal of themselves as just and recognized that fellow citizens did the same. Yet there is a fundamental difference in how *A Theory of Justice* and, two decades later, *Political Liberalism* conceive of that ideal. In the former, Rawls argues we are just from a desire to live up to a certain *ethical ideal* of what it means to be a liberal *person*; in the latter, we are just out of a desire to live up to a certain *political ideal* of what it means to be a liberal *citizen*. The first ideal (of the liberal person) is comprehensive, and covers many aspects of our character and the kind of life we want to lead; the second ideal (of the liberal citizen) is limited by comparison, and concerns only how we see ourselves in our capacity as members of liberal democracy.

Rawls's argument for an ethical ideal of the person in *A Theory of Justice* reaches its crescendo in the last hundred pages. There he spreads his wings and explains why a way of life based on the principles of justice and institutions he had spent the previous four hundred pages exploring is good and desirable. I will examine his assertions in part II of this book. For now, suffice it to say that in those final sections of *A Theory of Justice*,

Rawls well and truly hustles, laying out the most expansive set of reasons this side of Plato as to why his reader should personally want to be just (that is, just in the liberal way he describes). Some pertain to the obvious benefits of living in a society that strives to be a fair system of cooperation. Yet he also presents a whole other spectrum of reasons as to why being liberal is appealing and enhances our own everyday life. He speaks of the pleasures of friendship, joy of joining all kinds of social associations, relief of open dealings with others, contentment of learning our true needs, reprieve from envy and resentment, satisfaction of aligning self-interest with morality, and even felicity of realizing our true nature as free and equal beings. The spire of Rawls's monumental *A Theory of Justice* is a hymn to a liberal way of life.

All of that might persuade Rawls's readers who already see themselves along the lines of the liberal subject he portrays. "Sign me up!" they'd exclaim. But what about those who don't? Liberal democracies include all manner of reasonable citizens who, while they affirm equal and reciprocal rights for their fellow citizens, would not recognize—and may well not want to recognize—themselves in the ideal of the liberal person Rawls depicts. If we can imagine Rawls as a traveling salesman carrying his wares from door to door, many citizens might not want the way of life on offer. "Thanks but no thanks," they would say before closing the door, "it's just not for me."

With that polite but firm refusal, Rawls's project in *A Theory of Justice* hit a wall. For what to do? Imposing an ethical ideal on a diverse citizenry is out of the question. Doing so would violate core liberal commitments, such as freedom of conscience. On the other hand, presuming that the vast majority of a diverse citizenry would, of their own desire and accord, converge on the ethical ideal of the just liberal person is, to recall Rawls's word, unrealistic. The cathedral thus had a structural flaw and could not guarantee its own stability. It could neither demand nor assume that its members would find a liberal way of life appealing. The only option was to go back to the drawing board. This time Rawls would start from a frank acknowledgment of the terrain that any solid liberal edifice must be built on: moral and religious pluralism.

In the Shadow of Political Liberalism

Depending on where you stand, a recent turn in political theory and intellectual history can seem fruitful or decadent, innovative or sclerotic. For fifty years, Rawls's writings have been scrutinized with almost Talmudic attention. With hundreds of thousands of pages written about it, you might well wonder if there is anything more to say. Hasn't all the juice been squeezed from this lemon? But in the past five years, new zest has been added: the history of Rawls studies! Before you roll your eyes, consider this. If Rawls's impact on political philosophy is as substantial as is widely believed, then a history of the reception and influence of his work is in great part the history of contemporary Anglo-American political philosophy itself.[14]

The main work on this topic is Katrina Forrester's *In the Shadow of Justice* (2019). At once generous and critical, Forrester shows, first, how Rawls developed his ideas in relation to a particular historical milieu (a midcentury moment of prosperity and optimism), and second, how those ideas were studied to a fault well after the relevance of that milieu had passed (and the United States had entered the civil strife and stagflation of the 1960s and 1970s, and then the deregulation of the 1980s and 1990s). To quote an already classic line, Forrester says that her book tells a "ghost story, in which Rawls's theory lived on as a spectral presence long after the conditions it described were gone."[15]

Whether *A Theory of Justice* is a ghost story for a philosophy of living well today is an issue to settle later (clearly my answer will be no, but it's complicated). Here, however, I propose a Forrester-style argument with respect to Rawls's more recent *Political Liberalism*. It too has profoundly shaped political philosophy. And it too was written in relation to a historical context that has since shifted. While in many respects still correct and necessary, it has also become constraining and blinkering.

Let me build my case from a deep insight by Forrester. Over and above all the concepts he invented, she says, Rawls's real legacy is to have established the "problem-space" of contemporary political philosophy—broadly speaking, the kinds of questions, topics, methods, and approaches that the mainstream of the discipline debates and pursues.[16] Problems in philosophy (and mathematics as well as the natural and social sciences) don't just exist "out there" on their own. They need to be formulated and stated—created, in a word. Indeed, the real fireworks of thinking happen when someone poses a genuinely original question that opens new lines of inquiry.[17]

Political Liberalism is a major work of political philosophy precisely because it created a substantial problem for philosophers, political scientists, and jurists. "How is it possible," asks Rawls, "for there to exist over time a just and stable society of free and equal citizens, who remain profoundly divided by reasonable religious, philosophical, and moral doctrines?"[18] Bits and pieces of this problem had been posed before. "How is it possible for there to exist over time a just and stable society?" is nearly timeless and certainly cross-cultural. "Of free and equal citizens" is an addition tacked on by generations of democratic and liberal political thinkers. But "who remain profoundly divided by reasonable religious, philosophical, and moral doctrines" is new. The inclusion of "reasonable" is why.

Never before had it been asked how citizens, who may well disagree on nearly every aspect of the good life, can come to agree—and crucially, agree for the right kind of moral reasons (which are not based on self-interest *or* controversial moral, religious, or philosophical doctrines that fellow citizens could reasonably reject)—on a shared framework for the public social world. That problem had to be invented. And if with the benefit of thirty years of hindsight it seems obvious and urgent, then all the more credit to political liberals who first discerned the real issue for plural societies.

The problem I quoted from *Political Liberalism*, a work originally delivered as lectures at Columbia University in 1980, appears in the second paragraph of the first lecture. Rawls, in other words, had barely begun to clear his throat. Yet already in that problem the entire outline of his later philosophy can be discerned. He only needed to uncover it. Granted, he had lots of uncovering to do. Nearly six hundred pages long, *Political Liberalism* is a cathedral in its own right. Still, far from merely stating a query to pursue, that single sentence contains a program of research—one that thanks to its own merits and Rawls's eminence has come to establish the primary *subject, purpose, solution,* and *limits* and *sins* of Anglo-American political philosophy for the past several decades, and is still holding strong.

Consider the italicized words of the previous sentence. The *subject* of political liberalism is front and center in the quoted problem of *Political Liberalism*: free and equal citizens divided by religious, philosophical, and moral doctrines. Given that subject, the *purpose* of political liberalism is to devise a just and stable framework for a public social world marked by pluralism. How? Well, if these citizens will never agree about what constitutes the good life, then the obvious *solution* is to take that divisive issue off the table, and focus instead on what all reasonable citizens can share and support. Political liberals, in other words, solve the problem of pluralism by drawing a bright line between two things they insist should never be confused. To one side of this line are the various moral, philosophical, and religious doctrines that citizens hold ("comprehensive doctrines," to use Rawls's term). To the other side is a fair framework of social and political institutions that must be justified to all citizens using values and ideals that are independent of these comprehensive doctrines ("a political conception of justice," to use Rawls's phrase). Finally, this bright line puts firm *limits* in place as to what political philosophy should and should not do. Specifically, liberal political philosophers should not try to derive or justify a framework for the public social world in terms of a particular religious, philosophical, or moral doctrine (doing so would be called "comprehensive liberalism" and can be considered a venal *sin*). And they certainly should not use that framework to promote or favor a particular doctrine (doing so would be called "perfectionist liberalism" and is truly a mortal *sin*).[19]

It is delicate to claim that political liberalism is the orthodoxy of Anglo-American political philosophy. Clearly, not everyone is busy commenting on Rawls, nor do most political philosophers explicitly claim the mantle of political liberalism. What I mean is that the general enterprise Rawls describes—proposing and justifying liberal norms and institutions, minding the fact of reasonable pluralism, and insisting that liberalism is not, and should not be, a philosophy of life or comprehensive worldview—is taken for granted as what contemporary political philosophy is and does. Some philosophers carry out this project in relation to the core public institutions of liberal democratic countries. Others apply it to a wide range of different topics, including international law, religion, migration, education, the environment, development, health care, parenting and childhood, and marriage. But make no mistake, political liberalism is the lingua franca of the field.[20]

LEGO People

When I teach political liberalism to undergraduate students, I bring a prop: LEGO pieces. I have two kinds with me. First, a handful of basic bricks that I've already combined into a long rectangle (roughly twenty by five by five centimeters). Second, five LEGO people purchased just after the 2014 *LEGO Movie*: a construction worker, an astronaut, Batman, a cool female figurine named Wyldstyle, and Shaquille O'Neal.

When in my lesson I need to introduce a key idea from Rawls's later work, out come the LEGO bricks. "Here," I say, holding up the rectangular structure, "is what he calls a political conception of justice." This term, I explain, refers to a set of moral values that citizens agree should inform and regulate their fundamental political and socioeconomic institutions. In a liberal democratic society, these values include tolerance, fairness, and equal freedom for all citizens, and should inform and regulate such institutions as the political constitution; the legal system of trials, property, and contracts; the system of markets and economic relations; and the family.[21]

Teaching Rawls with LEGO is not entirely gratuitous. He uses a positively LEGO-like metaphor to describe the main feature of the political conception of justice: its freestanding quality, meaning its independence from any particular moral, religious, or philosophical comprehensive doctrine. "To use a current phrase, the political conception is a *module*, an essential constituent part, that fits into and can be supported by the various reasonable comprehensive doctrines that endure in the society regulated by it."[22] Just like LEGO, the modular political conception can be clicked into and detached from the comprehensive doctrines of the citizens who support it.

Now come the LEGO people. Holding them up, I introduce them as citizens of a liberal democratic society, each of whom has a different comprehensive doctrine: a Christian (the construction worker), romantic (Batman), philosophical naturalist (the astronaut), meritocrat (Wyldstyle), and Muslim (Shaquille O'Neal). Next, this is key, I remove the hair or hat from each figure (save for Shaq, who is already bald) to reveal what every LEGO figurine has on top of their head: a small cylinder that can be connected to other pieces. Finally, I complete my extended analogy by clicking the heads of the LEGO persons (the comprehensive doctrines) into the rectangular block (the political conception) so that each figure forms a kind of column to support the overall edifice. Voilà, Cathedral 2.0.

Cathedral 2.0 is much stabler than its predecessor. Unlike *A Theory of Justice*, it does not implausibly depend on citizens adopting a liberal comprehensive doctrine (or way of life). Each citizen instead decides for themselves how the liberal political conception relates to their comprehensive doctrine. "It is left to citizens individually," Rawls states, "to settle how they think the values of the political domain are related to other values in their comprehensive doctrine. For we always assume that citizens have two views, a comprehensive and a political view; and that their overall view can be divided into two parts, suitably related."[23] Rather than the comprehensive *ethical* ideal of the person from *A Theory of Justice*, members of a liberal democratic society are said to want to live up to a much more limited *political* ideal of the citizen—informed by "the values of the political domain" Rawls mentions just above—which they personally determine how it relates to their overall comprehensive doctrine.

Political liberals make a big deal of the freestanding nature of the political conception. As they should. It is their core article of faith: a conviction that it is wrong and illiberal to justify public institutions, many of which are backed by coercive state power, with doctrines that fellow citizens could reasonably reject. Yet what political liberals only rarely make explicit is that on their model, freestandingness is a two-way street and applies to comprehensive doctrines as well. To his credit, Rawls states it up-front. "We assume," he writes in the introduction to *Political Liberalism*, "that each citizen affirms *both* a comprehensive doctrine and the [shared] political conception, somehow related."[24] And a few pages later, he says, "I assume all citizens to affirm a comprehensive doctrine to which the political conception they accept is somehow related."[25]

Picture my LEGO structure one last time. In your mind's eye, detach the construction worker from the political conception. Now do the same for all the other figures and lay them out side by side. I shudder to think what this would mean in real life; separating these doctrines from the political conception would mean they are no longer connected to or tempered by liberal values and institutions. Bracketing that worry, my point is simply that political liberals take it for granted that everyone's comprehensive doctrine is intelligible, or at least identifiable, outside its relation to a liberal political conception. From this point of view, everything is modular. The political conception can and should be detachable from all comprehensive doctrines, which for their part are themselves *more or less* detachable from the political conception.

More or less, I hedged. Political liberals do acknowledge that a liberal political conception will affect comprehensive doctrines. As Rawls observes in an important remark, "A reasonable and effective political conception may bend comprehensive doctrines toward itself, shaping them if need be from unreasonable to reasonable."[26] When connected to the political conception, then, the construction worker is a *liberalized* Christian, and Batman (thank God) is a *liberalized* romantic.[27] Yet this is as far as Rawls and his model are prepared to go. A liberal political conception can—and in a stable regime, will—inform, shape, modify, temper, and guide comprehensive doctrines. Nowhere in his later philosophy, however, does he suggest that someone can be liberal top to bottom in the sense that the values and ideals contained in the liberal political conception *are* their comprehensive doctrine, with nothing behind or beneath it. No LEGO figure is so welded to the political conception that if you were to wrench it off, it would fall apart in your hands.

Comprehensive Liberalism

Actually, one such figure may seem inseparable from a liberal political conception: what political liberals call a "comprehensive liberal." As my own notion of a liberal way of life is itself a comprehensive doctrine—and covers, as per Rawls's definition, "what is of value in life, the ideals of personal character, as well as ideals of friendship and of familial and associational relationships, and much else that is to inform our conduct, and in the limit to our life as a whole"—I need to explain how our notions of comprehensive liberalism differ.[28] The difference boils down to how political liberals and I understand the relationship, and in particular, *the direction of* the relationship between a liberal comprehensive doctrine and a liberal political conception.

Let me explain. Whenever Rawls or his followers discuss comprehensive liberalism, two great philosophers are trotted out as models: Kant and John Stuart Mill. These are mighty thinkers indeed. Both created philosophical systems that span metaphysics, epistemology, morality, psychology, and aesthetics. What makes them comprehensive liberals? Two things, according to political liberals. First, their conceptions of the good life revolve around ethical ideals—autonomy for Kant and personal freedom for Mill—that are historically, politically, and philosophically associated with liberalism. Second, in their respective political philosophies, they use those ethical ideals to design political principles and institutions for a just and decent society. What is more, they hold that those principles and institutions should openly and actively promote their ethical ideals. On this picture of comprehensive liberalism, then, a liberal political conception is generated out of a particular comprehensive doctrine. To put it in a formula, the direction of the relationship flows this way: comprehensive doctrine → liberal political conception. Or to use Rawls's term, the relation is *deductive*. "Someone who affirms Kant's doctrine," he explains, "regards that [comprehensive doctrine] as the deductive basis of the political conception and in that way continuous with it."[29]

Take the case of Mill. He looked around at his Victorian world and was immensely depressed. The romantic in him was saddened by the fact that he was surrounded by social-climbing sheep who suppressed any genuinely individual desire or ambition for fear that doing so would make them stand out in the crowd. The utilitarian in him was angered that these sheep were in turn wolves, and ready to apply social pressure to their neighbors as well as perpetuate a moral and cultural economy that benefited no one. Confronted with this bleak landscape, what did Mill do? From his utilitarian-cum-romantic worldview, he projected a liberal polity of equal rights and moral courage capable of "giving full freedom to human nature to expand itself in innumerable and conflicting dimensions."[30] This liberal genius, in other words, deduced an entire political conception out of a prior worldview and tasked it to promote his vision of the good life.

Ghost Story

Let's return to the problem that started us off. Rawls wrote *Political Liberalism* in the 1980s because his earlier theory of justice could not accommodate the fact of moral and religious pluralism. He recast his system to provide a satisfactory answer to this problem: "How is it possible for there to exist over time a just and stable society of free and equal citizens, who remain profoundly divided by reasonable religious, philosophical, and moral doctrines?"

Given this problem, it is clear why Rawls needs to presume that citizens of liberal democracies hold two distinctive views: a comprehensive doctrine about what is good and valuable in life, *and separate and separable from it*, a political conception made of values and principles for a shared liberal democratic framework. To put it another way, it is obvious why *Political Liberalism* is peopled with LEGO figures. Its purpose is to ensure that a liberal theory of justice is not tied to a specific worldview.

This aspect of political liberalism (the book and especially the strand of contemporary political philosophy based on it) is a ghost story: something that may have once been true but now lives off its own prestige and inertia. Perhaps when this theory was formulated thirty years ago, liberal values and attitudes may have been located in, and confined to, a domain called the political or public sphere. But those days are long gone. Decade by decade, year by year, and day by day, liberal ideals and sensibilities have spread to every nook and cranny of the background culture of liberal democracies. Love it or hate it, we all swim—we positively marinate—in liberal waters. And here is my critique: the firewall that political liberalism draws between comprehensive doctrines and a liberal political conception obscures this changed landscape.

With LEGO figures who can be clicked into and unclicked out of a shared political framework as its one and only subject, political liberalism has a special knack for frustrating critics and allies alike. Old fish conservatives are unsure whether political liberals are culpably innocent or diabolically clever. Can liberals really not see how pervasive their ideology has become? And allies, at least those of us inclined to identify liberalism as our own comprehensive doctrine, also have cause for irritation. For the philosophers best placed to tell us who we are not only have designed a theory that does not say, but, to rub salt into the expectation too, patiently explain why the request is beyond the remit of political philosophy.

The way political liberalism conceives of comprehensive liberalism distills what is outdated and ghostly about it. I repeat: political liberals are correct to insist that liberals of all stripes should not want or use the state to favor their doctrine. I do not object to political liberalism on normative grounds.

But the theory falters empirically. The trouble is that virtually no one today is a comprehensive liberal—more precisely, virtually no one has *come to* their comprehensive liberalism—in the way it describes. On this model, a comprehensive liberal is someone who has independently developed their own sophisticated comprehensive doctrine, and from that basis, worked out and deduced a political conception from it.[31] That may be true of certain rare geniuses. Kant did it by combining Rousseau's philosophy with Pietism; Mill did it by blending utilitarianism with romanticism. And some scholars today still attempt to generate updated liberal political conceptions from ever-evolving comprehensive doctrines.[32] But the blunt version of my objection is that 99 percent of the people who would identify as comprehensive liberals did not arrive at their doctrine in that way. The representative formula of comprehensive liberalism is no longer, as per political liberalism, comprehensive doctrine → liberal political conception. The direction has reversed: liberal political conception → comprehensive doctrine in the sense that a liberal worldview and way of life are soaked up from living in what is effectively a liberal monoculture—that is, a world in which liberal values saturate the public *and* background culture. Neither LEGO figure nor Comprehensive Liberal (with a capital C and L, as per the rare geniuses from the pages of *Political Liberalism*), we who are liberal all the way down lack adequate models to understand how we came to be who we are.[33]

A Letter from Judith Shklar

On November 10, 1986, Rawls received a letter from Shklar. She had just finished reading his H.L.A. Hart Memorial Lecture, titled "The Idea of an Overlapping Consensus," an early work from his political liberalism period. The two were dear friends, and Shklar had the courtesy to not pull punches. She opens with a bit of sugar: "Dear Jack, I have now read your Hart Lecture at least once and plan to do so again, before long. As always I am enormously impressed by the clarity of the exposition and your conceptual ingenuity." From there the letter turns critical, and in a paragraph cuts more deeply than other interlocutors could with an entire essay:

> The one issue that does puzzle me is the basic assumption on which you build your edifice: the implicit values of an actual political society. The task you then set for yourself is to draw out these intimations and make them explicit. The burden of

historical proof then becomes very heavy. You cannot evade the demand for demonstrably accurate historical evidence to show that these are indeed the latent values. How latent? How widely shared? How deeply held and by whom at what times? Remember that most of your fellow citizens just now think that the Declaration of Independence is too radical for them. And while this is a good time for the First Amendment, it is not always so. One can say that only religion is safe, because no one cares about it that much any longer, and in a way what is left is all Protestant anyhow. Finally your account of the conflicting beliefs and ideologies that can overlap may be out of date. It is not religion and even ideology that now separates us, but race, language, gut-loathing and ethnic incommunicability. Does your model fit that reality, or only one in which tolerance of creedal diversity was in question? My point is simple. If you base your case on history, then contemporary history, which is what the best social science is, must provide you with a far less speculative ground to start from. Those latent values have to be accounted for every bit as much as more overt ones.[34]

There is a feast of details for those who wish: the dismissal of religion as something no one cares about, how it has all become Protestantism anyway, that the best social science is contemporary history, and what ethnic incommunicability means. But stepping back, Shklar's letter makes two big criticisms. The first is substantive: Rawls is far too sanguine in thinking that most citizens of liberal democracies do, in fact, support its core values. Let's put this criticism to the side. Because methodologically, Shklar raises a more fundamental objection: Where is the proof for anything Rawls asserts? Liberal values, he assumes, are embedded in the public culture of mature democracies.

That, however, is a historical claim to be demonstrated with empirical evidence. The trouble is, Rawls offers little to none. And without such proof, we have no way of knowing whether the edifice of political liberalism is just another cathedral in the sky.

Perhaps both thinkers are right. Rawls, I believe, is correct that liberal values are anchored in the public culture and self-conception of citizens of mature liberal democracies. And Shklar is certainly correct that he doesn't empirically demonstrate it or even seem to feel the need to. Her objection must be reckoned with—particularly for the sake of my own argument, for I have extended Rawls's method. He locates liberal values in the public culture of liberal democracy, whereas I claim that they have spread to our background culture as well. Liberalism, to recall my refrain, is the water we swim in. To be convincing, however, I need to do what Rawls didn't and make good on the burden of proof. The next two chapters, which I regard as the heart of the book, are my attempt to do so.

5

Six Ways Liberalism Shapes
Us (and Vice Versa)

IT IS RARE for a senior professor to be fired from their job. University administrators typically find it easier to eliminate an entire department, redeploy its staff elsewhere in the institution, and then claim to lack a suitable new position for the professor in question. Yet something similar happened just a few years after I arrived at the University of Sydney.

Professor Barry Spurr, chair of poetry and poetics, was effectively forced to resign in October 2014, two months after recent emails he had sent to friends and colleagues were leaked. In those emails, he describes First Nations Australians as "human rubbish tips," refers to Nelson Mandela as a "darky," and laments that "one day the Western world will wake up, when the Mussies and the chinky-poos have taken over." Spurr defended himself by claiming that these emails were not to be taken seriously and part of a "whimsical game" in which colleagues tried to one-up each other with extreme statements. The university didn't buy it. Two weeks after the emails were leaked, and on the back of public protests organized by staff and students, Spurr was placed on suspension. Shortly thereafter, he was gone for good.[1]

Why was Spurr forced to leave? His hateful statements, obviously. But we can be more precise. He was gotten rid of, I want to say, because he swore.

Liberal Outrage: Swear Words

This chapter illustrates in greater depth my claim that liberalism is the water we swim in. The idea is that far from being confined to the public or political sphere, liberal values, ideals, sensibilities, and practices have taken over the background culture of contemporary liberal democratic societies. So ubiquitous is liberalism that it has performed that special trick of disappearance achieved only by omnipresence: to have become invisible by infiltrating everything.

A quick test will show what I mean. When you read about Spurr's emails, did you think to yourself, "Wow, what a piece of shit"? If so, I think you're a liberal (whether you're nothing but liberal is only for you to decide). Such a reaction, so natural and seemingly spontaneous, is the product of a long acculturation, two centuries in the making, and so successful as to be mistaken for plain decency. Yet there is nothing plain about it, and in this chapter I call attention to aspects of everyday life that while seemingly remote from anything to do with liberalism, can, with just a little effort, be shown to be unimaginable without it.

Sometimes the impact of liberalism on our sense of self is straightforward. This section on swear words is a case in point: liberal values directly inform our moral sensibility. Sometimes, however, the influence of liberalism is more diffuse and unpredictable. Each section of this chapter highlights a different way that liberalism shapes us and uses a cultural artifact as a focal point: a high five between tyrants to uncover what shocks us; a TV show to reveal the questions we consider meaningful; a joke to express what we find funny; work and parenting to put a world of practices on display; and the most popular genre of pornography to expose new deformations of the self. My strategy in this chapter is akin to a sweep of the hand, a gesture to everything around us, as if to suggest, "Look, don't you see it too? Nothing in this shared culture of ours that each of us, like it or not, navigates on a minute-to-minute basis would make the least bit of sense were we not already steeped in liberal notions." Perhaps you'll dispute certain examples. Here or there, the connection to liberalism may seem tenuous. But if I convey an overall impression of how extensively liberalism informs our shared mainstream background culture (and thus our day-to-day lives), I will have met my goal.

As you'll soon discover, I persistently use a set of words that may seem problematic: *we*, *us*, and *you*, as if I presume to know who you are, where you come from, and what you care about. I also draw on my own reactions and experiences to represent what we collectively think and feel. This may strike readers as out of step with the times, not to mention with a contemporary strand of liberalism, in which claims are so often prefaced by long identifier strings ("as a white, straight, cisgendered, middle-class male, I think that . . ."). What gives *me* the right to speak for *you*? Nothing, of course. But remember what I am out to accomplish: to excavate and describe a shared sensibility underpinned by liberalism. If I hold myself out as exemplary and speak in the first-person plural, it is not because I take myself to be special or authoritative. To the extent that *I* am able to represent *you*, it is only because, whatever our differences, *we* have been raised in and drilled by the same mainstream—or hegemonic, if you prefer—moral, political, and cultural regime.[2]

I begin with low-hanging fruit: the nature of swear words today. Nothing illustrates the attunement of liberals quite like it. The clever title of an excellent book can get us started: Melissa Mohr's *Holy Sh*t: A Brief History of Swearing* (2013). With two words, she summarizes the long history of unsayable words in Western civilization: "Over the centuries these two spheres of the unsayable—the religious and the sexual/excremental, the Holy and the Shit, if you will—have given rise to all the other 'four-letter words' with which we swear. A history of swearing is a history of their interaction and interplay."[3]

Using abnormal and pathological phenomena to investigate what is normal and healthy is a time-honored method in anthropology, sociology, biology, and medicine. So too in linguistics and cultural history: the words a society labels taboo shed light on what it considers sacrosanct. They are symptoms of what we value, and their history reveals great transformations about what is violable and inviolable. The worst words in Roman civilization, for example, were about sexual passivity. The big three are getting fucked (*futuo*), being a cunt (*cunnus*, in the sense of a receiving sexual organ), and being a sissy/bottom (*cinaedus*, in the sense of the receiving partner in male-on-male sex). What does this show? That, above all else, Rome valued the ideal of the free, active, dominating, self-controlled male citizen. Fast-forward to the Middle Ages where religion is supreme and everything changes. Obscenities are freely used, even in religious texts and services. But religious oaths and curses—"swear words" to bind oneself and call on God to witness that binding—are highly charged and even dangerous. Badly or falsely done, an oath threatens yourself and your community, and even injures God.[4]

Where do we stand now? Until recently, so-called Western culture remained caught in a Victorian era dominated by worries over etiquette, decorum, and taboos about the body. When in a 1972 stand-up routine, George Carlin famously rattled off the seven words that couldn't be said on TV—shit, piss, fuck, cunt, cocksucker, motherfucker, and tits—he voiced a cultural consensus whose time was nearly up.[5] By the second decade of the twenty-first century, these are no longer our swear words, and they have lost their power to shock and incense most people. Spurr wasn't fired for words like *shit* or *fuck* (or alternatively, *goddamn* or *Jesus Christ*). Most of my colleagues would be out of a job were that the case. He used qualitatively different language: slurs, derogations, and racial and sexual epithets.

Mohr is aware that the reign of holy and shit is at an end. Yet she does not fully appreciate the extent of the shift, nor identify its cause. "The twentieth century," she observes, "witnessed the beginning of sexual obscenity's decline and the rise of a new kind of obscenity, racial epithets, which are now some of the most taboo words in the English language."[6] Certainly, racial epithets are part of the picture, and the fact that I need to write "the N-word" expresses this. Still, the reality is that slurs of all kinds are our new profanity: words that essentialize and convey contempt for subgroups of people, whether in terms of race (chink, spic, cracker), mental acuity (retard), physical disability (cripple, spazz), sexual orientation (faggot, dyke), gender (bitch, cunt), and age (even a tame phrase like "OK boomer" starts to creep into this category). These words are designed to demean and dismiss. As Steven Pinker says with respect to the N-word, which can be adapted to other slurs I listed above, "to hear [the N-word] is to try on, however briefly, the thought that there is something contemptible about African Americans, and thus to be complicit in a community that standardized that by putting it into a word."[7]

Or for an insider's account of how such terms come to be internalized and devastate one's sense of self-worth (in this case, around sexuality and disability), look no further than the most famous stand-up comedy routine of recent years—one that puts the entire genre into question: Hannah Gadsby's *Nanette* (2018). Gadsby was born and bred in Tasmania, Australia's rural southern island state. In the first part of her set, she jokes about growing up lesbian in a place where she was routinely mistaken for a man. In the second part, she explains how she made her name as a comic by subverting the slurs she was attacked with. All of this builds to the third part, though, where she states her need to quit the game. "I built a career out self-deprecating humor," she says. "I don't want to do that anymore. Because do you understand what self-deprecation means when it comes from somebody who already exists in the margins? It's not humility. It's humiliation. I put myself down in order to speak, in order to seek permission to speak. And I will simply not do that anymore."[8] This is the terrible power of slurs: to make someone hate themselves.

What accounts for the transformation of our swear words? Not democracy. The United States was an apartheid democracy—an illiberal democracy—from its founding until the civil rights era and slurs flourished. Things started to change only quite recently. Here is when linguist and cultural critic John McWhorter locates the shift: "[It] occurred as Generation X, born from about 1965 to 1980, came of age. These were the first Americans raised in the post–civil rights era. To Generation X, legalized segregation was a bygone barbarism, and overt racist attitudes were ridiculed and socially punished in general society. Racism continued to exist, of course, in endless manifestations, but it became 'complicated'—something to hide, to dissemble about, and among at least an enlightened cohort, something to check oneself for and call out in others, to a degree unknown in perhaps any society until then."[9]

The post–civil rights era is, properly speaking, the liberal era of US politics and culture. It is when the freedom, integrity, and especially self-respect of *all* citizens became a matter, *the* matter, of public concern. John Rawls is clear about this. Self-respect is the single most important good that liberal democracies must strive to ensure for all of their members. Without a sense of our own value and confidence that our ends are worth pursuing, nothing seems worth doing.[10] For that reason, a just liberal polity makes preserving the conditions for citizens to acquire and maintain a healthy sense of self-respect its number one priority.

A slur is a missile aimed at self-respect. It diminishes a person's value, dismisses their goals, and undermines their confidence. Slurs, in short, attack the fundamental liberal commitment to guarantee that in a society that sees itself as a fair system of cooperation, every citizen must be able to acquire and maintain a strong sense of their own worth. And so if you condemn slurs no matter who they are aimed at (that is, your indignation is not limited to your in-group), and if you are provoked by them in a way no other word has the power to do, then you are liberal in at least this respect. What else could account for your visceral spark of anger, your flush of outrage? Liberalism has a hold on you. Perhaps a deep one. Research shows that swearing, both giving and receiving, activates a different region of our brain than almost any other function of language. Swear words erupt, McWhorter tells us, "from the more emotional, impulsive parts of the brain, more squawks than labels."[11] When critics attack liberalism for being too "cerebral," this is not what they have in mind. But liberalism has wormed its way into our brain and changed what lights it up.

Liberal Shock: A High Five between Tyrants

Liberalism has also gotten under our skin. I am someone who is rarely shocked. Disappointed by the world? Often. Disgusted? Sometimes. But shocked? Almost never. Recently, however, I was. The occasion was a ten-second clip of Saudi crown prince Mohammed bin Salman and Russian president Vladimir Putin flashing big smiles and high-fiving before a 2018 meeting at the G20 summit in Argentina. They were celebrating two recent assassinations that everyone suspected they had ordered: of *Washington Post* journalist Jamal Khashoggi (murdered and dismembered in the Saudi consulate in Istanbul) and the former Russian spy Sergei Skripal and his daughter in London (poisoned by perfume, though they survived the attack). What shocked me wasn't the deeds themselves. Tyrants will tyrannize. It was the openness and publicity of the celebration. This was no fist bump behind closed doors; it was jocularity for the cameras. Cruelty took a bow on the international stage.[12]

Liberalism has a long-standing relation to the prevention of cruelty. In *Ordinary Vices* (1984)—a desert island book of mine, and the text I recommend to students who want to take a deeper dive into political theory—Judith Shklar locates the origin of liberalism in a particular moral sensibility: hatred of cruelty, understood as the infliction of pain on the weak by the strong for the purpose of fear and intimidation. Why is cruelty so wrong? Because it destroys freedom and unseats judgment, which is especially intolerable for liberals, who value agency and self-determination so highly. No one can think or act reasonably in a climate of fear. That is why forerunners of liberalism (particularly Montesquieu and the Federalists) took it upon themselves to design political and legal systems to hinder cruelty and mitigate fear: "To put cruelty first is not the same thing as just objecting to it intensely. . . . Justice [for liberals] itself is only a web of legal arrangements required to keep cruelty in check, especially by those who have most of the instruments of intimidation closest at hand."[13]

Bin Salman and Putin's high five slapped this tradition in the face. They signaled not just that they would kill their opponents and critics but also that going forward, they could do so openly and with impunity. Cruelty was back as a publicly avowed principle and technique. If that shocks rather than merely depresses you, this reaction too is a liberal inheritance. We liberals thought the world—or at least its public face, the tribute of hypocrisy that vice pays to virtue—was one way, but it turned out to be another.

I am reminded of a similar episode. At a 2015 rally, Donald Trump infamously mocked *New York Times* reporter Serge Kovaleski, who suffers from a congenital condition. Many people, critics and allies, were not surprised. That's just Trump being Trump. Yet it did shock one observer. When Meryl Streep accepted her Lifetime Achievement Award at the 2017 Golden Globes, she said this in her speech: "There was one performance this year that stunned me. It sank its hook in my heart. Not because it was good. There was nothing good about it. But it was effective and it did its job. It made its intended audience laugh and show their teeth. It was that moment when the person asking to sit in the most respected seat in our country imitated a disabled reporter, someone he outranked in privilege, power, and the capacity to fight back. It kind of broke my heart when I saw it."[14] This is a liberal reaction, unthinkable—unfeelable— without a vast network of institutions and mores in place to protect the weak from the predations of their political superiors.

Liberal Questions: *The Good Place*

The common theme of our discussion of swear words and public cruelty is that what truly outrages liberals are harms people do to one another. Ensconced as we are in this sensibility, it can be difficult to notice how new and radical it is. Here again

Shklar is helpful. She explains why a liberal morality that abhors cruelty is such a departure from tradition and religion.

> To put cruelty first is to disregard the idea of sin as it is understood by revealed religion. Sins are transgressions of a divine rule and offenses against God; pride—the rejection of God—must always be the worst one, which gives rise to all the others. However, cruelty—the willful inflicting of physical pain on a weaker being in order to cause anguish and fear—is a wrong done entirely to *another creature*. When it is marked as the supreme evil it is judged so in and of itself, and not because it signifies a denial of God or any other higher norms. It is a judgment made from within the world in which cruelty occurs as part of our normal private life and our daily public practices. By putting it unconditionally first, with nothing above us to excuse or to forgive acts of cruelty, one closes off any appeal to any order other than that of actuality.[15]

What we have here is the horizontalization of morality. Sin, which offends a Being on a different (vertical) plane of existence, diminishes in importance; what starts to really matter are temporal (horizontal, or "mundane," in the sense of worldly) interpersonal harms. This does not mean that the forerunners of liberalism were irreligious. It is possible to argue, as Locke did, for example, that harming other people (or even ourselves) is wrong because we are the property of God, created equal, and not free to destroy what does not belong to us. Yet—and here I compress a long and complicated history—as time goes by, and religion separates (is "disestablished") from law and politics, retreats to the private sphere, and is made increasingly marginal to popular culture, more and more does Shklar's statement become a truism. Cruelty and harm, along with what she calls "ordinary vices," done to others is wrong in and of itself.

Once this happens, many things change. When morality sheds (or just plain forgets) its vertical dimension, being a good person comes to mean not harming others. Being a great person means doing nice things for them as well. That's all there is to it: a radically horizontal vision of good, evil, moral relationship, virtue, decency, depravity, excellence, and flourishing. True, this process took a long time to come into its own. Michel de Montaigne proclaimed his hatred of cruelty nearly five hundred years ago. Yet this moral sensibility has been making its way through Western culture ever since, and only just recently, reached an apotheosis in the Netflix sitcom *The Good Place*.

Bear with me. *The Good Place* is the rarest of things: a television show that makes moral philosophy cool and popular. We've met its creator and showrunner before: Michael Schur, who cocreated *Parks and Recreation*. The fifty-three episodes of *The Good Place* aired from 2016 to 2020, and enjoyed commercial and critical success. Ever a prickly bunch when it comes to popularization, even academics praised the show for presenting sophisticated moral theories in fun, entertaining, and emotionally compelling ways.[16]

The premise of *The Good Place* is that a woman dies and arrives in heaven (aka, the good place). This afterlife is nondenominational and reserved for only the very best people. The twist? She is not a good person and quickly realizes she doesn't belong there. On being introduced to her soulmate—himself a recently deceased moral philosopher—she comes up with a plan for him to teach her how to become good.

The Good Place is an exemplary liberal artifact for what it says, and crucially, what it does not say. Consider the criteria for admission into the heaven of *The Good Place*. To get in, you had to have been a top "point earner" during life on earth. Certain acts accrue positive points, and others negative points. The show never specifies the precise mechanics. It doesn't provide a comprehensive table of good or bad acts, spell out principles of evaluation, or indicate what point total is required. But in the background of one of its first scenes, on-screen for only a few seconds, the viewer glimpses a sample list of good and bad acts, along with the point uptake for each.

[Good acts:] Sing to a child (+0.50); end slavery (+814292.09); fix broken tricycle for child who loves tricycles (+6.59); remember sister's birthday (+15.02); step carefully over flower bed (+2.09); save a child from drowning (+1202.33); pet a lamb (+0.89); plant baobab tree in Madagascar (+9.40); hug sad friend (+4.98); purify water source (village): pop>250 (+271.82); remain loyal to Cleveland Browns (+53.83); maintain composure in line at water park in Houston (+58.40); politely tolerate stranger recounting *New Yorker* article at cocktail party (+12.19).

[Bad acts:] Fail to disclose camel illness when selling camel (−22.22); commit genocide (−433488.07); harassment (sexual) (−731.26); be commissioner of professional football league (American) (−824.55); steal copper wiring from decommissioned military base (−16); poison a river (−4010.55); rev a motorcycle (−64.49); disturb coral reef with flipper (−53.83); root for New York Yankees (−107.09); stiff a waitress (−6.83); blow nose by pressing one nostril down and exhaling (−1.44); buy a trashy magazine (−0.75); use the term "bro-code" (−8.20); use "Facebook" as verb (−5.55); overstate personal connection to tragedy that has nothing to do with you (−43.79); ruin opera with boorish behavior (−90.99); tell a woman to "smile" (−54).[17]

There is much here to distract a philosopher. The weighting of acts, for example. Is ending slavery (+814292.09) really twice as good as committing genocide (−433488.07) is bad? There is the issue of quantitative commensurability: What sense does it make to say that fixing 184 tricycles (+6.59 each) is morally equivalent to saving 1 drowning child (+1202.33)? And what about intentions—do they count for nothing? Staying on track, however, the point to emphasize is that the moral imagination represented by this list conforms exactly to Shklar's theory that the only thing that matters is the good or harm we do to other finite beings. Apostasy and blasphemy carry no negative points; boorishness and meanness do. Being a good or bad person according to *The Good Place* is entirely a matter of how well or poorly, humanely or instrumentally, decorously or grossly, and generously or cheaply we treat our fellow creatures.

We now arrive at the crucial issue of what the show leaves out and does not talk about: deep religious and metaphysical questions. Imagine that, freshly deceased, you arrive in the good place. Presented with a list of good and bad acts of this kind, you might have a few questions. Who came up with it? Why was it created? Come to think of it, why was *I* created? Who or what made the cosmos, earth, the good and bad places, the humans in them, and the angels and demons who administer it? Not once—literally never—are questions of this kind raised in *The Good Place*. I do not intend this as a criticism of the show, as if to suggest it suffers from a glaring oversight. To the contrary, its writers and performers have created a world where the absence of such questions feels natural (or otherwise put, seems remarkable only on reflection). It is a triumph of sorts: a postmetaphysical show set in the afterlife! Traditionally deep questions are not so much repressed as not on the map to begin with. This universe, along with its humor, pathos, charm, and relatability, starts and finishes with the question of how we should treat one another.

This aspect of a liberal worldview and way of life confounds conservative and religious critics. Can it really be the case, they half wonder and half scoff, that the "big questions" that have gripped the human imagination since the dawn of time have ceased to be interesting? "Much of the secular intelligentsia seems content with a basic incoherence in its worldview," states Ross Douthat, opinion columnist for the *New York Times*. "[They seem] content with an agnosticism that treats the essential questions about the nature of the universe and the destiny of man with a weary 'Who's to say?' sort of shrug."[18]

That sounds about right. Sure, we liberals have our wobbles. A tragedy or sudden illness may for a time lead us to wonder about cosmic justice or the endurance of the soul. We're only human, not to mention distant yet still literate ancestors of those deeper comprehensive doctrines. But most of the time such matters are not live for us. For good reason: religious and metaphysical questions are not encoded into a liberal political conception, or the background culture it inspires. The source of a liberal way of life, in other words, passes over such questions in silence. Consequently, so do we. We have not been taught to ask them. Yet neither are we convinced that we need to. An atheist—someone whose comprehensive doctrine denies transcendence and attacks religion—vigorously shakes their head when asked about immortality or providence. We liberals merely shrug, indifferent and unconcerned.

What do we care about? When we are introduced to Eleanor Shellstrop, the hero of *The Good Place*, she is a train wreck of a person. Her motto is "I don't owe you anything, you don't owe me anything," and appropriately, she dies on earth while shopping for Lonely Gal Margarita Mix for One. The moral arc of the show consists of Eleanor unlearning this worldview in the afterlife. Like *Parks and Recreation*, *The Good Place* wears its

liberalism on its sleeve. A key text it returns to time and again—
as both doctrine and prop—is T. M. Scanlon's now-classical
work of liberal theory, *What We Owe to Each Other* (1998). Schur
goes so far as to identify it as the "spine" of the show.[19] Scanlon,
like his teacher Rawls, is a contractualist thinker who argues that
moral life consists of abiding by principles no one can reasonably reject. That may strike some people as arid and abstract.
Not Schur; he grasps its human and even redemptive power. His
remarks during a panel discussion on *The Good Place* hosted by
the University of Notre Dame are worth citing at length:

> The only thing you can actually count on is that there are
> other people around you, the only joy you can be sure you
> can get is by embracing human relationships with other
> people, trying to make them as good as you can, trying to
> treat people with dignity and respect, hoping that they
> do the same for you. That's the best we can do, if you take into
> account what is knowable.
>
> Theologians would disagree with me, and they would say,
> "You don't do this for other people, you do it for Something
> else [here Schur points upward, as if to God above], and
> other people are the beneficiaries of this." . . . I'm going to
> find some meaning not from *That* [Schur points upward
> again] but from *this* [Schur points around to his panelists and
> the audience]. That, in essence, is what contractualism is to
> me. It is in essence what the show has become: an argument
> for humanism, an argument for the respect that we should
> pay to the idea that we have to interact with other people,
> and what's the best way to do that.[20]

Schur says "contractualism" and "humanism," but he should
have used a word that is broader than the former and narrower
than the latter: liberalism. For the question he poses, and the

one that unites all of his work, is the one liberals have always asked: How can we live well and generously in this world? This question and its horizon is all we have. Lucky for us, it is also all that we want.

Liberal Humor: A Joke by Dave Chappelle

All of this makes liberals seem awfully high-minded: we pour our hearts and souls into treating each other with dignity and respect, and in so doing, become our best self. Maybe that's true, sometimes, on our best days. But it is the least interesting aspect of what I'm trying to say. The real point is that the horizontal ethics I have described—with its liberal ideas in tow, including society as a fair system of cooperation, each person as owed dignity and respect, and individuals as free to live their lives within reasonable limits—sucks up all the oxygen of public conversation and popular culture. Whether these ideas are accepted or rejected, earnestly claimed or ironically played with, we talk and think about little else.

Comedy is an excellent site to consider my claim. In truth, it's the perfect site as comedy is unrivaled when it comes to revealing the tacit expectations of our moral order—"the banana peel in the coal mine," Jon Stewart calls it.[21] And what happens when we look for even five minutes at any top performer (as judged by the number of YouTube views or Netflix specials)? Nearly every joke presupposes or riffs off liberal ideas. I am not just talking about political satirists such as Stephen Colbert or Sacha Baron Cohen who mock the cruelty and hypocrisy of officials. They are only the most explicit. For the bread and butter of comedy today is of a kind: observations on how the great themes of horizontal ethics—including identity, belonging, sexuality, romance, friendship, parenting, aging, illness, violence, work, wealth, and respect and disrespect—play out, in ways hilarious and tragic, within the context of a society that professes (yet fails) to be a fair system of cooperation, and by individuals, like you and me, who aspire to be free and generous (yet know deep down that in so many ways we are not).

Care for an example? Here is a joke that plays with liberalism in every phrase. It is by a comic many consider the greatest of all time, Dave Chappelle. Be warned, it is lewd. To save myself embarrassment, let me state that I have not picked it to be edgy. I picked it to be pedantic. I will break it into two parts.

I had a friend from high school. Now, in high school, this guy was a thug, he was a fucking dope-boy, he did it all. He's a wild dude, people used to be very scared of him. And then after high school, word on the street was he had come out the closet. I personally didn't believe it. I bring him up because last year, he calls me out of the blue, like "Yo, what's up man? I got your number from so and so. I heard that you gonna be in New York doing a show. Can I get some tickets?" I said, "Fuck yeah, get some tickets, man. How you been?" . . . I was about to hang up and couldn't resist it, I was just like, "Hey nigga, I heard you was gay. What's going on with that?" And I wish I didn't ask. Cause he sounded like he was dying to talk about that shit, and he had a long story about it. And it's not that I didn't care; but I was, you know, I don't like talking on the phone, I was watching TV at the same time, so I wasn't really paying attention like I should. But I was trying to sound supportive. I didn't really know what to do, so I was just mumbling shit throughout this conversation, and I'd just be like, "You know, nigga, you gay man, you just gay." This went on for a while, then finally I had to say something definitive to get him off the phone, and I was like . . .

Let's pause here. The "liberal" part of this bit so far isn't that Chappelle's old friend, despite his rowdy ways, came out as gay. That's just stage setting. The humor lies in how Chappelle handles himself. First, as someone who assumes, more or less correctly, that nowadays it is socially acceptable to ask a distant acquaintance point-blank about his sexuality. And then as someone who stupidly forgets that there is more to this conversation than his own prurient curiosity. That's the joke so far: Chappelle should have known that asking this particular person, with his particular past, about being gay would elicit a more than perfunctory response. But he didn't stop to think, and is now caught feeling bored and impatient with a conversation that he himself initiated about deeply personal issues of identity and authenticity. The joke, to put it leadenly, is to have claimed a liberal privilege (asking about a friend's sexuality) without acknowledging its corresponding duty (listening to him). Chappelle continues,

And I was like, "Hey man, you know what? Don't let people get you down, alright. And the next time someone tries to make you feel bad about yourself, just remember 'Everybody fucks funny to somebody.'" He didn't like that shit. He's like, "What the fuck does that mean? You saying I fuck funny, motherfucker?" I said, "Nah. That's not what I'm saying. I'm saying everybody's different." He said, "You didn't say 'different,' nigga, you said 'funny.' What's so fucking funny about the way I fuck?!" And I said, "Hey man, I fuck feet." He said, "What?" Oh this is not a joke ladies and gentlemen, I get women to squeeze their feet together like this [here Chappelle makes a diamond shape with his hands] and I fuck 'em, right in that little space in their feet. But you can't build a community behind that shit. There's no flag for us. That shit made him laugh.[22]

A liberal platitude, often repeated yet seldom believed, is that all difference is good difference. How you practice your religion, how you raise your kids, or how you have sex is as worthy, excellent, and beautiful as the way I do—and it is on this basis of mutual recognition that rights and respect for our choices are built.[23] Chappelle runs in the opposite direction to get to the same destination. Like a good liberal, he embraces moral perspectivism: the idea that claims of value and normalcy depend on a person's perspective. But he flips it. Everyone is *abnormal*— "funny"—to someone else. Particularly when it comes to sex, all of us are amused and a little grossed out by each other—and it is on this basis of mutual opacity that rights and respect for our choices is built. Never before has the phrase "hey man, I fuck feet" been uttered in a spirit of pragmatism and grace, but there it is. Homosexuality is weird, just as heterosexuality is, and so is a foot fetish, as are whatever ways you and I have sex, and we can all laugh and carry on in shared absurdity.[24] Chappelle's joke is a lesson, a homily as to how liberal pluralism might work in the real world. It is also a microcosm, one to test for yourself with any popular clip on YouTube, of the state of comedy today. Liberalism is the backdrop, and frequently the direct object, for what we laugh at, with, and about.

Liberal Practices: Life in the Meritocracy

My examples of liberal waters have so far been based on the same model: a signature liberal idea finds expression in this or that part of our background culture. To recap, slurs have become our swear words thanks to a liberal concern for self-respect; public cruelty is shocking because it instills a climate of fear that debilitates freedom; horizontal liberal values shift the kinds of deep questions that occupy us; and liberal truisms become the raw material for what makes us laugh. This list is not in the least exhaustive. If liberalism is omnipresent, there are countless illustrations.

Yet usually the ways liberalism impacts our background culture are messier than what I have covered. Of particular significance are instances when liberalism links up with a different ideology or social system to make a surprising, frequently illiberal hybrid. Neoliberalism is the best known, and critics have examined its fusion of liberal and capitalist values.[25] Another is contemporary populism, which loudly and sincerely draws on the notion of society as a fair system of cooperation for its members, and *only* its members, to urge rigidly closed borders and strong nationalism.[26] The next chapter explores such hybrids with the concept of *liberaldom*—a word I use to describe a world, such as our own, where liberal values are publicly and personally professed, yet that is manifestly illiberal in so many ways (that is, unfree, unfair, and ungenerous).

To prepare for this discussion, the present chapter concludes with two extended examples of how liberalism can go awry in the sense of sustaining illiberal (and frankly, depressing and dark) parts of our background culture. That these are murky and treacherous waters is no reason to look away. We need to be honest about how compromised our liberal democracies are. We also need to reckon with how personally compromised we are as liberal subjects. As we will see in the next chapter, half the tragedy of liberaldom is that in separating us from our own values—and worse, teaching us to ignore or even positively desire that separation—we liberals deny ourselves the gifts and felicities that our own way of life affords. Liberaldom is the ethical equivalent for liberals of shooting ourselves in the foot.

My next examples preview how that happens. Both concern the relation between liberalism and meritocracy. Meritocracy is the idea that political power, social prestige, and economic wealth should be vested in individuals strictly based on their talent, effort, and achievement. Going by recent academic literature, this notion seems to have fallen on hard times. Several excellent books have attacked meritocracy for entrenching social and economic inequality, destabilizing politics, and making everyone caught up in its machinations (which is effectively every single person in modern societies) anxious and smug, or else dejected and humiliated.[27] Still, there is no denying that its hold over us remains powerful. A good indicator is that alternative schemes to distribute political, social, and economic advantage seem barbaric and inefficient. Should family or breeding determine who gets what? How about race or caste? No, we recoil; that's wrong and crazy. Talent, effort, and achievement must be our standard. Only that way will distributions of power, prestige, and wealth be rational and efficient (the best rise to the top), freedom and responsibility be vindicated (our fate is in our own hands), and inequalities be just (we get what we deserve).

What does meritocracy owe to liberalism? Its condition of existence, for starters. A restricted type of meritocracy may be possible in illiberal societies; for instance, a political (see ancient Greece), bureaucratic (see ancient and contemporary China), or mercantile (see medieval Europe) elite that admits members only from certain strata of society. But full-fledged meritocracy, where *anyone* can rise or fall, requires equal rights and real equality of opportunity. These are uniquely liberal ideas and institutions, and however much meritocracy ends up derailing liberalism, it can only grow on that soil.

Meritocracy owes another crucial debt to liberalism: its notion of selfhood. Meritocracy's motto—"you can make it if you try"—depends on a prior liberal principle: that individuals are not defined by their social ascriptions (such as race, sex, class, or religion), and are free to formulate and pursue their own interests and conception of the good.[28] True, that principle need not necessarily lead us to pour our time and energy into personal achievement and social climbing. But as Alexis de Tocqueville observed long ago, it certainly incentivizes it. When class and background no longer ensure wealth and social standing, the preponderant passion of liberal democracy—"the most imperious of all needs"—is not to sink in the world.[29] And so begins the race and thus are lives spent. Here is how Daniel Markovits portrays the contemporary meritocrat in his extraordinary *The Meritocracy Trap* (2019):

> People who are required to measure up from preschool through retirement become submerged in the effort. They become constituted by their achievements, so that eliteness goes from being something that a person enjoys to being everything he is. In a mature meritocracy, schools and jobs dominate elite life so immersively that they leave no self over apart from status. An investment banker, enrolled as a two-year-old in the Episcopal School and then passed on to Dalton, Princeton, Morgan Stanley, Harvard Business School, and finally to Goldman Sachs (where he spends his income on sending his children to the schools that he once attended), becomes this résumé, in the minds of others and even in his own imagination.[30]

This passage is demoralizing for so many reasons. With respect to social justice and dream hoarding, take the parenthetical comment near the end about how our übermeritocrat will confer on his children every advantage he has had, thereby securing dynastic succession of power, prestige, and wealth. The outcomes are devastating. In the United States, by the age of eighteen a child from a rich family will have had five thousand more contact hours with parents and enrichment activities than a child from a poor family (and the latter will have had eight thousand more hours of screen time). In terms of dollar value, the investments made to develop human capital in a rich household amount to a traditional inheritance of ten million dollars per child. Finally, almost unbelievably, the academic gap between rich and poor students now exceeds the gap between white and Black students in 1954, the year in which the Supreme Court declared racially segregated educational facilities unconstitutional. Economic inequality today generates more educational inequality than US apartheid did.[31] The *MIT Technology Review* claims that for fifty dollars, it will soon be possible to purchase a DNA test to predict academic prospects.[32] Truth is, a zip code already provides this information. It would be unfair to baldly claim that rampant inequality is the house that liberalism built. Yet it would be disingenuous to deny its hand in it. Compounded over time, unregulated equality of opportunity entrenches vast inequalities. Liberal freedoms have paved the road to injustice.

There is another aspect of this passage to consider: the sad, hectic life of the meritocrat himself. Cry me a river, you might retort. Poor Mr. Meritocrat, having to go from Dalton to Princeton to fabulous wealth in finance. Still, every moment of his waking life has and will be arranged as an unending tournament. This affects his self-conception: he sees himself as an asset to invest in. It affects his relationships: other people, from his coworkers to his spouse, are investors in the venture that is him (and he in theirs). Most of all, it affects his practices: every stage of life is organized by intensive training and labor in elite institutions, and tasks and challenges likely not chosen by him, to the point that his lived reality and curriculum vitae blend into one. And this, I suspect, is something we've all tasted. If you've been helicopter parented to within an inch of your life; if you've ever wondered whether you have real talent or are just an excellent sheep; if your sense of self-worth is worryingly bound to recognition of professional achievements and being in demand; if every time you're asked "how are you?" you answer "super busy!" out of both truth and vanity; if your mental energy is a mix of planning how to get ahead and fretting about falling behind; if you exercise not only for health or pleasure; if you've ever dismissed someone's idea or opinion out of sheer credentialist snobbery; or if you've experienced guilty pleasure when dropping your kid off at childcare—then you know firsthand how meritocracy coils itself into ambition, self-esteem, and personal identity. There are no villains here, only a malignant system that passes for common sense. Meritocracy keeps the hamster wheel spinning. But it could never have been set up, much less acquired its virtuous veneer, without liberalism. Personal freedom and equality of opportunity—where's the harm in that?

Liberal Deformations: Pornography Today

Every society and culture has its own ideal of love, attraction, and marriage. Liberals are no exception. Authentic and lasting romance is for us based on attraction, of course, and also mutual esteem, admiration, friendship, and reciprocity. Lovers must really, deep down, see and meet one another. As in so many things, *Parks and Recreation* distills this liberal ideal to its essence. When Leslie Knope exchanges wedding vows with her fiancé, here is what she says: "The things you have done for me to help me, support me, surprise me, to make me happy, go above and beyond what any person deserves. You're all I need. I love you and like you."[33]

The ideal of loving *and* liking has a long genealogy. In arts and letters, it can be traced from rom-coms and reality dating shows to classical Hollywood screwballs to Elizabeth Bennett and Mr. Darcy, and all the way back to John Milton, who first argued that the "chiefest and the noblest end of marriage" was for spouses to delight in each other's company as well as engage in "meet and happy conversation."[34] In politics and philosophy, ever since Mary Wollstonecraft and John Stuart Mill made their respective cases, feminists have contended, first, that authentic romance must be anchored in friendship, and second, that the conditions for friendship between the sexes need to be secured through equality in law and education.[35]

Even in an age of Tinder and Bumble, romance doesn't just spontaneously happen. It takes place against a background of institutions and established expectations. For meritocratic elites, that context is overwhelmingly college—sometimes as a site and stage of life, and more generally as intermarriage between graduates. By 2010 in the United States, 25 percent of couples were composed of two college graduates—an impressive figure given that only 30 percent of US adults have college degrees.[36] Economists, with typical sentimentalism, have named this practice "assortative mating."[37] In the olden days, and still in many nonliberal cultures, elite intermarriage was and is arranged. Today it is voluntary. Young meritocrats go on the hunt for their equal, someone worthy of their own accomplishments and drive: a partner to love and like, in a spirit of friendship and shared adventure, provided, of course, that they pass the necessary background checks.

Which brings me to the topic of this section. Pornhub.com is the tenth most visited website in the world. That may not surprise you, but perhaps this does: when sorted into all-time most viewed videos, whether in the United States or globally, one genre dominates. It is step-incest (or "fauxcest"), meaning sex between family members who are not biologically related to one another, such as stepbrothers and stepsisters; stepsisters; stepsons and stepmothers; and stepfathers and stepdaughters (stepbrothers is also a popular genre on Pornhub's gay videos). The count is not even close. As of March 2023, of the most popular 100 videos, 3.9 billion views were for step-incest videos and 3.1 billion views were for *all* other videos combined. Make no mistake, step-incest pornography is mainstream; it may even be majoritarian.[38]

Call me naive, but I refuse to believe that most pornography viewers in the United States have an incest fetish. There must be another explanation. And given the premise of this book—that every major element of the background culture of liberal democratic societies is intelligible only when viewed in relation to liberal values and ideas—it is incumbent on me to provide one. I need to account for not just the good of our world but the bad, weird, and ugly too: things that either distort liberalism (such as meritocracy) or are such clear reactions that they make no sense without being situated in relation to a constant and hostile reference to liberalism.

Step-incest porn falls into that latter category. Almost every video in the genre follows the same plot. First, partly for legal reasons and partly to remove the ick factor of real incest, there is an explicit declaration of nonbiological ties, such as "*Step*bro, what are you doing home?" or "I can't stay in the same hotel room as my *step*son!" Second, and this is key, prior to the sex, a few narrative minutes are always devoted to persuasion or coercion. Step-incest videos never start out with both characters desiring one another as sexual partners. One of them always needs to be brought to that view: sometimes by seduction, and most often by blackmail, bribery, wheedling, pleading, or deceit. The methods

are as various and sordid as the human imagination: to threaten
to tell a secret or call the cops, pay off a loan, request sexual instruction, beg, impersonate, and much else. All of them, however,
turn sex into an ill-gotten gain. The taboo being busted, in other
words, is not the prohibition on incest. It is merit: the idea that
reward should track talent, achievement, and effort.[39]

Step-incest porn is objectionable for many reasons—as
wrong, creepy, or gross; for me, it is most of all sad. This is porn
for and about losers and frauds. A moment ago we looked at
elites, the winners of the meritocratic tournament. What about
the other side of the equation? What about those who weren't
educated by fancy institutions, fail to get a glossy job, don't live
in a glittery city, and above all, aren't invited to the assortative mating party of attractive and accomplished singles? Meritocracy
churns out losers just as surely and in much greater quantity.
And that inspires feelings of disappointment as well as potentially humiliation and shame. As Michael Sandel states, "For
those who can't find work or make ends meet, it is hard to escape the demoralizing thought that their failure is their own
doing, that they simply lack the talent and drive to succeed."[40]

Enter the antihero of step-incest porn. The same stock character, he is almost always white, bored or bummed out, watching TV or playing video games, or on his phone. Along comes
a female into his field of vision, and he leaves his stupor to cajole
or compel. The attraction is not that she is related to him by ties
of marriage; it is that she is there, in the same time and space,
and he doesn't have to go out into the world. He doesn't love
her; he doesn't like her; there is no meet and happy conversation. She is simply something to do, a surface to cum on, and
best of all, he doesn't have to change out of his sweatpants.

In her book of the same title, Amia Srinivasan gives this
attitude a name: a "right to sex," a sense of entitlement by

"someone who is convinced he is owed sex."[41] These someones are so-called *incels*: involuntarily celibate men who are enraged by women who deny what they think is their due. Technically, the antihero of a step-incest video is not an incel. He has sex. Yet he is impotent in a deeper sense: stuck at home, with little to recommend him professionally to society or personally to a mate, and he knows it. Say what you like about the plumber or cable repairman of yore, at least he was out there in the world. But the idea that *this* (pathetic, incelish) guy gets laid is titillating for losers and winners of the meritocratic game alike. For the losers, he short-circuits the logic of achievement and effort that holds them back (and rightly or wrongly, is felt to be rigged to begin with). For the winners, he represents a reprieve from the bullshit of the hamster wheel they run without respite. Step-incest porn has something for everyone.

It gets worse. Step-incest porn trades off a challenge not only to meritocracy but also to liberalism itself. Today the issue of consent, for better and worse, has moved to the heart of the public debate about sex. Sex-positive liberals, out of respect for privacy and aversion to moralism, have by and large concluded that a lack of consent is the only ground on which to judge and regulate. But as Srinivasan observes, "When we see consent as the sole constraint on ethically OK sex, we are pushed towards a naturalisation of sexual preference in which the rape fantasy becomes a primordial rather than a political fact."[42] This is exactly what happens in step-incest videos. Searches on Pornhub for such overt terms as *rape, force, violence, violate,* or *assault* return no results. Softer forms of coercion, however, are fair game—*bribe, convince, reluctant, talk into, trick,* and so on. The bread and butter of step-incest porn videos, such coercions are based on bringing an initially unwilling partner to a state of consent, or preferably for this genre, not nonconsent. Within the mainstream, much more so than any kind of bondage-type videos, this is as near to nonconsensual pornography as you can get. And to repeat, it is the most popular genre by a mile. Yet is that surprising? When we look at the genre and what it does, most viewers are probably not actually hot for mommy, daddy, sister, and brother. Much more plausible is that we get off by seeing the ethical consensuses of our liberal age—about desert and effort, love and friendship, consent and desire—either openly abrogated or brought into a gray zone of negotiation and thrill.

Philosopher Ludwig Wittgenstein once wrote, "When we first begin to *believe* anything, what we believe is not a single proposition, it is a whole system of propositions. (Light dawns gradually over the whole.)"[43] That is what I have tried to show in this chapter. For many of us, liberal values and sensibilities are not confined to the realm of law and politics. Light dawns on the whole such that our most spontaneous reactions (offense, outrage, laughter, and much else) and intimate concerns (love, desire, friendship, ambitions, the deepest questions, and much else) are liberal through and through. But Wittgenstein never said that the system of propositions had to be consistent. Those who cheer Leslie and her fiancé in the morning may well consume step-incest porn in the evening; those who recoil from slurs and discrimination of all kinds may well send their children to private schools to ensure their advantage. In an ideal world, we liberals would be consistent. Yet that is not the one we live in. Our societies are not, properly speaking, liberal. We exist in liberaldom, and it is to this topic I now turn.

6

Pretend Liberals in
a Pretend Liberal World

NEAR THE END OF HIS LIFE, theologian Søren Kierkegaard
(1813–55) launched an attack on the Christianity and Christian
culture of his native Denmark that breached the bounds of civility and decorum. A subdued version had been brewing for a
decade. In such works as *Either-Or* (1843), *Fear and Trembling*
(1843), *Christian Discourses* (1848), and *Practice in Christianity*
(1850), he emphasized how demanding a Christian way of life is
and chided the watered-down version taught by the Church of
Denmark. In 1854, however, he entered open war with the establishment. The occasion was the death of Bishop Jacob Peter
Mynster, the top-ranking cleric of Denmark. Mynster had long
been family friends of the Kierkegaards (Søren to an extent, but
mainly his father and grandfather), and out of respect, Søren had
kept quiet. Yet when Mynster died, and when the encomiums
came rolling in—particularly from social-climbing priests looking to capitalize on Mynster's reputation—the gloves came off.

Kierkegaard's critique comes down to this: the Christianity
taught and practiced in his day is a joke. It is Christianity-lite, a
pale copy of the demands of the faith. Genuine Christianity

calls for the imitation of the life of Christ, with its universal love
and conscious unworldliness. Mynster and his ilk (which is the
entire Danish ecclesiastical order) preach fine words on Sun-
day, yet the way they live is just Epicurean or bourgeois philis-
tinism. Moderate pleasures and social respectability are their
thing. They play at Christianity, and Kierkegaard calls the social,
religious, and political world that is cause and effect of this play-
acting "Christendom" (*Kristenhed* in Danish, literally meaning
Christianness):

> Compared with the Christianity of the New Testament, it is
> playing at Christianity. . . . [W]hat does it mean to play? It
> means to counterfeit, to mimic a danger where there is no dan-
> ger, and in such a way that the more art one applies to it the
> more deceptively one can pretend as if there were danger. . . .
> This is the way Christianity is played in "Christendom." Dra-
> matically costumed, the artists [that is, clerics] make their ap-
> pearance in artistic buildings [that is, churches]—there is
> truly no danger at all, anything but; the teacher is a royal office
> holder, advancing steadily, making a career—and now he dra-
> matically plays at Christianity, in short, he is performing
> comedy.[1]

Kierkegaard published several polemics in newspapers (as well
as his own journal, *The Moment*) and railed against the priesthood,
those "silk-and-velvet pastors"—those "hypocrites," "counter-
feiters," "guild of swindlers," "blatherers," and "cannibals"—who
know how to "profit" from Christianity.[2] He even called for a
boycott of public worship, imploring churchgoers to walk out
and stop trying to make a fool out of God.[3] Whereas his work
is usually swathed in layers of irony, Kierkegaard's late criticism
of the church is striking for being so direct, relentless, and
personal.

But priests weren't the only problem. Christendom corrupts all, clergy and laity alike. Martin Luther once stapled ninety-five theses to a church door. Kierkegaard, sadly, needs just one: "The Christianity of the New Testament does not exist at all."[4] Thus comes Kierkegaard to fully inhabit his persona of the Socrates of Copenhagen. On the one hand, he buzzes around like a gadfly, reminding everyone that becoming Christian is a lifelong task, incompatible with their tranquilized existence.[5] On the other hand, adopting Socrates's famous posture, he admits that he himself is no Christian, only a "scrutineer" of what it takes to be one. Like Socrates who was wise because he was aware of his own ignorance, Kierkegaard has this advantage: by knowing his distance from a Christian way of life, he is the least un-Christian person in Christendom.[6]

Philosophizing with a hammer is nothing new. Socrates, Saint Paul, and Luther smashed the idols of their day, and Karl Marx and Friedrich Nietzsche will soon savage the same European culture that Kierkegaard attacks. Yet he differs from them in a key respect. They denounce the ideals of their reigning culture (whether Homeric, Hellenic, Roman Catholic, bourgeois, or Wilhelmian) as false and ignoble; they also offer up their life and/or work as heroic or salvific alternatives. Kierkegaard does neither. Christendom does not spread false doctrine. The trouble is that the godly doctrine it professes remains merely that: doctrine, without having been existentially appropriated. Every Dane claims to admire the life and sacrifice of Christ; there's a Lutheran church on every corner; yet no one is honestly Christian in desire or deed. Christendom is one big hypocritical joke; so too is every "Christian" caught in it, down to a soul. This is a world of deceit, self-deceit, and sanctimony that mocks the truth it is built on.

Becoming Liberal in Liberaldom

The reader may sense where I am going with this. If Kierkegaard's problem is how to become Christian in Christendom,
ours is how to become liberal in liberaldom.

What is liberaldom? The same as Christendom—a compromise. Christendom is a comfortable and semistable marriage
between Christianity, a secular state, and capitalist civil society.
It is also, in the words of a Kierkegaard scholar, "the craven capitulation to un-Christian values that threatens to destroy the
life of the spirit."[7] Liberaldom is similar. As we saw with John
Rawls in chapter 2, the core tenet of liberalism—as axiomatic
for it as "love the Lord your God with all of your heart and
all of your soul" and "love your neighbor as yourself" is for
Christianity—is that society is a "fair system of social cooperation over time from one generation to the next."[8] Liberaldom,
then, is a mixture of liberalism and other ideologies and systems, including capitalism (with its individualism, materialism,
and instrumentalism), democracy (with its latent populism),
nationalism and internationalism (with their patriotism and
often jingoism), and meritocracy (with its calculations of worth
and reward), as well as openly illiberal forces (such as racism and
patriarchy) dug into our institutions and attitudes. As much a
state of the soul as a state of affairs, liberaldom is liberalism
compromised, in both senses of the word: a settlement between
itself and other ideologies *and* a lowering of its standards. Liberaldom, we could say, is the craven capitulation to unliberal
values that threaten to destroy your and my spirit.

That we live in liberaldom and not liberalism is obvious. Any
critical work in the social sciences testifies that politically, legally,
and especially socially and economically, liberal democratic

societies fall far short of being fair systems of cooperation.[9] Even philosophers, who congenitally theorize about near-perfect societies ("cities of words," Plato called them), appreciate that injustice is not a problem at the margins but instead wrecks the core of liberal democratic societies.[10]

Excellent and gripping representations of liberaldom also come in video form. The best is the US drama *The Wire* (2002–8), which is a righteously angry show about how individuals and communities are formed and deformed by institutions of a crumbling liberal democracy.[11] If you can't spare three whole days to watch it, I recommend a fourteen-minute clip by the *New York Times*: "Liberal Hypocrisy Is Fueling American Inequality" (2021). It boils liberaldom down to its essence by looking at resistance to liberal policies—in this case, more egalitarian housing, taxation, and education—by so-called *progressive* (rather than conservative) politicians and voters. Christians who talk the talk but refuse to walk the walk are the stuff of Christendom. Ditto for liberaldom. "We are not living our values," the video concludes. "People who live in blue states [that is, states governed by the Democratic Party], people who profess liberal values, you need to look in the mirror. And you need to understand that [your blue states] are not taking the actions that are consistent with those values; not just incidentally, not just in small areas, but that in some of the most important policy choices we are denying people the opportunity to prosper, to thrive, and to build better lives, and it is happening in places where Democrats control the levers of policy."[12] "Liberalism," a political theorist observed thirty years ago, "holds out the promise, or the threat, of making all the world like California."[13] That remains true, though in a different sense nowadays. Inequality and dysfunction, not individuality and eccentricity, loom on the horizon.

Is liberalism to blame for liberaldom? Opinions vary. Recent studies by intellectual historians answer with a qualified yes. Specifically, they point to a juncture in the development of liberalism—the Cold War period—when leading liberal thinkers (such as Isaiah Berlin, Karl Popper, the later Judith Shklar, and Lionel Trilling) decided to decry the perfectionist and progressivist tendencies of their nineteenth-century forebearers as protototalitarian.[14] As Samuel Moyn puts it, what followed was a "kind of libertarianization of what liberalism stood for," reducing liberalism to the protection of individual freedoms and prevention of physical harm, and what is worse, leaving the welfare state intellectually undefended when neoliberalism came calling two decades later.[15] Still, the yes of these historians is qualified. Specific disastrous decisions by liberals may be partly to blame for the slide of liberalism into liberaldom, yet it needn't have happened, nor is it irreversible. The perfectionist and progressivist impulses of liberalism can—and indeed must—be redeemed if liberalism is to believe in itself again, attract a new generation of partisans, and reclaim the verve and futurity it once had.

Ideally, collective and individual perfectibility would go hand in hand in the way these critics propose. This is a long-term project, however, and I'm writing for the meantime: self-help for liberals in liberaldom.[16] My book is not about how to fix liberaldom; there are libraries full of proposals for how to try to do that.[17] It is about how liberals can live well in it. And the first step, as is frequently the case with self-help books, is admission: for "liberals" to recognize just how many of our decisions and desires are inconsistent with our professed commitments. I'll go first. My wife and I pay a great deal of money to send our daughter to private school. Our taxes support the public school system, and truthfully, we would happily agree to pay more.

That said, we are not willing to forgo the advantages she gains in teacher quality, facilities, curriculum choice, and reputational excellence. Now it's your turn.

Being liberal is hard work—arguably as difficult as being Christian. That may sound far-fetched. Christianity is notoriously demanding. Not only Kierkegaard says so. Shortly after comes Alfred Loisy and his quip that Jesus promised the kingdom of God and all we got was the church. Today we can consult David Bentley Hart, the most recent translator of the New Testament into English. "Most of us," he says referring to non-Christians *and* Christians alike, "would find Christians truly cast in the New Testament mold fairly obnoxious: civically reprobate, ideologically unsound, economically destructive, politically irresponsible, socially discreditable, and really just a bit indecent."[18]

Can a liberal way of life compete with that? Is it as hard core as authentic Christianity? Maybe not. Still, the quiet radicalism of liberalism can sneak up on you. In the previous chapter, we looked at how liberal commitments inform our instinctive and felt reactions to things and each other. When a philosopher such as Rawls comes along, then, and observes that the key moral intuition embedded in the public culture of liberal democracies is that society is a fair system of cooperation, we liberals sagely nod, "Yes, absolutely." But to continue with my metaphor of liberal waters, Rawls is something of a swimming instructor. He starts us off in the shallow end of the pool, water knee-high, feeling safe and comfortable with who we are and the limits of our commitments. He then gets us to take baby steps into deeper and deeper water. "Well," he says, "if society is a fair system of cooperation, you'll also grant that it should guarantee equal rights to basic liberties." "Naturally," we reply, and find ourselves waist-high. "How about providing the social bases of self-respect for everyone?" "Sure," now chest high. And so Rawls continues to lead us until, suddenly and surprisingly, we find ourselves in the deep end, treading waters we are not sure we agree with, yet recognize as continuous with our prior moral and political intuitions as well as personal identity.

Part II of this book uses Rawls to spell out what a committed liberal way of life looks like, what it does to our sense of self, how it can be cultivated, and crucially, why we should wish to do so. But let me give you a preview, drawn from a single section of *A Theory of Justice* ("The Tendency to Equality," §17). We'll see how politically and personally radical liberalism can be, along with how far we in liberaldom are from it.

An Aristocracy of All

We'll start at the shallow end of the pool. All liberals (and not only liberals) will agree that although every society has deep inequalities into which people are born, no one can be said to "deserve" their starting position, nor the ensuing advantages or disadvantages that compound it over a lifetime. What kind of twisted sense would it make to say that *this* child in Palo Alto, California, deserves to be born rich, whereas *that* child in Detroit, Michigan, deserves to be born poor?

Liberals have a stock answer to the problem of arbitrary social and economic advantage: the principle of fair equality of opportunity, the purpose of which is to ensure that social positions, such as jobs, are meritocratically allocated and that everyone has a genuinely fair chance to attain them. While waiting for our swimming lesson, then, we liberals stand in the pool chatting about which policies, institutions, and wealth redistributions will best ensure that the kid from Palo Alto and the kid from Detroit compete on a level playing field.

In comes our instructor. Rawls listens to our conversation with interest and asks two questions to start us off. Certainly no one deserves the *social* or *economic* advantages (or disadvantages) of their starting position. But what about *natural* advantages (or disadvantages), understood in terms of inborn talents and even the willpower to develop them? It is hard to argue that those are any more deserved. Just like social and economic advantages (or disadvantages), natural advantages (or disadvantages) depend on factors that are not up to us as individuals and are arbitrary from a moral point of view. I am not responsible for my initial genetic endowment, nor for the family and wider society I am born into that will (or won't) nurture my talents and willpower, nor for the kind of talents that my society values and rewards. And so we wade a little deeper into the pool, acknowledging that no one deserves their economic and social *or* natural starting position, nor the ongoing advantages (or disadvantages) that flow from it.[19]

Rawls now asks his second question—about the principle of fair equality of opportunity he heard us chatting about. Even if this principle worked perfectly (which it never does), should the priority of a liberal society really be to ensure that anyone has a fair chance to leave behind the less advantaged group they came from? Shouldn't the goal, rather, be to improve everyone's lot, especially the least advantaged? The issue is not primarily one of efficiency (namely, that it is better to help lots of people as opposed to a handful of talented individuals). It is moral. A just liberal society is solidaristic, in which "men agree to share one another's fate."[20] That means our fundamental institutions need to be justifiable to *all* fellow citizens, no matter where they are situated in it. More pointedly, if social, economic, and natural inequalities are built into and rewarded by the basic structure of our society, those inequalities need to be justifiable to everyone, including less advantaged people.

Liberals must believe in good faith that the worst off would be even worse off without certain social and economic inequalities in place.

Rawls is about to lead us into deep waters with one of his most famous ideas: the "difference principle." It is an integral part of the two fundamental principles of justice that, he claims, should underlie a liberal society. They are as follows, with the difference principle being (a) of the second principle:

FIRST PRINCIPLE. Each person is to have an equal right to the most extensive total system of equal basic liberties compatible with a similar system of liberty for all.

SECOND PRINCIPLE. Social and economic inequalities are to be arranged so that they are both: (a) to the greatest benefit of the least advantaged . . . and (b) attached to offices and positions open to all under conditions of fair equality of opportunity.[21]

With the first principle as well as the second principle (b), Rawls whisks us back to the shallow end of the pool. Liberals will readily agree, as per the first principle, that everyone should have the same package of fundamental legal and political rights. The rich do not get to vote twice, nor enjoy different legal protections. And the second principle (b) is what we were discussing among ourselves before our swimming lesson began. Offices (elected representatives or judges, for example) and positions (jobs or places at university, for instance) that enjoy greater responsibilities and rewards should be open to all citizens under fair conditions to attain them.

The second principle (a)—the difference principle—is a different story. It is controversial for demanding less of a liberal society than we might expect and more than almost any of us are prepared to give.

With respect to its (seemingly) lesser demands, the difference principle may seem disappointing. Why permit inequalities at all? Wouldn't it be fairer if everyone had the same social and economic resources? Shouldn't we also try to minimize inequalities that stem from the lottery of natural talents? No one, remember, deserves their starting position or the advantages (or disadvantages) it accrues. Why not just level them out?

No, says Rawls. First of all, it would be a nightmare to attempt to do so while respecting the first principle of justice. More importantly, strict equality would do more harm than good to people from less advantaged groups. If social and economic goods were equally distributed, talented individuals would be unlikely to cultivate their abilities, nor assume the risks that come with new projects and initiatives. If, on the other hand, we allow the economic system to reward talent and risk-taking, everyone benefits from more and better doctors and teachers (and engineers, scientists, chefs, actors, athletes, entrepreneurs, police, politicians, and so on) as well as enhanced innovation, efficiency, and opportunity.

The difference principle establishes the kind and amount of social and economic inequality that can be justified: only so much as benefits the least advantaged members of society (as indexed and measured by the least advantaged group, usually defined in terms of income). And don't forget, the difference principle works within a broader egalitarian framework that includes fair and progressive taxation (personal, corporate, consumption, and estate), regulation of markets, and adequately funded public institutions (including health, education, transportation, parks and recreation, and much else).[22]

Looked at through the lens of the difference principle, there can be no doubt that we live in liberaldom, not liberalism. As a fact to explain, the world as it stands makes much more sense if we recognize that its social and economic inequalities are geared to favor the *most*, not the least, advantaged members. How else to account for its shocking inequalities? Moreover, the idea that our liberal democracies reward socially useful talents and responsible risk-taking seems quaint. The best and brightest of my own generation have spent their lives figuring out how to keep eyeballs glued to screens. And ever since the global financial crisis of 2008 and its legacy of bailouts, we know that while profits are always privatized, risks, if sufficiently large and reckless, are socialized. Judged as a whole, contemporary liberal democracies are, with respect to their liberalism, just as false as 1850s Denmark was with respect to its Christianity.

A society based on Rawls's two principles of justice would be nearly unrecognizable. But the insight I wish to reach is that we (you and I), as individuals, would be nearly unrecognizable to ourselves if we took our liberalism seriously. Consider the difference principle once more, this time applied by the individual to their everyday life. Taking it to heart would amount to a revolution in how we think of ourselves. First, we would reject any notion that we somehow morally deserve the advantages that stem from our talents and hard work (and that the less fortunate deserve their hardships). Nothing is less generous—less liberal—than smugness and contempt for accidents of birth and fortune. Second, we would stop personally chasing after goods of wealth and status, unless to the benefit of the less fortunate. And by "stop" I don't mean "be restrained from" but instead to learn to regard such things with cheerful indifference. Third, we would treat our own talents as common assets—gifts that while they happen to be in your or my possession (and yes, acquired through perseverance and training), do not exactly belong to us.

People like this are few and far between. Straight is the gate and narrow is the way. One can be found, however, in a paragon of liberal culture: the Netflix reality show *Queer Eye*, specifically in the sixth episode of its sixth season. The premise of *Queer Eye* is that five members of the LGBTQ+ community—the "Fab Five," each of whom has a special area of expertise—travel around the United States to help some individual improve their lifestyle and become happier. The hero/patient of one episode in season 6 is Dr. Jereka Thomas-Hockaday, an educator who founded a medical school, the Central Texas Allied Health Institute, which offers training programs in pharmacy, patient care, phlebotomy, and surgical technology. Thomas-Hockaday can certainly use some tips to achieve a work-life balance. But when it comes to ethics and personal fulfillment, she's good. More than good, in fact; she is a living, breathing incarnation of the difference principle.

The mission of the Central Texas Allied Health Institute is to provide affordable medical education for people of color, especially those below the poverty line. Thomas-Hockaday traces her vocation back to her teen years, when her father had lung cancer, and she witnessed the inequities of the health system and how few carers were of color. Her professional life has been devoted to improving that situation. And when reflecting on her trajectory and accomplishments, she uses language that mirrors the difference principle, right down to seeing her talents as a common asset: "I am 100 percent knowing of who I am as an educated Black woman in this world, and the things that I want to do with the gifts that I have been given. Less than 1 percent of Black women in the United States have a doctorate degree. I feel a privilege to have it in front of my name. That's why I don't want to fail at this."[23] Now *that's* a liberal: she is cognizant of her gifts and achievements yet without a hint of pride, and her duty and good lie in making her society at least slightly fairer than it would otherwise be.

We might even call Thomas-Hockaday a natural aristocrat. In *A Theory of Justice*, Rawls remarks that aristocratic regimes, for all of their brutality and silliness, in some sense honor the difference principle. A decent feudal lord will dedicate his luck and talents (that is, his purported intelligence, learning, humanity, and bravery) to the less fortunate. Noblesse oblige is one interpretation of service and social responsibility, after all.[24] Rawls does not pursue this idea further in *A Theory of Justice*. But in an evocative passage in his *Lectures on the History of Moral Philosophy*, he observes that Immanuel Kant's moral philosophy aspires to "an aristocracy of all."[25]

Now one way to interpret this phrase in the context of liberalism is to pair it with similar expressions—such as the Protestant idea of a "priesthood of all believers" or John Stuart Mill's "society of sovereign individuals"—that emphasize freedom. An aristocracy of all is one in which autonomous individuals act on principles compatible with the freedom of others.[26] But a second and complementary interpretation is also possible. As we saw in chapter 3, early liberals such as Alexis de Tocqueville believed that being a liberal person was as much about generosity (*liberality*) as freedom (*liberty*). They also fretted that modern subjects are besieged by social forces (including democracy, capitalism, and nationalism) that make us closed-minded, intolerant, and stingy with our love, time, and money. And that, they concluded, is a disaster not just for our polities but for our well-being too. Restlessness and loneliness are not good ways to live.

A similar apprehension inspires the difference principle. Rawls is less explicit than Tocqueville about the spiritual dissatisfactions of modern life. Yet when we attend to what the difference principle actually does for our psychic well-being, it looks like a remedy for precisely those dissatisfactions. By not wishing for advantages unless to the benefit of the less fortunate, we are protected from many of the most corrosive vices of our culture, including ingratitude, envy, and what the ancient Greeks called pleonexia, to have and yet want more. Positively put, we become natural aristocrats: free and generous in thought, feeling, and action. From this perspective, living by the light of the difference principle is not supererogatory. It is self-interest properly understood.

Is this the right way to read Rawls? Egalitarian critics would protest. Two eminent philosophers, G. A. Cohen and Ronald Dworkin, pounce on Rawls's repeated assertion that the two principles of justice apply to (and are meant to assess and reform) the fundamental institutions of a liberal democratic society, not individuals or their actions.[27] The trouble is that a genuinely egalitarian society will never be realized if its principles are restricted to laws and institutions. "My own view," states Cohen, "is that *both* just rules *and* just personal choice within the framework set by just rules are necessary for distributive justice." And channeling his inner Kierkegaard, he adds, "I now believe that a change in social ethos, a change in the attitudes people sustain toward each other in the thick of daily life, is necessary for producing equality, and that belief brings me closer than I ever expected to be to the Christian view of these matters that I once disparaged." For these critics, Rawlsian liberalism represents an "evasion," an egalitarianism-lite that is ironically cause and symptom of what I have called liberaldom.[28]

In a sense, these critics are partly correct. The primary subject of Rawls's theory of justice is indeed the basic institutional structure of liberal democracies. In another sense, these critics are completely correct. Once Rawls takes his turn to political liberalism and adapts his theory for a pluralist democracy, he (and legions of followers) will no longer seek to persuade readers as to why they should want to become a liberal *person* (rather than just a liberal *citizen*) through and through. Yet there is a window in Rawls's thought—a large and important window—where these critics are badly mistaken: the third and final part of *A Theory of Justice*. There he describes in rich experiential detail the goods of a liberal way of life and why such a way of life is itself good. As we saw in chapter 4, he abandoned that line of argument once he realized it could not appeal to all of his readers, especially those who held different conceptions of the good. For our purposes, however, it does not have that liability. My book is not written for just anyone. It is a work of self-help for liberals. And for us, part III of *A Theory of Justice* is a treasure trove.

I have concluded this chapter with a preview of Rawls's vision of the goods of a liberal way of life: a free and generous way of being that rivals aristocracy in quality and ambition. Who wouldn't want that for themselves? Nearly everyone, is the short and sad answer. Liberaldom is not something "out there" in the world but rather anchored in a pattern of wants, aspirations, and habits built up over a lifetime. Unlearning it takes work and effort. Yet here too Rawls is ready to help. Our instructor will not abandon us in the deep end. He will, first, give a fulsome account of why we should want to swim in these deep waters. Second, he will teach us practical exercises for how to do that. Part II of this book continues the lesson.

Soulcraft for Liberals

7

Spiritual Exercises

PART I OF THIS BOOK concluded with a predicament called
liberaldom. It goes like this. On the one hand, we swim in liberal waters in the sense that our public and background cultures
are saturated with liberal values and sensibilities. That means
there are three types of people in the (liberal democratic)
world: those who are illiberal, and whose worldview derives
its energy and much of its content in reaction to liberalism;
those who are friendly to and influenced by liberalism, but hold
some other conception of the good life (such as a religion); and
those who are liberal all the way down. I do not talk about the
first (and explain why at the beginning of chapter 9); I addressed the second in chapter 4 (they are the LEGO people);
and the third is my real subject. The premise of this book is that
there are lots of us liberals all the way down, which is only to be
expected if I am correct about the omnipresence of liberalism.
What could be easier and more natural than being borne along
by the culture of our times?

On the other hand, the fact is that none of us truly live in
liberalism. We exist in liberaldom: pseudoliberal societies that
publicly profess liberal commitments, yet fail and often do not
even try to honor them. And the gut punch of liberaldom is that

we can't just blame it on other people. So-called liberals have all kinds of desires and behaviors that cannot be squared with who they take themselves to be. Hence the predicament: we are liberals, but not. Long ago, Aristotle uttered a cryptic phrase, at once acknowledgment and negation, "O my friends, there is no friend!"[1] Let us then say, "O my liberals, there is no liberal!"

Part II of this book works from within this predicament to address three questions. The first is descriptive: *What* does a liberal way of life look like? In chapter 3, we saw how nineteenth-century liberals reclaimed the old Latin words *liber* and *liberalis* as a political and ethical banner. A liberal citizen and person, they claimed, is free and generous in heart and deed, despite the pressures (timeless and historically modern) not to be. These two qualities—freedom and generosity, liberty and liberality—remain at the heart of a liberal way of life. Yet they need updating. Nineteenth-century liberalism, unlike its twentieth- and twenty-first-century successors, did not center on the idea that society should be a fair system of cooperation. That idea was barely embedded in its public culture and even less so in its background culture. For a liberal way of life to be fit for our times, we need to figure out what freedom and generosity look like from within the context of a society that sees itself as a fair system of cooperation.

The second question is motivational: *Why* would we want to lead a liberal way of life? This issue demands a no-nonsense reply. Being liberal is tough. It requires that we cease to strive for a whole series of goods that from the perspective of liberaldom seem obviously desirable, such as paying lower taxes or lavishing our kids with unfair advantages. If that is the ask, the payoff must be high. We need, in other words, to identify the intrinsic benefits of a liberal way of life—not in some distant aspirational future, but in terms of our happiness and well-being here and now. What new kinds of experiences does it afford? Which toxic emotions and expectations does it release us from? Any decent self-help book needs real answers to such questions.

The third question is practical: *How* do we cultivate a liberal way of life? The issue is crucial because short of waving a magic wand and transforming our societies, we need to learn how to acquire and sustain a liberal way of life amid the constraints and temptations of liberaldom. This chapter introduces the concept of spiritual exercises to address this last question. Spiritual exercises are practices an individual undertakes to bring about a comprehensive change in their way of living. Liberalism, I argue, has spiritual exercises all of its own that can be taken up by anyone who wishes to deepen a liberal way of life. But before I consider spiritual exercises in the context of liberalism, this concept must first be presented on its own terms. To do so, I turn to one of the heroes of this book from its early pages but not heard from since: classicist and philosopher Pierre Hadot.

Philosophy as a Way of Life

When I introduced Hadot in chapter 2, I mentioned that he was chair of history in Hellenistic and Roman thought at France's most prestigious institution, the Collège de France. But his path to becoming an eminent classicist of the twentieth century is more interesting than I let on. It was certainly not the destiny that he (nor his parents, I should add) envisaged for himself as a young man. Initially training to be a priest, his path was upended by what can only be called a series of "mystical" or "unitive" experiences (in the sense of feeling a deep oneness with the world and cosmos) that could not be reconciled with his faith.[2] He then set to study philosophy, and after flirting with the idea of writing a doctoral thesis on Rainer Maria Rilke and Martin Heidegger, specialized in ancient philosophy.

Only die-hard classicists are likely to take an interest in Hadot's early work. He spent twenty years of his life (from 1946 to 1968) translating and then writing a dissertation on Marius Victorinus, a nearly forgotten disciple of the great Neoplatonist Plotinus and who defended the consubstantiality of the three persons of the Trinity. But great discoveries can come from unexpected places. For it was during this time that Hadot struggled to solve a problem that quite inadvertently led to ideas that later made him famous. You see, the young Hadot was perplexed by a phenomenon well known to scholars of the ancient world: the presence of inconsistencies and even contradictions in classical authors. Was it plausible that the greatest minds of antiquity failed to notice what modern readers spot with only a little study? Surely not. There had to be a better answer. Here is how Hadot recounts his journey:

> I have always been struck by the fact that historians say, "Aristotle is incoherent" and "Saint Augustine writes poorly." And this is what led me to the idea that the philosophical works of antiquity were not written as the exposition of a system but in order to produce an effect of formation. The philosopher wanted to make the minds of his readers or listeners work, in order to improve their disposition. This is a rather important point, I believe. I did not begin with more or less edifying considerations about philosophy as therapy, and so on. No, it was really a strictly literary problem, which is the following: For what reasons do ancient philosophical writings seem incoherent? Why is it so difficult to recognize their rational plane?[3]

The change in perspective that Hadot describes calls to mind a gestalt optical illusion, those images where first you see only one thing (a rabbit or two faces) and then suddenly see another (a duck or vase). The rabbit in this case—that is, the thing we immediately see and at first assume is the entire picture—is the modern conception of philosophy. We tend to think that the purpose of philosophy has always been what it is today: a theoretical and systematic discourse to explain something about the world (or at limit, the world itself). "The aim of philosophy, abstractly formulated," says a distinguished modern philosopher, "is to understand how things in the broadest possible sense of the term hang together in the broadest possible sense of the term."[4] From this point of view, inconsistencies in a philosophical system look like errors that the author should have caught. Plato is a genius, certainly, but he or a discreet glossarist should really have ironed out the kinks in his doctrine.

Yet what if—and here is when the rabbit started to turn into a duck for Hadot—we paused to reflect on how and why these ancient texts were created. Perhaps they served a different purpose from what we moderns assume. Ancient philosophy, after all, was predominantly focused on conversation, produced and taught within the context of schools (the Platonic Academy, for example), and usually oral and only later preserved in writing. That means philosophical teachings were constantly being modified for audiences. Content was tailored to the needs of specific interlocutors, sophistication was matched to their level of prior instruction, and even the genre itself (and the ancients had many more to choose from than we do: from dialogue to meditation, consolation, confession, treatise, letter, and much else) was selected for the occasion. Where our modern eyes see error and inconsistency, the young Hadot's interpretative labors led him to spot effective pedagogy.

From this insight, Hadot needed only a few small steps to reach much broader ideas. He started with a strong contrast: unlike modern philosophy, which tries to *inform* people about something, ancient philosophy seeks to *form* them into a different kind of person.[5] He took, in other words, something that we assume works one way (call it philosophy as rabbit: a theoretical discourse to explain things) and showed how it can work in a qualitatively different manner (call it philosophy as duck: a formative practice to shape people).[6]

Next, building from this contrast, he proposed that ancient philosophy was understood and practiced as a way of life. In the ancient world, philosophy always started with a personal decision to live a certain kind of life—one defined by love and the pursuit of wisdom (*philosophia*, meaning a love of wisdom). An individual would pledge themselves to a school that explained, justified, and reinforced what it meant to live wisely. To be a card-carrying philosopher in antiquity, then, it wasn't necessary to come up with a single original idea. You only needed to want to live, and then actually try to live, a certain way.[7]

Three features of Hadot's conception of ancient philosophy (and philosophy as a way of life in general) are essential for my account of a liberal way of life. First, it is *therapeutic*. "The philosophical school is a medical clinic," Epictetus said.[8] If we were to go back to ancient Greece and Rome to ask a philosopher (that is, a lover of wisdom) why we should practice philosophy, they would have answered that something in our lives, or more specifically, something about ourselves (and how we think, feel, and desire) impedes our potential to flourish and live well. Were we perfect—were we "sages" in the language of the ancients—there would be no call for philosophy. Yet as presently constituted, warts and all, work on the self is required to achieve any measure of contentment, tranquility, and self-realization. This is how ancient philosophy presented and promoted itself: as therapy (*therapeia*, meaning healing) for individuals to overcome the default human condition of unhappy disquiet.

Second, philosophy as a way of life is *comprehensive* in the sense that it affects all aspects of a person's life. The goal of ancient philosophy was not to change people's opinions or ideas, narrowly understood. It sought to transform their whole existence as a method to relearn how to see—how to perceive, feel, want, and judge—the world. For that reason, Hadot does not shy away from drawing on language usually reserved for religion: "[Philosophy] is a conversion which turns our entire life upside down, changing the life of the person who goes through it. It raises the individual from an unauthentic condition of life, darkened by unconsciousness and harassed by worry, to an authentic state of life, in which he attains self-consciousness, an exact vision of the world, inner peace, and freedom."[9]

Third and unsurprisingly, philosophy as a way of life is *rare*. Thanks to centuries of later European culture, we have the impression that philosophy was simply in the air in the classical world, in its speeches, theater, sculpture, poetry, science, and more. That is a mistake. The ancient philosopher is an odd duck and out of step—deliberately and often willfully so—with their milieu. They choose to tear away from the everyday, and for every Crito or Glaucon who devotes themselves to philosophy, there exists a thousand ordinary Athenians who want nothing to do with it. And who can blame them? If to a philosopher, the life of normal people looks like "madness, unconsciousness, and ignorance of reality," just imagine how the philosopher looks to them—a contrarian whose entire existence protests the received wisdom of the day.[10] Such a figure is as rare as a Christian in Christendom or a liberal in liberaldom.

Spiritual Exercises

Hadot developed his conception of philosophy as a way of life in a series of books on ancient thinkers (Marcus Aurelius and Plotinus), synoptic treatments of ancient philosophy, and accounts of modern authors (Johann Wolfgang von Goethe and

Ludwig Wittgenstein) who renew the tradition of philosophy as a way of life. I am not alone in esteeming these works as models of scholarly precision, accessible presentation, and human purpose. Philosophers and historians widely credit him with founding the study of philosophy as a way of life.[11] His writing also reached a much wider nonacademic audience—proof of which are the many touching letters he received from readers expressing gratitude for having changed their lives.[12]

Hadot himself was always on the lookout for conceptions of philosophy as a way of life from beyond antiquity. This includes cross-civilizational perspectives in Chinese and Indian philosophies.[13] It also includes applications to contemporary contexts. As his friend and colleague Arnold Davidson reports, "We had innumerable discussions about, and Hadot was passionately interested in, the ways in which the notions of spiritual exercises and philosophy as a way of life could be applied and extended to unexpected domains."[14]

Part II of this book takes up Hadot's invitation and constructs a way of life from the liberal tradition. As before, John Rawls will be our guide, and I propose that many of his signature concepts can be interpreted and practiced as spiritual exercises. Rawls is not, of course, the first and last word on all things liberal. Spiritual exercises could be worked up from other thinkers, thus giving a different shape and texture to a liberal way of life. Many Cold War liberals, for instance, could profitably be read along these lines.[15] So too could libertarians who privilege personal freedom rather than the social democratic ethos I develop in this book.[16] Liberalism is a broad enough tradition to support contrasting and even conflicting ways of living.

The reason I favor Rawls, you will recall, is that he derives the fundamental principle of liberalism—society as a fair system of cooperation from one generation to the next—from the public and background culture of mature liberal democracies. My wager is that the liberal way of life found in his work is likely to resonate with our own self-conception and the kind of person we aspire to be. Poet A. K. Ramanujan once said that in India and Southeast Asia, "no one ever reads the *Rāmāyana* or the *Mahābhārata* for the first time. The stories are there, 'always already.'"[17] I exaggerate only slightly when I claim something similar for Rawls. Once you push past the forbidding technicality of his system, reading him for the first time can produce an uncanny effect of recognition in the sense of knowing again or recalling to mind.[18]

Regardless of which thinker inspires us, spiritual exercises are indispensable for a liberal way of life. Consider a line I quoted from Hadot a moment ago: "[Philosophy] is a conversion which turns our entire life upside down, changing the life of the person who goes through it." Conversion is a loaded word. We tend to picture it along the lines of a sudden reversal or decisive illumination, as when the scales fall from the eyes of Saul of Tarsus and up rises Paul the Apostle. Yet it need not be so dramatic. Conversion simply means, as Hadot explains in another piece, a change of "mindset," which can range from modifying a particular opinion to transforming one's whole personality.[19] Deep personal transformation can, I suppose, take the form of a sudden and lasting reversal (though I've never seen it outside art and literature). But conversion can also be a slow and gradual process—one in which, day by day, we work to effect the change we want to become. Two steps forward and one step back along a lengthy winding road strikes me as more plausible than being knocked off one's horse.

This is where spiritual exercises come in as tools to help someone who commits to a way of life—be it secular or religious—to get and stay there.[20] "Spiritual exercises," says Hadot, are "voluntary, personal practices intended to cause a transformation of the self."[21] Four criteria are packed into this short definition, each of which must be satisfied for an activity to count as a spiritual exercise. Spiritual exercises are *voluntary* and freely taken up. Spiritual exercises are *personal*, such that one's own person is a matter of care and concern. Spiritual exercises are *practices*, meaning that they are embodied regular activities. And spiritual exercises are *transformative*, the goal of which is to alter the person practicing them.

What kinds of exercises are we talking about? They vary from school to school in the classical world. But suppose you wake up one fine morning a Stoic, circa late second century. Your first spiritual exercise of the day would be a premeditation in which you mentally rehearse the potential adversities of the hours to come to better bear them should they happen. Marcus Aurelius, emperor that he was, braced himself every morning with these words: "Today I will be meeting with interference, ingratitude, insolence, disloyalty, ill-will, and selfishness—all of them due to the offenders' ignorance of what is good or evil."[22] In the same vein, you could add a negative visualization in which you imagine you lose everything that you love and hold dear so as to contemplate impermanence. After these solitary exercises, you later meet and dialogue with a friend or teacher, which for Stoics were occasions for spiritual activity. Maybe the conversation dwells on physics and your place in a rationally ordered cosmos, or maybe the discussion steers toward ethics and the need for coherence in your wider pattern of actions; either way, you acknowledge your place within a larger whole and remember the need to harmonize with it. Finally, to finish the day and prepare for the next, you examine your conscience to observe where your thoughts and deeds have fallen short of a philosophical ideal.[23]

As a day in the Stoic life shows, a wealth of spiritual exercises exist. Hadot discusses many more but nowhere provides an exhaustive list. Thankfully, his interpreters put one together, including meditation, observation, contemplation, premeditation of evils, examination of conscience, confession, reframing one's perspective, mastering passions, abstinence, teaching, counseling, dialogue, dialectical inquiry, reading, writing, and rhetoric.[24] All of these are techniques for the self to work on the self. And to be clear, spiritual exercises are not supplements or top-ups to the theoretical core of ancient philosophy. Ancient philosophy is spiritual exercise all the way down, and its core teachings in logic, ethics, and physics serve to justify the choice of a philosophical life as well as specify what it requires in everyday life.[25]

There are, then, a million and one spiritual exercises. Still, as Hadot often observes, if you get right down to it, perhaps only a single attitude, a single philosophical choice and stance, underlies and inspires all the various spiritual exercises of the ancient world. "Generally speaking, I personally tend to conceive of the fundamental philosophical choice as an overcoming of the partial, biased, egocentric, egoist self in order to attain the level of a higher self."[26] Many admirable traits can be ascribed to this higher self, all of which are hard-won fruits of spiritual exercises: a universal outlook to keep narrow self-interest at bay; impartiality ("luminous indifference," to use Hadot's preferred phrase) to temper a preference for those near and dear; personal integrity to remain true to our principles and achieve moral coherence; a feeling of oneness with humanity; and a big-souled generosity for people and projects we might otherwise neglect. And in an important interview comment, Hadot mentions one more grace acquired through spiritual exercises: objectivity.

The problem of scientific objectivity is extremely interesting from the point of view of spiritual exercises. Since Aristotle, it has been recognized that science should be disinterested.

To study a text or microbes or the stars, one must undo one-self from one's subjectivity. [Some scholars] will say that is impossible. But I nevertheless think this is an ideal that one must attempt to attain through constant practice. Thus the scholars who have the rare courage to recognize that they were mistaken in a particular case, or who try not to be influenced by their own prejudices, are undertaking a spiritual exercise of self-detachment. Let us say that objectivity is a virtue, and one that is very difficult to practice. One must undo oneself from the partiality of the individual and impassioned self in order to elevate oneself to the universality of the rational self. I have always thought that the exercise of political democracy, as it should be practiced, should correspond to this attitude as well. Self-detachment is a moral attitude that should be demanded of both the politician and the scholar.[27]

In calling for objectivity and self-detachment in democracy, Hadot touches on a great problem of political and moral philosophy: the relationship between the government of the self and the government of others. For the ancients, it was axiomatic that statecraft required prior soulcraft on the part of leaders.[28] Anyone unable to control their own impulses had no business running the city. The same goes, Hadot says, for democracy. The issue is even amplified in democracy in that all citizens wield political power, such that not only politicians must acquire virtues of self-detachment and other-mindedness for our polities to flourish. Democracy requires us all to pick up our game.

Yet what if we looked at the relationship between virtue and politics the other way around? Rather than ask, as Hadot does here, which virtues are *required for* liberal democracy, we could investigate which virtues are—or more broadly, which way of life is—*imparted by* liberal democracy. Part II of this book is titled "Soulcraft for Liberals," yet it could just as well be called "Soulcraft through Liberalism." It may sound off-putting, if not downright alarming, for any political ideology to connect itself to soulcraft. Did Isaiah Berlin teach us nothing when he warned that positive liberty—the freedom of the higher self from the lower self—should never be promoted by the state?[29] That's the stuff of authoritarians and collectivists! Yes, it is. But I am not asking for the state (or any public institution) to promote or favor a liberal way of life over others. I only suggest that liberalism has the same spiritual heft and latent resources from which to craft spiritual exercises, as any rival philosophical or religious way of life. That is not a possibility Hadot considered: that a viable way of life lies hidden in plain sight, everywhere in our (and his own late twentieth-century French) public and background culture. Perhaps he couldn't. Unlike Søren Kierkegaard, who sees breaking away from one's society (Christendom) in terms of plunging deeper into its own values (Christianity), the ancient philosophers who inspire Hadot saw that kind of break in terms of an alternative way of life, a leap into some other kind of morality (Socrates contra Homer, or Christianity contra Hellenism, for example). And so while Hadot provides crucial tools, our path lies with Kierkegaard, Rawls, and the standing problem of how to become liberal in liberaldom.

8

What Does a Liberal Way
of Life Look Like?

IN THIS BOOK, I've canvassed many examples of a liberal way of life. I started with a party on the beach, and from there moved to more serious and inspiring cases, from liberal heroes (such as Leslie Knope and Jereka Thomas-Hockaday) to liberal ideals of character (freedom and generosity, liberty and liberality), liberal moral and aesthetic sensibilities (including a sense of justice and hatred of cruelty), and myriad sites of background culture informed and deformed by liberalism and liberaldom (offensiveness, outrage, humor, ambition, romance, sexuality, parenting, and more). To understand what a liberal way of life consists of, there is not exactly a need for additional examples. We need an explanation of what ties the ones we have together. What makes these things more than a collection of random stuff?

This chapter formulates an elegant answer to this question—elegant in the sense of parsimony, explaining a lot with a little. It lays out three ideas at the heart of a liberal way of life, all of which stem from the conviction that a liberal society is (or should and must be) a fair system of cooperation. The first is reciprocity, the cardinal value of liberal democracy. The next two are qualities of character: freedom and fairness. One value (reciprocity) and two virtues (freedom and fairness) are all it takes to connect the illustrations I've considered so far, and reveal liberalism as the fun, rewarding, and fulfilling way of life it can be.

Defenders and critics of liberalism will protest. As we saw in chapter 4, many liberals claim that out of respect for pluralism, questions of the good life should politically and philosophically be stricken from liberal discourse. Critics go the other way. They recognize the extent to which liberal notions of the good infiltrate everyday life, but decry it as a disaster. For them, liberalism is a blob that absorbs each of our relationships—from "place, to neighbourhood, to nation, to family, and to religion"— and sucks them dry of meaning, purpose, and passion.[1] Finally, even thinkers friendly to liberalism as a legal and political system, and who also acknowledge that it might strive to be a comprehensive value system, conclude that it is too thin a gruel for anyone with serious moral commitments or spiritual aspirations.[2] A motley crew if ever there was one, these voices are united by the belief that liberalism is not, should not, or cannot truly be a viable way of life.

I am not of that opinion. Neither, I suspect, are you—at least not if you are liberal all the way down in the manner I've described. Part II of this book is written for us and animated by three questions. This chapter answers the first: *What* does a liberal way of life look like? The next chapter answers the second: *Why* would we want to lead a liberal way of life? The final three chapters on spiritual exercises answer the third: *How* do we cultivate a liberal way of life? The refrain of part I of this book is that we swim in liberal waters. Part II changes tack. My advice is that if you see yourself in the liberal way of life I set out, dive in. The water is just fine.

Growing Up Liberal

In this chapter, we rejoin our guide (our guru, dare I say) to a liberal way of life, John Rawls. This may be a good place to remind ourselves why. Why is my account so bound to this thinker?

The answer is not that he is some sort of liberal god or has the best ideas, whatever that would mean. His special status is due to his method. As you will recall from chapter 2, Rawls does not launch his grand theory of liberalism by defining the term directly, nor does he start from first-order moral principles about how society should be organized. His opening gambit is instead to consult the major documents and artifacts in the public culture of a liberal democratic society (in his case, the United States), and from there, reconstruct its fundamental ideas and commitments. He starts, in other words, by observing rather than speaking.[3] And it is by observing our shared public culture that he derives his—which is to say, *our*—fundamental idea of society as a fair system of cooperation from one generation to the next. No matter our more specific views and beliefs, Rawls feels confident that his readership will be not just familiar with this idea but steeped in it too. This is how he hooks his theory of liberalism into our own self-conception and the kind of citizen and person we want to be.

Part I of this book doubled down on Rawls's method. If liberalism now saturates the background (and not only the public or political) culture of our times, then what Rawls said fifty years ago will be even truer today: our self-conception is likely to be liberal through and through. Many of us have been raised in societies where liberal ideas and sensibilities are the background framework of personal, professional, and political life. It is on this point that I wish to bring Rawls back in. Why? Because the most psychologically astute and sociologically rich sections of *A Theory of Justice* are about growing up in a liberal democratic society, surrounded by its institutions, and learning to see oneself in its norms and values. Rawls, in other words, tells a coming-of-age story that may well resonate more in our day than it did in his.

If you are unfamiliar with the structure of *A Theory of Justice*, a quick overview is helpful. The book is divided into three parts. Part I ("Theory") establishes general principles for a just society. Part II ("Institutions") lays out an institutional scheme for those principles. And part III ("Ends") describes what kind of person is produced by those principles and institutions. Most readers do not read the whole book through. While understandable given that the book is over five hundred pages long, it is also a shame. Part III is the widest ranging and the one Rawls liked best.[4]

Part III focuses on an issue that I raised in chapter 4: social and political stability, and whether a society based on his principles of justice could reliably reproduce itself from one generation to the next. Is it realistic, Rawls asks, to expect that the principles and institutions laid out in parts I and II of *A Theory of Justice* could take root in the lives of members of liberal democracy? Fine principles and institutions are of no ethical or political use if they fail to interest and vivify ordinary people (and not just moral heroes and saints).

To address this question, Rawls did something smart and creative. He ventured past his familiar terrain of moral, social, and political theory for insights from the field of developmental and childhood psychology. Some of his sources are still widely read today (Sigmund Freud and Lawrence Kohlberg, for example), and others less so. Yet the overall effect of this literature was to focus Rawls's attention on what people *who grow up in* a liberal democratic society would be like. Specifically, key sections of part III of *A Theory of Justice* examine how, from infancy to adulthood, individuals are socialized by domestic, educative, religious, professional, and political institutions underpinned by liberal values.[5] When Rawls thus asks if members of liberal democracy will come to support liberal principles and institutions, he is not talking about people in general (for instance, two thousand people randomly plucked from a global database) but rather about those who have been raised within—who have spent their lives swimming in—a liberal society. He wants to know how, whether, and why *liberals* might come to give full-throated support to liberal ideas and institutions.

A word of warning: if you haven't read the relevant sections of *A Theory of Justice*, it's best to lower your literary expectations. They don't have much dramatic tension or flair. Yet they read almost as if Rawls had set out to write a Bildungsroman, that is a coming-of-age story about the moral and emotional maturation of a young person.

Starting from early childhood, Rawls tracks an individual through the stages of life to show how he (that is, his fictional individual) comes to learn the norms and acquire the desires that we (that is, Rawls's readers who have grown up in a liberal democratic society) can be presumed to already have. Granted, no one's journey through life is going to be quite as smooth as the one in Rawls's story. His *persona dramatis* is a little too blessed, and passes from a loving family to meaningful friendships and a rewarding profession to become a man with a moral backbone. Realistic or not, what matters is that this lucky individual and Rawls's readers can both be expected to have acquired deep in-their-bones knowledge of the single moral idea that underlies virtually all institutions, associations, and relationships in a liberal society: reciprocity.

Reciprocity

"[My] theory of right and justice," Rawls observes, "is founded on the notion of reciprocity which reconciles the points of view of the self and of others as equal moral persons."[6] The idea of reciprocity is everywhere in *A Theory of Justice*. A society that sees itself as a fair system of cooperation is a scheme for mutual benefit. It also underlies his theory of selfhood and how liberals perceive themselves in all manner of personal, professional, and political contexts.

Reciprocity may sound grubby, a principle of the you-scratch-my-back-I'll-scratch-yours variety. It sounds, in other words, like everything liberalism has a bad reputation for: egoism, calculative rationality, a morality for the Poloniuses and "last men" of the world.[7] But one way to think of Rawls's philosophy is that he elevates reciprocity to an ennobling principle of psychology—in terms of giving others their due and fair share (of rights, respect, and riches) as well as asserting the validity of our own claims and expectations. That makes reciprocity balanced between altruism and impartiality, on the one hand, and mutual advantage, on the other.[8]

It is relevant that Rawls derives his conception of reciprocity from the work of the grandfather of the Bildungsroman genre, Jean-Jacques Rousseau's coming-of-age treatise, *Emile—or On Education* (1762). *Emile* is a wonderful, weird, and depressing book. Wonderful because it is Western philosophy's first and only attempt at a full-blown manual for coming of age; weird because it requires a nearly omniscient and omnipresent tutor to succeed; and depressing because its author never raised a child, having abandoned all five of his own to an orphanage.[9] Despite that enormous moral failing, and bitterly ironic for it, *Emile* founded the field of child-centric pedagogy: the idea that every child enters the world with a distinctive temperament, and the goal of education is to enable them to grow according to their unique nature and rhythm.[10]

Rawls drew much inspiration from *Emile*. His moral theory shares Rousseau's highest-order aim: to explain how a person can live the best life for themselves and retain their personal integrity while living in modern society.[11] Moreover, his political theory assumes Rousseau's mission—from *Emile* and *The Social Contract* (also 1762), which Rousseau insisted be read in tandem— to arrange the institutions of a social world so that humankind's worst vices would not arise.[12] He had even planned to use a quote from *Emile* as the epigraph for *A Theory of Justice*: "Those who expect to treat moral and political philosophy as separate things will never understand anything about either."[13]

Yet it is Rawls's theory of the self that most bears Rousseau's fingerprints, and he takes from *Emile* the single principle that underlies the psychology of *A Theory of Justice*. As appropriate for a Bildungsroman, Rawls introduces it in a passage on childhood development and how children learn to love their parents:

> The parents, we may suppose, love the child and in time the child comes to love and to trust his parents. How does this change in the child come about? To answer this question I assume the following psychological principle [of Rousseau's]: *the child comes to love the parents only if they manifestly first love him.* Thus the child's actions are motivated initially by certain instincts and desires, and his aims are regulated (if at all) by rational self-interest (in a suitably restricted sense). Although the child has the potentiality for love, *his love of the parents is a new desire* brought about by his recognizing their evident love of him and his benefiting from the actions in which their love is expressed.[14]

The idea is this: young children, says Rousseau—anticipating the tradition of developmental psychology that follows him, from Freud to Jean Piaget, Kohlberg, Abraham Maslow, and Jacques Lacan—do not yet know how to love or hate. They have needs and instincts that can be met or not, along with attendant feelings of satisfaction or frustration. For love and hate to come into being, two additional things are necessary. First, the child must be able to perceive, however inchoately, the intentions of other people (in this case, their parents). Second, their parents must manifest their intention to help or harm the child. Only when intentions are manifest and perceived can love and hate be born. "We seek what serves us," writes Rousseau, "but we love what wants to serve us. We flee what harms us, but we hate what wants to harm us."[15]

Rawls makes a meal of this principle, going so far as to call it a psychological law. It marks, as we have just seen, the beginning of love. It also marks the beginning of something equally important: a sense of self-worth. For with the feeling that you are loved comes a series of affirmations. "Someone cares about me" is only the first, which with nurturing and a growing sense of confidence, may well bloom into "I am worthy of love" and "I matter." (Of course, the negatives can flow just as swiftly and destructively: "No one cares about me," "Maybe I'm not love-able," and "I don't matter.") Parental love leads the child to self-respect and affirms their own sense of self-worth. With luck, this disposition will last a lifetime.

Rawls does not stop with this family scene. The protagonist of his Bildungsroman grows up, goes to school, makes friends, gets a job, and becomes an active citizen. What do we find? Versions of the same psychological law at each stage of life. Its most general version reads, "We acquire attachments to persons and institutions according to how we perceive our good to be affected by them. The basic idea is one of reciprocity, a ten-dency to answer in kind."[16]

Liberalism didn't invent reciprocity. Answering like with like is human nature (and more than human nature).[17] Yet liberal-ism is the first social and political system that strives to realize this value, here on earth, for *all* of its members. No premodern regime or ideology dreamed of it, nor does democracy on its own, except when alloyed with liberalism. And if collectivist movements (such as democratic socialism) take on this mantle, and providing they respect civil and political liberties while pursuing social and economic equality, then they are simply the kind of liberal regime that Rawls believes best realizes his principles of justice.[18]

It is easy to lose sight of how extraordinary liberalism is. It teaches every single one of its members that they matter, and that every citizen—you *and* me: you no more than me, and me no more than you—has a legitimate expectation to be treated reasonably and fairly by the basic institutions of our society. Reciprocity for all is the radical moral adventure of liberalism and has profound psychological effects.

First, in response to Rawls's fundamental question in part III of *A Theory of Justice*, we have an answer as to why citizens of liberal democracies might learn to love and support liberal principles and institutions. Because if these principles and institutions do their job, then as per Rousseau's law, they have with evident intention loved and supported us. These principles and institutions, in other words, engage our affections because they extend and consolidate the reciprocity at the core of the most fundamental experiences and relationships of our lives. Our family loves us, so we learn to love; our friends like us, so we learn friendship; our colleagues depend on us, so we learn mutual trust; and our fundamental institutions care for us, so we develop what Rawls calls a "sense of justice": a capacity and desire to understand, apply, and act from the principles of justice that underlie those institutions. No wonder, then, how resentment festers when this reciprocity is not honored. Betrayal by a liberal polity is more than a political harm. It is a psychic injury, an undermining of who it has officially and repeatedly led us to believe we are.[19] It is enough to make people think they hate liberalism when what they really reject is liberaldom.

The second psychological effect of having reciprocity enshrined in the fundamental institutions of a liberal democratic society is that it (that is, the ideal of reciprocity) has the potential to spread to all aspects of our lives. Now, strictly speaking, this needn't happen. Liberalism only mandates that in our capacity as *citizens*, we are free and equal. Out of respect for self-determination and pluralism, it lets people make up their minds if that's how they want to think of themselves through and through.

Some won't, of course. It is possible to compartmentalize that self-conception to a particular domain (call it the political—the public sphere of citizenship), and elsewhere seek out relationships (such as marriages or friendships) or associations (such as churches or professions) that do not enshrine reciprocity as a first principle. Granted. Yet isn't it natural and likely that for most people who grow up in a liberal democratic society, this self-conception will spill over into other areas of life? From essential constitutional documents to the pervasive rights talk of our culture, from the earliest instruction in civic education to the wall-to-wall of twenty-four-hour news, from ads that tell us that we deserve a vacation to human resources codes of conduct for respectful workplace relations, from calls of the American dream and Australian "fair go" to cries of "tax the rich!" and "fuck the 1 percent!" we are engulfed in a public and background political culture that declares our mutual freedom, equality, and dignity at every turn. Why wouldn't reciprocity become the default lens for how we understand and carry ourselves?

Think of it this way. This book is about leading a liberal way of life, yet it may seem as if there are basic questions that liberalism can't answer: Should I have children? How should

I raise them? Should I prioritize a career over friends? What kind of job won't leave me feeling drained? What is love? If liberalism lacks the resources to answer questions of value and meaning, then it is not a viable conception of the good life.

But let's take a closer look at one of these queries: Should I have children? Few conceptions of the good will ever give a direct answer to a question like that. Some strands of religion might: "Yes! Go forth and multiply!" or if you're an aspiring monk, "No! That would break your vows!" Nevertheless, short of highly prescriptive doctrines, most conceptions of the good leave a lot of room for individuals to figure out what suits them.

A conception of the good provides a framework to deliberate life's big questions, not a direct answer to them. My claim throughout this book is that liberalism can be—and for a great many readers, already is—your framework. A woman raised in a liberal society, and who is thus thoroughly schooled in reciprocity, is likely to have her own career aspirations. That might lead her to wait until she is professionally established to have kids. Or she might resent her deadbeat husband who doesn't do any household chores (which he should given liberal expectations of reciprocity) and think to herself, "I can't deal with a kid on top of that." Or a couple might think twice about bringing a child into the world given the environmental costs to future generations. A liberal way of life won't prescribe an answer to this or most any fundamental question. It would be illiberal if it did! It does, however, set out ideas to guide deliberation of matters of the deepest personal concern.

No one needs to be confined to liberal ideas to make big life decisions. If, to stay with Rousseau, you have a romantic vision of raising a child in the astonishing style he recommends, well, all power to you. Liberalism doesn't provide a single set of answers to all of life's questions. That said, we are only ever one person. Unless we make a conscious effort to hold them apart, the practical wisdom we've gleaned from Rousseau (or the Bible, Bhagavad Gita, Yukio Mishima, Simone Weil, Cormac McCarthy, or any other pre- or nonliberal influence you can name) will be swirled up with our liberal selves. In the course of my everyday life, it's not as if I freely hop from one perspective to another, as if to say, "Well, as a liberal I think this, but my study of Rousseau has led me to conclude that." There's just the semicoherent miasma that is me.

But here's the thing: it is not a fair fight between these influences. Even if I were to read Rousseau for an hour every day, my fifteen other waking hours are spent soaking up liberal waters. The options facing us, then, are threefold. You can forget you ever read this and keep bobbing along—with no judgment from me because anyone who affirms a comprehensive doctrine distinct from liberalism (and is sympathetic to liberalism) will be in this boat (in that their liberalism and comprehensive doctrine will blend in countless ways). You can, as many do today, take an antiliberal stance, and try to root out all traces of liberalism in you and your community. Or you can claim liberalism as an existential option and see where it takes you.

Liberalism as an Existential Option

The term *existential option* is one of Pierre Hadot's favorite descriptors for ancient philosophy.[20] Both words are significant. *Option* conveys how philosophy in the ancient world always starts with a decision to lead a certain kind of life. *Existential* emphasizes how comprehensive and demanding this way of life is. Ancient philosophy is not something that tinkers around the edges of our beliefs and behaviors. It involves a vision of the world that requires personal transformation.

The term is not in Rawls's vocabulary. Yet existential option captures the profound effects that a conception of justice can have on our personality. Consider the analogy he develops between choosing a profession and sincerely affirming the principles of justice that underlie the basic institutions of liberal democracy:

> When an individual decides what to be, what occupation or profession to enter, say, he adopts a particular plan of life. In time his choice will lead him to acquire a definite pattern of wants and aspirations (or the lack thereof), some aspects of which are peculiar to him while others are typical of his chosen occupation or way of life. These considerations appear evident enough, and simply parallel in the case of the individual the deep effects that a choice of a conception of justice is bound to have upon the kinds of aims and interests encouraged by the basic structure of society. Convictions about what sort of person to be are similarly involved in the acceptance of principles of justice.[21]

Person, says Rawls in that last sentence. Not citizen, not member of a liberal society, but person—who someone is through and through.[22] This is not a one-off expression. Part III of A Theory of Justice is all about personal transformation and the acquisition of new desires and life goals. The child who loves their parents is not their earlier self who had merely liked or needed them. Neither is someone who takes liberal principles of justice to heart, which is exactly what we should expect from an existential option. They will be a changed person, with a different way of being in the world and new aspirations for who they aspire to become. To speak more precisely, if they claim a liberal conception of justice as an existential option, they will acquire two virtues that permeate their way of living: freedom and fairness.

The Free Self

We begin with freedom. On top of being abstract and prone to abuse, the word also takes on different meanings according to the kind of conversation it is located in. In metaphysics and morality, debate swirls about free will and whether individuals are really free to do what they want. In religion, the issue is how a higher power constrains and/or enables our choices.

In politics, the question is simpler: In what sense are citizens free, and how is freedom enshrined in fundamental institutions?[23] For liberals, this last question matters. Throughout this book, I have insisted that liberal values are ubiquitous in the background culture of liberal democracies. Yet we mustn't forget that the political domain is the home base (the mothership, as it were) of liberalism—the place where it is officially housed and radiates into the background culture. A liberal political conception, Rawls states, provides citizens "with a way of regarding themselves that otherwise they would most likely never be able to entertain."[24] To see what freedom means in liberalism, then, we need to attend to how the subject is represented in its political conception.[25]

As with all things liberal, the notion of society as a fair system of cooperation and its ideal of reciprocity is our touchstone. Everything stems from it. If society is a fair system of cooperation, it means that within reasonable limits, its members are free to pursue their own conception of the good. That, in turn, leads to an insight that is crucial for how liberals understand themselves in the political domain and beyond: liberalism is a uniquely nonteleological ideology.

This is not as complicated as it sounds. Nonliberal social and political ideologies understand the purpose of their major legal and political institutions (what philosophers call "the right") in terms of maximizing some particular conception of the good life, worldview, or excellence (what philosophers call "the good"). In a word, nonliberal ideologies are teleological: they seek to further a particular good that is defined independently of the right. To cite the most extreme example, Adolf Hitler pronounced, "*Right* is what is *good* for the German people."[26] But what Hitler expresses with terrifying semantic economy is true for nonliberal ideologies in general. Illiberal democracy seeks the good of an exclusive people, oligarchy of an elite, and communism of an economic class. Utilitarianism maximizes the satisfaction of rational desires. And perfectionist ideologies (which are many and varied, and include ancient political theory, all theocracies, and many First Nations worldviews) identify prior standards of human excellence to promote.

Liberalism flips this formula. It puts the right before the good, and neither specifies the good independently of the right nor interprets the right as maximizing the good. Barring exceptional circumstances such as war or humanitarian disaster, we accept that collective goods mustn't override basic individual liberties and respect for persons. Reasonable citizens also agree that their own personal conception of the good, no matter how correct-seeming or ardently desired, cannot require the sacrifice of someone else's happiness. In fact, interests that require the violation of equal rights are declared to have no value, and routinely canceled and deplatformed.

Nothing in my account of the nonteleological nature of liberalism is original. Any textbook on political ideologies says the same: the common denominator for any regime that calls itself liberal is to guarantee equal rights for citizens to pursue their own good in their own way.[27] But Rawls has a gift for drawing out the implications of seeming truisms, in this case about how citizens in liberal democracy conceive of and enjoy their freedom. Specifically, he claims that we think of ourselves as free in three respects.[28]

First, citizens in liberal democracy regard themselves as free to form their own conception of the good, and crucially, revise or change it if they so desire. Apostasy is not a crime, and no one is fated to the worldview they once held. "As free persons," says Rawls, "citizens claim the right to view their persons as independent from and not identified with any particular such conception with its scheme of final ends."[29] Citizens in liberal democracy, then, have two distinct identities. On the one hand, we have a moral identity, sourced in whatever conception of the good we hold. On the other hand, we have a political identity, sourced in a liberal political conception that guarantees equal rights and freedoms. And however unthinkable it may be to view ourselves outside our moral identity, liberal citizens are aware that we would continue to have rights, interests, and the power to pursue other conceptions of good no matter our relation to these convictions. This is the first sense of liberal freedom: I am not—or more precisely, I am not only and not inevitably—my conception of the good.

Second, citizens in liberal democracy regard themselves as "self-authenticating sources of valid claims."[30] With this wordy phrase, Rawls means that liberalism empowers every citizen to make claims on public institutions to advance their conception of the good. My status in a social hierarchy is irrelevant when it comes to voting, a fair hearing in court, access to education, buying things at the same price as everyone else, and so forth. This second sense of liberal freedom is a primal cry: I matter! I have a right to be counted and heard no matter who I am or what I believe in.

Third, citizens in liberal democracy regard themselves as capable of taking charge of their own affairs and goals. Liberals have a special horror of paternalism, and given that citizens are free to form and revise their own conception of the good, we also see ourselves as competent to assess and adjust our life plans accordingly. We are not, as Rawls puts it, "passive carriers of desires," and no one (outside special situations of parenthood or guardianship) is entitled to make those decisions for us.[31] This is the third and final sense of liberal freedom: I am responsible and self-directed.

These three senses of liberal freedom—I am not my conception of the good, I matter, and I am responsible and self-directed—are direct consequences of liberalism putting the right before the good. They are the freedoms liberal citizens have in their capacity as liberal citizens. Now Rawls's point is that all citizens in liberal democracy have this set of freedoms and the political self-conception that comes with it. He also says (and must say, because of these freedoms) that it is up to each individual person to reconcile their political identity as citizens with their moral identity based on whatever conception of the good they hold. A Christian or Muslim, for example, must determine for themselves how their liberal freedoms sit with their religious convictions.

My account has an importantly different focus than what we find in Rawls. Unlike him, I am not talking about *all citizens* in liberal democracy. I am only concerned with *liberals all the way down*. And my point is that we liberals do not, like everyone else, simply put the right before the good. For us, the right *is* our good. The liberal conception of the person, with its characteristic freedoms and enshrined in a liberal political conception, is central to who we aspire to be through and through. It is who and how we are. Indeed—and I say this with gratitude, not resignation—we have little else.

Here is an illustration of what I mean. It comes from an extraordinary Bildungsroman of the twenty-first century: Tara

Westover's *Educated* (2018). This is a memoir by someone exposed to liberal ideas and values uniquely late in life. Born in 1986, Westover was raised and homeschooled in Idaho in a Mormon survivalist family that allowed little contact with the outside world. The extremity of her upbringing is shocking. She learns to read only from the Bible, Book of Mormon, and speeches of Joseph Smith and Brigham Young; she first hears of the Holocaust only as a young adult; she is put to work in her father's scrapyard that can only euphemistically be described as dangerous; and she suffers brutal abuse at the hands of her brother. A vignette from her childhood tells you all you need to know. When she comes down with a bad case of tonsillitis, her parents, who own a business mixing herbal tinctures for "God's pharmacy," instruct her to stand in the sun with her mouth open so that the healing rays can work their magic, which she does, for a whole month.

To make a long story short, through grit and courage Westover educates herself, gains admission to Brigham Young University, and from there goes on to complete a doctorate in history at Cambridge University. The climax of the memoir comes when her parents pay a visit during her studies. They come with a mission: to cast the devil out of her and return her to the family fold. She knew in advance why they were there, having seen them succeed in something similar with her sister. Yet even after all of her struggles, Westover remained torn as to whether she would allow the exorcism. She doesn't in the end, and here is her reason:

> [My father] was offering me the same terms of surrender he had offered my sister. I imagined what a relief it must have been for her, to realize she could trade her reality—the one she shared with me—for his. How grateful she must have felt to pay such a modest price. I could not judge her for her choice,

but in that moment I knew I could not choose it for myself. Everything I had worked for, all my years of study, had been to purchase for myself this one privilege: to see and experience more truths than those given to me by my father, and to use those truths to construct my own mind. I had come to believe that the ability to evaluate many ideas, many histories, many points of view, was at the heart of what it means to self-create. If I yielded now, I would lose more than an argument. I would lose custody of my own mind. This was the price I was being asked to pay, I understood that now. What my father wanted to cast from me wasn't a demon: it was me.[32]

Westover does not spell out where she learned this "one privilege" to "construct [her] own mind." I doubt it was from any single source. She read authors filled with this message (including David Hume, Rousseau, William Godwin, Mary Wollstonecraft, and John Stuart Mill).[33] Studying abroad surely contributed. But it also had to be from living, for the first time, in a world saturated with liberal values. I say so because the reasons she gives for refusing to submit are a veritable précis of the three freedoms of the liberal person. First, her reasoning starts from the premise that she is not fated to the conception of the good she was born into; second, her power and right to self-create are sourced in herself along with the fact that she, as an individual person, matters and can make claims on her own behalf; and third, she claims responsibility and self-direction over her life ("custody," in her words).

Westover is the liberal subject incarnate. So am I, and perhaps so are you. Bravery is required in her case. In the face of the self-abnegation demanded by her family, she needs to stake liberal freedoms, not only to fend them off, but to establish for herself who she is and wants to be. Yet what we (Westover, me, and perhaps you) have in common is that liberal freedom *is* our conception of the good. For us, liberal freedoms are more than legal rules and political parameters to pursue some other conception of the good life. Those freedoms, and the liberal political subject that is their substratum, are the prereflexive framework we use to navigate the world, and when pressed or questioned, the kind of person we explicitly take ourselves to be.

Ask yourself, Am I someone who lives, let's say, with a touch of irony and self-reflexivity, holding most of my commitments provisionally until something more convincing or interesting comes along (freedom 1)? At the same time, do I take it for granted that not just institutions but also my friends, family, co-workers, and spouse will (or at an urgent minimum, should) listen to and treat me with respect, and vice versa (freedom 2)? Finally, do I value personal independence and assume that how I live is mainly a matter for me to figure out (freedom 3)? Those are not narrowly political freedoms for liberals. They are who we are. Or rather, they are half of who we are. Because in addition to freedom, a genuine liberal way of life is defined by fairness.

The Fair Self

Late in life, Rawls wrote a short, unpublished autobiography titled "Just Jack." *Jack* was what friends and family called him, and *just* was a play on the meanings of *justice* and *simply*. In contrast to his tranquil decades as a Harvard professor, his youth was eventful and at times tragic. On two separate occasions as a child, he passed fatal illnesses to his younger brothers (diphtheria to Bobby Rawls in 1928, and then pneumonia to Tommy Rawls in 1929) and developed a stammer from the trauma. In 1944, he enlisted as an infantryman, was nearly killed in battle, and decorated with a Bronze Star for bravery. Yet in telling his life story, Rawls singles out a seemingly minor occurrence: his first and only "real" job. While an undergraduate at Princeton in 1941, he had wanted to go on a sailing trip with friends and expected his family would pay. To his chagrin, his father had other ideas, telling Jack to get a job if he wanted a holiday. He did, and the experience was formative.

Jobs were hard to find in those days. The depression was beginning to ease by that time, of course, but the best I could do on short notice was a twelve-hour job—6 a.m. to 6 p.m., 6 days a week—in a doughnut factory somewhere in downtown Baltimore, whose location I have conveniently repressed. I was the helper of an older man named Ernie who operated one of the mixing machines. He had been there for eighteen years and had three children to support, and it seemed he'd be there forever, breathing flour dust all his life. . . .

Ernie was decent and considerate, and never spoke harshly to me. He seemed resigned to the fact that he would always have that sort of job. There was no prospect of advance, really, or much hope of anything better for him. As for me, I decided to look elsewhere. There must be jobs easier than this, I thought, and twelve hours a day breathing flour dust was too much. . . .

I came to feel very sorry for Ernie. Often I've felt my days at the doughnut factory and Ernie's decency and stoicism in view of his fate—or so it seemed to me—made a lasting impression. So that was how most people spent their lives, of course not literally, but to all practical purposes: pointless labor for not much pay, and even if well paid it led nowhere. Even business and law struck me as dead ends. While trying not to forget the plight of the Ernies of this world, I had to find my place in life in some other way. Did these things influence me in proposing the difference principle years later? I wouldn't claim so. But how would I know?[34]

Who am I to gainsay Rawls? Still, his theory of justice makes a lot of sense when viewed through the prism of this experience.

A major accomplishment of his political philosophy is to have reconciled two seemingly incompatible liberal traditions: a US strand based on personal freedom with a European strand based on social welfare.[35] The term he used to bridge them is *fairness*, the exact quality missing when a person like Ernie must toil endlessly at a job that a college student like Jack can quit after six weeks because he finds it difficult and demeaning.

Fairness is a multilayered word, untranslatable into other Indo-European languages. Unlike the term *justice*, it lacks a bombastic tone. That may surprise parents of young children, whose first moral utterance is so often a primal cry of "that's not fair!" With age, however, they learn that on top of equity, fairness signifies grace and attractiveness as well as gentleness and kindness. Those are not qualities associated with social and political institutions. Yet Rawls places fairness at the heart of his vision of the good society, good citizen, and good life. Or more precisely, he leads us to see that we already believe that fairness should be at the heart of these things, and with our acceptance secured, proposes principles of justice to specify what fairness requires of our institutions and ourselves. I cited these principles in chapter 6, yet they are sufficiently important to list once more. A liberal will see them not as external constraints on conduct but instead as guides for living well:

FIRST PRINCIPLE. Each person is to have an equal right to the most extensive total system of equal basic liberties compatible with a similar system of liberty for all.

SECOND PRINCIPLE. Social and economic inequalities are to be arranged so that they are both: (a) to the greatest benefit of the least advantaged . . . and (b) attached to offices and positions open to all under conditions of fair equality of opportunity.[36]

Freedom and fairness are the signature virtues of a liberal way of life. It may be tempting to map them onto the principles of justice, such that freedom would correspond to the first principle and fairness to the second. But that wouldn't be accurate, either institutionally or existentially. Institutionally speaking, the basic liberties of the first principle are equal and reciprocal, and thus have fairness built into them. Moreover, the fairness of the second principle must honor the basic liberties.

Existentially—that is, from the perspective of a liberal way of life committed to the principles of justice—the two virtues are also inseparable. Freedom, we will see, is realized through fairness and fairness is freely practiced. That, at any rate, is the case I make in the coming chapters. I will have more to say about fairness than freedom. This is not because freedom is any less important but rather because it is more tempting to deviate from fairness, particularly in liberaldom, where Rawls's two principles of justice are far from realized. In chapter 6, I discussed certain attitudes that come from taking fairness to heart, such as a rejection of moral desert and willingness to regard one's talent as a common asset. With my Rawlsian spiritual exercises, I will uncover many more, and ones that stem from a liberal commitment to, as Rawls puts it, "share one another's fate."[37] But before I explore the attitudes and exercises of fairness in detail, I must address a prior question. Why should we want to share in one another's fate in the first place? What's in it for me and you? Why should Jack care about Ernie? And why, to pose the tougher question, should Ernie care about Jack?

9

Seventeen Reasons to Be Liberal

BY NOW YOU may have guessed that I'm a fan of liberalism. Still, the hard truth is that many worthy human goods do not flourish in liberal soil. Bravery, solidarity, loyalty, filial duty, compassion, oneness with nature, noninstrumental concern for nature, enthusiasm, and forgiveness are not well nourished by a culture centered on reciprocity. Piety, deference, and self-sacrifice fare even worse. And so while this chapter makes the case for why a liberal way of life is good, it is important to keep in mind who I am trying to convince and why.[1]

This book is not written for readers who are hostile to liberalism, not because they are beyond the pale, but because their supreme values relegate those of liberalism to second-class status or worse. If respect for hierarchy is central to your moral universe, what can I say to recommend fairness that is not already broadcast from every official channel of liberal democracy?[2] Or if the kind of personal freedom promoted by liberalism strikes you as nothing deeper than the "logic of the supermarket," how compelling will a defense of autonomy be?[3] Conversations with illiberal people are certainly possible. But for a liberal worldview to take hold, we must be frank about what it requires: elevating (liberal) values currently held in low regard and lowering (il-, non-, and aliberal) values currently held in high regard. This kind of revaluation is beyond the scope of any one book.

My intended audience is fence-sitters: people who, like me, support liberalism and are unable to nominate an alternative conception of the good for themselves, yet hesitate to fully plunge into our own values. I'm writing, in other words, for would-be liberals in liberaldom. Neither fish nor fowl, we tiptoe around ourselves. The advantages of our reticence are obvious. We need no reminder as to how we profit from quietly tilting the tables of reciprocity in our favor, subtly gaming fairness so that our loved ones benefit, and exercising our freedom in all sorts of ways that are not entirely symmetrical. Yet there is a cost to our cleverness: we fail to enjoy the felicities of the way of life we profess. I don't mean this in a wishy-washy sense, as if we're losing a warm fuzzy feeling that comes from doing the right thing. I mean that we deny ourselves the very goods our way of life is designed to deliver. Like someone who only buys low-fat cheese thinking they're so smart and prudent, we need to stop and ask, What are we even doing? This chapter will identify the benefits and blessings of a liberal way of life. We need to see what we stand to gain.

Liberalism and the Care of the Self

Great works of philosophy are filled with scoundrels and reprobates. Plato gave us Gyges, who could slip on a magical ring to do evil unseen; Montesquieu invented the sumptuous Uzbek, equal parts irony and cruelty; David Hume presented a rascal, the "sensible knave," able to sniff out loopholes in any obligation; and Søren Kierkegaard painted the bourgeois *gentilshommes* all around him. John Rawls too was fascinated by malign figures, and in his teaching drew up typologies of the philosopher's "rogue gallery."[4] His published work, however, targets a specific villain: the "unreasonable person." This is someone who may be perfectly rational and adept at pressing their own advantage, yet unwilling "to honor, or even to propose, except as a necessary public pretence, any general principles or standards for specifying fair terms of cooperation."[5]

Unreasonable people come in all shades. At the unscrupulous end of the spectrum are straight-up rule breakers who, if assured they can get away with it, will lie, cheat, and steal. But we shouldn't focus on this hardened minority. Much more common are those who follow and take advantage of the rules of their society, even if they know full well that those rules are unfair and cannot be squared with the principles of justice they profess in the abstract.

Let me offer an example. In Australia, if you make more than $45,000 per year (which is when a higher tax rate kicks in), you can divert a fixed amount of extra income toward your retirement fund, which will be taxed at a much lower rate (15 percent as opposed to 34.5 percent or higher, up to 48 percent). This is a significant tax concession for higher-income earners. Virtually everyone I know who can take advantage of it does, and of course, no rule is broken. The problem is that the rule itself is unreasonable, especially in an Australian context marked by baby boomer wealth, asset inflation, and intergenerational injustice.[6] It fails the test of reciprocity, is legislated by the privileged for the privileged, and is one tiny instance of the everyday ways that advantaged people leverage their wealth, status, and connections to beget more advantage. Most unreasonable people are not moral monsters. We can be models of decency.

How best to appeal to unreasonable people who profess to being liberal? One strategy is to call a spade a spade and reproach them for being, well, *unreasonable* and selfish. I take a different approach. To the unreasonable, I say this: you are being *irrational* (in the sense of imprudent and heedless) and missing the advantages of a liberal way of life. My emphasis, in other words, falls less on the fact that unreasonable liberals fail to care for other people than that they do a poor job of caring for themselves.

The phrase "care of the self" is not my own. In academia, it was popularized by philosopher and historian Michel Foucault. In his later work (itself inspired by Pierre Hadot), he shows how classical Greco-Roman civilization had a distinctive conception of morality, which he called *le souci de soi-même* (care of, or concern for, the self—with *souci* in French having both meanings). It was based on encouraging individuals to attend to, work on, and improve themselves for their own sake. As Foucault states in an interview, "What we have here is an entire ethics that pivoted on the care of the self and gave ancient ethics its particular form. I am not saying that [in general] ethics *is* the care of the self, but that, in antiquity, ethics as the conscious practice of freedom has revolved around this fundamental imperative: Take care of yourself."[7]

Caring for others and caring for yourself is not an either/or proposition. Moral motivation is often a mixture of both. More to the point, ancient philosophers believe that a selfish person is fated to misery: beholden to their desires, unable to dwell in the present, and without the least knowledge of friendship, love, and uncalculative sociability.[8] From this perspective, the best and most immediate reason to care for others is to care for yourself. Living your best life and becoming your best self is the goal. Helping others, says Foucault with sly exaggeration, "comes as a supplementary benefit."[9]

Rawls does not press his case quite as stridently as Foucault. Yet he mounts a similar (ancient-style, if you like) defense of a liberal way of life. In chapter 4, I introduced his argument for the stability of a polity based on his two principles of justice. Stability is best guaranteed when a large majority of citizens have a desire to live up to a certain ideal they have of themselves as just people and citizens. And here is the crucial point: when it comes to convincing citizens as to *why* they should want to be just (or more technically, *why* they should want to be the kind of reasonable person who makes a sense of justice supremely regulative of their life plans), Rawls consistently appeals to their self-interest in the expansive sense of demonstrating why a liberal way of life is excellent *for the individual themselves.*

How so? On the one hand, he shows how a commitment to liberal principles of justice frees us from all kinds of corrosive emotions. A liberal way of life is as protected from "special psychologies"—Rawls's word for such gremlins of the soul as envy, spite, jealousy, hostility, rancor, entitlement, pride, and grudgingness—as any other.[10] On the other hand, he describes in loving detail the great goods of a liberal way of life. A genuinely liberal person is stalwart yet fun, self-reflexive yet cheerful, impartial yet committed, and independent yet grateful. When it comes to selling his theory of justice and persuading ordinary citizens why they should want to be reasonable, Rawls's main tactic is not to harp on about moral rightness or draw out the practical benefits for the polity. He recommends a liberal way of life for the self-cultivation it affords.[11]

In aligning liberalism with care of the self, I seem to be playing right into the stereotype of liberals as caring only about their own welfare and private comfort. So let me state loud and clear that a liberal way of life does not detract from, or hold itself out as a substitute for, collective action geared to realizing social justice. To the contrary, it requires progressive political engagement.[12] To see why, I need only highlight a famous stipulation that Rawls makes at the outset of part III of *A Theory of Justice*. There, just as he is about to launch his campaign for a liberal way of life, he stipulates that his discussion will be limited to what he calls a "well-ordered society"—one that honors, and is publicly known to honor, liberal principles of justice.[13] Rawls, in short, confines himself to the context of an ideal just society. Why? Because only within the context of a just society is it straightforwardly rational (that is, consistent with one's own self-interest) to be and act reasonably (that is, to propose and honor fair terms of cooperation). Such an ideal world has no unfair rules or sanctioned injustices to tempt me. It also mitigates collective action problems, for if I can be assured that everyone else acts reasonably, it becomes that much more rational for me to do so as well.

Stipulating a just society to align morality with self-interest (and care for others with care of the self) makes for a neat theory. But Rawls elides the problem at the bottom of my book—a problem of and for nonideal theory: Why be liberal *under conditions of liberaldom*?

Take the tax concession from a moment ago. If everyone who qualifies takes advantage of it and siphons off tax revenue, I need truly compelling reasons—compelling enough to overcome the direct hit to my retirement savings—as to why I shouldn't do the same. This book tries to answer that kind of dilemma with an array of reasons as to why we should want to hold fast to our liberal commitments. But I'm the first to admit that it's an uphill battle. The sometimes more intangible benefits of a liberal way of life come, in this case, smack up against money lost. Such acute trade-offs are minimized for Rawls's hypothetical citizens living in an ideally just society. Their rules are fair and their fellows just. Yet that is precisely why collective action is imperative for real-world liberals. If we politically mobilize, campaign for changes to this and countless other unfair rules, and inch a little nearer to a just, well-ordered society, then a liberal way of life becomes that much more rational, that much more enticing. On top of living in a society with enhanced social stability, a more resilient social fabric, and warmer civility, we secure peace of mind for ourselves. For the closer we get to a just society, the more we get to live a liberal way of life qualm-free, not nagged (or at least, nagged less loudly and insistently) by the rational voice inside our heads calling us fools for being reasonable.

The Benefits of Being Liberal

Let's get down to brass tacks. What are the advantages—the *existential perks*, I will call them—of a liberal way of life? To set up our spiritual exercises, here is a list of the benefits of a way of life based on reciprocity, freedom, and fairness. The next three chapters will take up and expand on each of these seventeen perks in this order:

1. The most iconic representation of justice is as blindfolded. Accordingly, *impartiality* is a key liberal virtue: an ability to see the world and other people from beyond my narrow positional interests.
2. *Autonomy*, that much-vaunted liberal quality, is closely related to impartiality in that it means to be and act in a way that is not determined by my narrow positional interests.
3. Together, impartiality and autonomy work to *lessen the hold of pride and snobbery*—highly destructive emotions wherein I think of myself as distinct and superior, along with myriad anxieties.
4. Impartiality and autonomy also help me to step outside myself and be a little less gripped by the *me*-ness of me. That makes liberals *light, ironic, fun, and playful*.

5. Often, though, all lightness and irony aside, our positional interests tempt us to claim things we know we shouldn't. If we remain true to liberal commitments of fairness and reciprocity, we learn *stalwartness and self-restraint*.

6. We also come to *lessen frustration and rage at our society* by understanding why such things, however ardently desired, are not ours by moral or legal right.

7. We can even feel *gratitude* for living in a society that officially supports its members, including me and my loved ones, to learn our tastes, develop our talents, and find our purpose.

In the following chapter, I will unpack this first set of perks with the spiritual exercise of the original position, which has impartiality and autonomy at its core. The next spiritual exercise, reflective equilibrium, centers on self-coherence and personal integrity. With it, I will draw out a second set of existential perks:

8. Unlike other conceptions of the good, a liberal way of life is entirely based on the official public morality of our times. That means liberals have a real chance at *self-coherence*. So long as we live in reasonably healthy liberal democracies, our personal and public moral commitments need not conflict, which is a standing possibility for other conceptions of the good life.

9. But because liberalism is hegemonic, pretense and fakery are frequently rewarded. To avoid this temptation, liberals must strive to make *avoidance of hypocrisy* central to how we actually live.

10. That's easier said than done. Self-coherence can be elusive, and when our ideals and conduct fail to match up, a liberal way of life should *foster humility along with a reluctance to judge and scorn others*.

11. At its best, a liberal way of life might even *unify the self*. This is no mean feat, and consists in aligning, in lived experience, the right and good, the reasonable and rational, and the just and desirable.

12. If we get good at this alignment, we might even become *graceful*, fulfilling the requirements of justice with pleasure and relative ease.

The first twelve existential perks belong to the general attitudes and dispositions of a liberal way of life. The remaining five more directly concern our relation to other people. Late in his career, Rawls developed a concept of "public reason," which is a way of speaking with and listening to fellow citizens on matters of public concern that respects them as free and equal people. As with his earlier theory of justice, he extols public reason in part by identifying the qualities of character that follow from it. What is striking for our purposes is how many of its perks are happy and joyful.

13. None are more so than a *delight in others*, which is what liberals feel when we recognize ways of being in the world, potentially very different from our own, as committed to common principles we share. Liberals try to see and admire what others are most proud of in their own ways and ideals.

14. We also make room for doctrines we don't understand. Liberals care greatly about fairness and reciprocity, but not at all about the epistemic truth of other worldviews. Judgmental in some but not in all respects, a liberal way of life has a *live-and-let-live attitude of tolerance*.

15. When we do judge, though, even harshly, we *keep civil and cool*. Considerateness and reasonableness are built into our worldview, and we can justify no other way of treating fellow free and equal citizens.

16. All of this to say that liberals believe in reasoning in good faith with citizens of differing and even opposing points of view. We see the world not as a zero-sum conflict between inimical perspectives. *Cheerfulness* (or public cheerfulness at any rate, namely, cheerfulness in and about the public) is thus a liberal temperament.

17. Finally, as an ultimate perk, liberalism has the power *to redeem everyday life* by gracing it with moral purpose. Happy and worthy of happiness, a liberal way of life can be good in all senses of the word.

Liberals are often accused of being shrewd dealers, presenting ourselves in the best light all the while squeezing out personal advantage. We plunge everything in the "icy water of egotistical calculation," said Karl Marx and Friedrich Engels long ago.[14]

Let's play along with this persona to conclude. This chapter posed a question: Why be liberal? To answer it, I opened a ledger with two columns. The reasons in the negative column are of a kind: the fruits of deviating from our liberal commitments, including wealth, power, privilege, and prestige. But I also filled in an affirmative column with seventeen reasons, which are just as self-interested in the broad sense of enhancing our experience and character. Needless to say, this latter column is not exhaustive. Feel free to add additional perks. And if your own liberal way of life takes a different point of departure than Rawls and social democracy, please revise accordingly. Still, the message I want to get across is that we can't have our cake and eat it too. Liberaldom has its wages, and we can't consistently deviate from liberal values and still reap the rewards of a liberal way of life. A choice and commitment must be made.

10

How to Be Free, Fair, and Fun

SPIRITUAL EXERCISE 1

TO SEE THE WORLD with the eyes of God—this, John Rawls says, is what liberalism can do. Liberalism, huh? Secular, godless, and some might say soulless liberalism can do that? Yes, it can. All it takes is one simple exercise.

What Is the Original Position?

Each of the next three chapters follows the same course. I will identify a spiritual exercise from Rawls's work and show how to practice it in everyday life. Next, I will explain how it delivers the existential perks listed in the previous chapter: perks 1–7 for the original position, 8–12 for reflective equilibrium, and 13–17 for public reason. By the end, my hope is to have illustrated what a liberal—a free and generous—way of life can look like, why it is worth striving for, and how to start cultivating it straight away.

I begin with Rawls's most famous idea of all: the original position. It is what philosophers call a "thought experiment" and designed for citizens to clarify for themselves which principles of justice should regulate the fundamental institutions of a liberal democratic society.[1] Since spiritual exercises are a practical business, let's try it together. I'll break it down into four steps.

The original position is a meditative exercise done on one's own. Step one, then, is to find a comfortable seat or lie down on your couch. With practice, you can learn to do it on the fly as well as in situations requiring a decision or course of action.[2] For now we'll take it nice and easy.

The exercise begins in earnest with step two. Close your eyes and imagine that you are with a group of people. For the sake of a manageable mental image (though Rawls doesn't specify a number), picture ten other people, none of whom you've met before.

Step three is the crucial twist. Neither you nor anyone else in the group knows your own identity. You don't know your sex, gender, social class, religion, ethnicity, talents, conception of the good, or anything else that might differentiate you from the other people. As Rawls famously puts it, you are situated behind the "veil of ignorance."[3] If you'd like to visualize this step, turn everyone including yourself into stick figures (androgynous stick figures, as it were).

We proceed to step four. It is up to you, along with these imagined people—none of whom know anything about themselves either—to choose and agree on principles of justice to regulate the fundamental institutions of society. Your job, in other words, is to imagine yourself as a free and equal person, deliberating alongside other free and equal people, to select highest-order principles of right and justice for your society.[4] Yet thanks to the veil of ignorance, you must do so without any positional factors to skew the decision-making process.

If you're feeling brave, go ahead and try to reason out step four on your own. But spoiler alert, the setup of the original position is designed to deliver a specific result: the two principles of justice we have encountered before (near the end of chapters 6 and 8, and that together make up Rawls's liberal conception of justice, "justice as fairness"). Rawls reckons that it would be extremely reckless to choose any others given the veil of ignorance. If you don't know whether your conception of the good is favored by society or not, then ironclad equal rights to form and revise it are self-evidently desirable (principle 1). Moreover, if you don't know where you stand in a social and distributional hierarchy, then equality of opportunity and support for the least fortunate are almost as necessary (principle 2). Compared with a utilitarian conception of justice that maximizes aggregate happiness but can ride roughshod over individuals, or a perfectionist conception of justice that uses public power to promote specific notions of the good life, Rawls thinks that choosing something like his two principles is really no choice at all.

Don't be intimated by step four is my point. Unless you're a professional philosopher, it needn't launch you on sophisticated computations.[5] Quite the opposite, it serves as an instantaneous reminder of the "no duh!" variety. Once you suspend knowledge of who you are, rights to equal liberty along with guarantees of fairness and reciprocity are a foregone conclusion—a gimme really. In fact, step four dots the i's and crosses the t's of the much more consequent step three: agreeing to don the veil of ignorance in the first place and entertain questions of fundamental justice without reference to how you and your loved ones stand to gain or lose.[6]

Open your eyes. You've just completed the original position. Four steps, that's all there is to it. Perhaps it seems underwhelming. The original position is merely a hypothetical exercise, after all. There is no question of convening citizens in a town square. Nor are governments committed by meditations. But sincerely and repeatedly practiced, it can upend your life. Don't believe me? Let's turn to the final paragraph of *A Theory of Justice*.

The Mountaintop

The original position raises a microcosm of the question from the previous chapter: Why be liberal? Because from a certain perspective, it looks like self-sabotage.

Allow me to speak bluntly. Suppose in the real world, you are a relatively advantaged member of society. Suppose like me, you are a white, upper-middle-class, able-bodied heterosexual male in a Western capitalist liberal democracy. Why, from a self-interested point of view, should I ever entertain an exercise that brackets my positional advantage? In the present state of affairs, I enjoy more than my fair share of what Rawls calls "primary social goods," which includes rights, liberties, opportunities, income and wealth, and the bases of self-respect.[7] Disgraced or not, a remark by the comic Louis C. K. is painfully apt. On whether it is better to be Black or white in the United States, the answer is obvious: "I'm not saying that white people are better. I'm saying that being white is clearly better. Who could even argue? If it was an option, I would re-up every year. 'Oh yeah, I'll take white again absolutely, I've been enjoying that. I'll stick with white, thank you.'"[8] To suspend knowledge of my whiteness—or maleness, upper-middle-classness, and the rest—in reflecting on which terms of social cooperation to affirm might seem positively irrational.

Rawls's reply to this imagined skeptic (who lurks in all of us, of course) is laced throughout the third and final part of *A Theory of Justice*. It reaches a crescendo in its concluding paragraph. There he steps back to reflect on what he's really been talking about for hundreds of pages. Why, he asks, is the original position and the change in perspective it brings about so important? His answer is stunning:

> Finally, we may remind ourselves that the hypothetical nature of the original position invites the question: why should we take any interest in it, moral or otherwise? Recall the answer: the conditions embodied in the description of this situation are ones that we do in fact accept. . . . Once we grasp this conception, we can at any time look at the social world from the required point of view. It suffices to reason in certain ways and to follow the conclusions reached. This standpoint is also objective and expresses our *autonomy*. Without conflating all persons into one but recognizing them as distinct and separate, it enables us to be *impartial*, even between persons who are not contemporaries but who belong to many generations. Thus to see our place in society from the perspective of this position is to see it sub specie aeternitatis [from the perspective of eternity]: it is to regard the human situation not only from all social but also from all temporal points of view. The perspective of eternity is not a perspective from a certain place beyond the world, nor the point of view of a transcendent being; rather it is a certain form of thought and feeling that rational persons can adopt within the world. And having done so, they can, whatever their generation, bring together into one scheme all individual perspectives and arrive together at regulative principles that can be affirmed by everyone as he lives by them, each from his own standpoint. *Purity of heart*, if one could attain it, would be *to see clearly* and *to act with grace* and *self-command* from this point of view.[9]

This paragraph inspired my book. When I encountered it years ago, I kept rereading it and wondering to myself, "Is this Rawls?"

and then more significantly, "Is this liberalism?" How can the original position do all of that? Then it hit me: it's a spiritual exercise. Recall that in chapter 7, I gave Pierre Hadot's definition of spiritual exercises as voluntary, personal practices meant to bring about a transformation of the individual. The original position satisfies the criteria in letter and spirit. It is *voluntary* in that there is no obligation to take it up. It is *personal* in that it is a device of self-clarification that we adopt on ourselves and our social world. It is a *practice* that can be consciously and regularly adopted. And it is *transformative*, magnificently so: autonomy, impartiality, a God's-eye point of view, purity of heart, grace, and self-command are all to be won. The original position is no mere thought experiment, if that means testing a hypothesis or gauging the consequences of a viewpoint. It is a spiritual exercise, equal to any from antiquity.

Impartiality and Autonomy

Not all readers of Rawls have been as enamored with the final paragraph of *A Theory of Justice*. A prominent philosopher, for example, dismissed it as a "high-pitched homily."[10] I disagree with "high-pitched." But "homily" is on the right track; it does read as a (quasi or functionally) religious discourse intended for spiritual edification.

At its center are two graces (or perks, as I'm calling them) imparted by the original position. The first is *impartiality*, and here the original position is in distinguished company. Virtually all spiritual exercises of ancient philosophy sought to help individuals reach past their egoistic subjectivity to a universal and disinterested point of view. The methods were many and various: climb a mountain to see the world from on high; reflect on how you are an infinitesimal grain of sand in the cosmic ocean;

philosophize with others to escape your own blinkered point of view; or pretend that you're dead and beyond all needs and desires. Whatever the approach, the goal is to pass from a self who consults only their own interest to one open to other people and the universe.[11]

The original position works the same way. It is an exercise in letting go of our own all-too-dear situated self and its whole texture of attachments (to family, friends, class, profession, and more). By suspending knowledge of our preferences and social position on issues of fundamental justice, we leap into an unselfish and unsentimental perspective. That makes the original position a view from everywhere, not nowhere. We shed the partial self to ascend to the impersonal self, the one we share with all of our fellows, now and in generations to come, sub specie aeternitatis.[12] Indeed, to step into the original position is to make what Hadot calls *the* fundamental philosophical choice by seeking to overcome "the partial, biased, egocentric egoist self in order to attain the level of a higher self."[13]

Impartiality represents one-half of the liberal personality: liberality and generosity. *Autonomy*, the second grace imparted by the original position, represents the other: liberty and freedom. Autonomy has a storied history in liberal thought. There are many conceptions in the historical and contemporary literature. Leading contenders include the capacity to govern oneself, a personal ideal of integrity and authenticity, and a set of rights to ensure sovereignty over oneself.[14] With the original position, autonomy takes an austere form: not letting one's opinions and conduct on matters of justice be determined by arbitrary factors. My sex, native talents, and race and ethnicity are the dumb luck of nature. And my wealth, education, and conception of the good are, in fundamental respects, by-products of my social position and the compounded (dis)advantages of history. That is why Rawls created a spiritual exercise to recover my independence from the contingencies of nature and society at any time, simply by reasoning according to its procedure.

Think of the original position as a temporary escape hatch from your own identity. The moment you step through it, you set aside tradition and authority, the opinions of others, and calculations of personal gain and advantage. You become free of all of that. This is its negative work. The positive follows automatically: you engender, all on your own and from your couch, the morality you claim to profess. What is more, if you get good at it, and learn to integrate this perspective into your identity and routines, you then start to act in the real world from principles that would be chosen if your nature as a free and equal person were the decisive determining element.[15] For Rawls (and contractualists more generally), this is the meaning of autonomy: a capacity to obey a law that you give to yourself. The original position enables you to act and want to act from principles that match the kind of (liberal) person you take yourself to be.

The objective of the original position is not to cut oneself off from social ties as an isolated individual. Nor is it to distance oneself from the morality of our own time. The purpose is instead to take a deeper dive into that morality—that is, the morality of our own background and public liberal culture—and not permit ourselves to be distracted or swayed by our social position. We plunge, if you like, into the idea that society should be a fair system of cooperation. And if we do so regularly and cultivate what Hadot would call a "real" rather than "notional" commitment to that idea, we find ourselves exposed to and perhaps eventually committed by the principles behind our own most considered judgments.[16] That process is transformational. We disengage from our social position; we reengage with our social position; and in that ever-renewed activity, we become impartial and autonomous.

Trickle-Down Perks

Impartiality and autonomy are the main graces imparted by the original position. But flowing out from them are a series of "trickle-down" perks, as it were.

The first is to *lessen the hold of pride and snobbery*. Rawls's aversion to pride is well known.[17] We saw in chapter 6 that this aversion underpins his two principles of justice (and the difference principle especially). It is also on vivid display in his undergraduate thesis, "A Brief Inquiry into the Meaning of Sin and Faith" (1942). There the young Rawls defines pride as seeing oneself as "distinct and superior," and his denunciation of it is the only scornful passage I'm aware of in his oeuvre: "So you were an educated man, yes, but who paid for your education; so you were a good man and upright, yes, but who taught you your good manners and so provided you with good fortune that you did not need to steal; so you were a man of a loving disposition and not like the hard-hearted, yes, but who raised you in a good family, who showed you care and affection when you were young so that you would grow up to appreciate kindness—must you not admit that what you have, you have received? Then be thankful and cease your boasting."[18]

Snobbery is even worse. To the sanctimony of pride it adds meanness—the habit and pleasure of making inequality hurt. In *Ordinary Vices*, Judith Shklar shows how harmful this vice is for liberal democracy. It rips the social fabric of any society that proclaims the equality of its members. It also injures the snob themselves, particularly their capacity for self-respect. "To be afraid of the taint of associations from below is to court ignorance of the world," says Shklar. "And to yearn for those above one is to be always ashamed not only of one's actual situation, but of one's family, one's available friends, and oneself. Snobbery is simply a very destructive vice."[19]

It would be one thing if pride and snobbery were easily banished. Unfortunately, they have an insidious power, particularly for those who benefit from inequality. Who doesn't want to believe that they have earned their privilege? This is where the original position comes in. Every time we enter it sincerely— with purity of heart, as Rawls would say—pride and snobbery are taken down a notch. By donning the veil of ignorance, we reaffirm that with respect to our deepest moral conviction (that is, society as a fair system of cooperation), we are not distinct and superior. And by selecting the two principles of justice, we remind ourselves that we owe, and not just are owed, fairness and reciprocity. In fact, to weed out pride and snobbery, you don't even have to go through the steps of the original position. Just remember why Rawls created it in the first place: to select principles of justice to regulate the fundamental institutions of society, precisely because of the "profound and pervasive influence" that those institutions have on everyone's life prospects.[20] Hooray for you if you're educated, upright, and loving. Just cease your boasting and don't confuse being born on third base with having hit a triple. And if sometimes you slip, and pride and snobbery get the better of you, well, not to worry—there's an exercise for that.

I will be brief about the next perk as I have indirectly covered it in previous chapters: a liberal way of life can be *light, ironic, fun, and playful*. We simply need to combine two pieces of the puzzle. In chapter 5, I claimed that comedy today is largely about liberalism. In part that is because liberalism is the culture of our times. But it is also because liberals are naturally funny.

Why? Because of what I observed in chapter 8: a principal meaning of freedom for liberals is the capacity to step back from, evaluate, and revise our conception of the good. That makes us natural-born ironists. Consider what Richard Rorty, master theorist of liberal irony, says in an interview. "Let's say that tolerance is the ironist's main social virtue, and flexibility her main private virtue. Tolerance has to do with people who are different. Flexibility has to do with the ability to redescribe oneself. [Friedrich] Nietzsche and [Marcel] Proust were specialists in doing the latter."[21] With practice, the original position can make little Nietzsches and Prousts of us all by, first, confronting us with our own contingency, and second, teaching us how to step back from it. "Fun times" is not a phrase often associated with the original position, yet it imparts all the building blocks for a playful temperament: self-reflection, concern for others, appreciation of pluralism, and the ability to slip in and out of ourselves. Not taking oneself too seriously or absolutely is the first step toward lightheartedness.

Yet sometimes we do. Sometimes, despite knowing better, we are sorely tempted to assert our needs absolutely and take ourselves all too seriously. An objection made by economists to the original position is relevant. John Harsanyi claimed that the psychology of parties behind the veil of ignorance was too cautious and that a rational actor might be willing to gamble on a more unequal distribution (of rights, wealth, opportunities, and the social bases of self-respect) on the chance that they would be favorably situated once their social position was revealed.[22] "Too cautious to be bourgeois" is what another critic witheringly said of Rawls.[23]

Let's play out the thought. Suppose I roll the dice in the original position and lose. What would that show? According to Rawls, to gamble on something so fundamental signals that

I failed to take my own religious, philosophical, and moral convictions seriously. Perhaps I don't even understand what real religious, philosophical, or moral conviction is.[24]

Now suppose my bet pays off, and when the veil is lifted, I find myself advantageously situated. Well, that reveals something else: I'm happy to benefit from an unjust distribution even though others are treated unfairly. And if we remember that the original position is a hypothetical exercise, it becomes more sinister. In real life, no one who steps into the original position is actually in the dark about who they are. The veil of ignorance is not a real (*Men in Black*–style) amnesia device. To gamble, then, on the "hope"—which is to say, the certainty— that I will benefit from an unequal distribution reveals that in fact, I know perfectly well that I'm already in the dominant social group, and what's more, premeditatively unreasonable and ready to execute an unfair distribution for others.

Not a pretty picture, is it? Yet it's business as usual in liberaldom for its privileged members. Any number of unreasonable courses of conduct are at our fingertips, all sanctioned by law and stamped with social approval. What can the original position do? Two things—if, unlike our gambler, practiced in good faith.

The first is good old-fashioned consciousness-raising. Whenever we step into it, the original position may confront us with the unsettling truth that our decision or action—or at the limit, our plan of life—clashes with our moral convictions. The second is one of our perks: provided we stay true to the principles specified in and by the original position, we learn *stalwartness and self-restraint*. As Rawls states, "When we knowingly act on the principles of justice in the ordinary course of events, we deliberately assume the limitations of the original position."[25] The original position is at once hypothetical and not—a spiritual exercise to practice in the comfort of home, yes, and also carried into the real world through our conduct and character. Its limitations (that is, the reasonable constraints it imposes on practical reasoning), in other words, are not merely thought but lived as well. And that takes, and at the same time inculcates, what Adam Smith calls the "awful virtues" (or what, somewhat differently yet more enticingly, Stephen Macedo names "executive virtues").[26] Stalwartness, self-restraint, resolve, diligence, and patience require discipline. But the original position is fortifying, and by helping us to resist temptation and caprice, can change how we feel about the claims and demands of others.

Which leads to our next perk: *to lessen frustration and rage at our society*. Ours is an age of anger, much of it apt.[27] Now in one sense, the original position positively foments anger. Whenever we look out from it, all we see is liberaldom staring back—in our institutions, the conduct of others, and worst of all, ourselves. That makes it a machine to produce righteous indignation.[28] It sensitizes us to injustice precisely because it defines justice and injustice in a way that is at once exorbitant (what society lives up to the two principles of justice?) yet also ordinary (what reasonable person denies that society should be a fair system of cooperation, roughly along the lines of the two principles of justice?).

At the same time, the original position is designed to defuse a different type of anger, which I'll call *self*-righteous indignation: frustration and even rage at the impact that the norms, laws, and policies of my society have on *me, my* life plans, and *my* notion of the good life.

The decade ushered in by COVID-19 produced a meme to capture this type of anger: the Karen. The meme itself is fraught, tangled as it is in sexism, ageism, racism, and antiracism, particularly in the context of US history.[29] Still, it gets at something real—a me-first, "I'd like to speak to your manager" entitlement that sees social rules and norms as so many impositions on me and my freedom. Squabbles over physical distancing and vaccine mandates neutralize the meme, comfortably splitting the field into us reasonable citizens over here and all of those (male and female) Karens shouting about their "RighTs" and "LibERtY" over there.

But let's push past our comfort zone, shall we? If my default point of view centers on my own plans and welfare, then I'm likely to be irate and Karenish much of the time. My society won't seem like a home but instead a maze of obstacles that get in my way. I may, for example, begrudge every dollar in tax taken from me. I may also resent the fact that so many fellow citizens think and act differently from me, and that my country doesn't feel like a community. If I'm a person of privilege, the claims of the less fortunate may even strike me as so much whining and special pleading. It's the little things too. Every second spent waiting in line at the Department of Motor Vehicles will feel like slow death. And whenever I check the sales tax on a receipt, I'll mutter a *WTF* under my breath. An inner Karen is hard to keep down.

Here we can avail ourselves of the original position as a reframing exercise, which consists in recontextualizing one's experience and concerns within a wider cosmos or whole.[30] Consider the first principle of justice, guaranteeing equal liberties for all. To accept it (which is to say, to enter the original position and acknowledge it as an outgrowth of our moral convictions) is to accept moral and religious pluralism too, and the fact that a modern society can never be a community based on a shared conception of the good. The original position deflates this expectation, and in so doing, releases us from inevitable frustration.[31] It can even come to the rescue at the Department of Motor Vehicles. In his book *This Is Water*, David Foster

Wallace tells us that if you pay attention to the right thing, then even at the supermarket during peak hours, "it will actually be within your power to experience a crowded, hot, slow, consumer-hell type situation as not only meaningful, but sacred, on fire with the same force that made the stars: love, fellowship, the mystical oneness of all things deep down."[32] I haven't gotten quite that far myself. But the next time you go to get your driver's license renewed, think to yourself, odd as it may sound, everyone here is a free and equal citizen. At minimum, you'll enter the headspace of commiseration, where other people aren't nuisances to outfox and cut ahead of. You may even marvel at their decency, the dignity of equals recognizing equals in a situation designed to test human patience.

Rawls has a name for the anger-diminishing power of the original position: "reconciliation." The idea (*Versöhnung* in German) comes from Georg Wilhelm Friedrich Hegel and consists in showing how, broadly speaking, the institutions of liberal democratic society are rational and have evolved the way they have for good reason. The goal is simple and profound: to lead us to intellectually and emotionally grasp our own society as a home, a place that is good to us, and perhaps most important, *of* us—one in which we feel that we are somehow part of the process of creating it. Rawls is fond of a famous saying of Hegel's: "When we look at the world rationally, the world looks rationally back."[33] When we do so, the argument goes, we accept and affirm our social world rather than merely resign ourselves to it. We even become, to cite another fine line from Hegel, able to "delight in the present."[34]

Contrary to the current zeitgeist, I believe there are causes for delight. There is so much we take for granted in our liberal democratic world, so many fragile fruits of civilizational labor that we mistake for the human condition: freedom of speech and belief, the emancipation of women, friendship between the sexes, peaceful transfer of power, unprecedented longevity, Wikipedia, olive oil in every supermarket, and the list goes on. *Gratitude*—felt daily thanks—seems to me the right response and is the final perk of the original position. For if we look out from it and sincerely believe that the social and political order (at least to some extent) satisfies (at least some of) the principles of justice, then we reveal this order to ourselves as decent and worthy of devotion. This is a heartening thought. The original position, to adapt the words of one commentator, "can help us to understand and affirm the very puzzling judgment that God is said to have passed upon the world."[35] Ingratitude is not, in the end, the deadliest enemy of gratitude. Cynicism is—and if we conclude that the contemporary liberal order is a scam and lacks goodness, then that conclusion will infect all of our thoughts and attitudes.

Reconciliation must be evoked with care.[36] Easily does it slide into apologetics and ideology. Between, then, the yes-saying of reconciliation and gratitude, and the no-saying of cynicism, lie the thoughtful positions we might have on the state of our liberal democracies. It was no coincidence that none of my examples of reconciliation evoked the difference principle or social equality. Here, as we all know, real-world liberal societies have an abysmal track record, and for what it's worth, if I could wish one reform into existence to bring us out of liberaldom, it would be comprehensive tax reform (and were I a citizen of the United States, public financing of elections). Rawls never seriously wrote about less than perfectly just societies. As we have observed many times, he works from within ideal theory, and postulates a "well-ordered" society in which the two principles of justice are effective and publicly recognized as such. Yet he did provide an idea that can be adapted to the predicament of living in liberaldom. He called it reflective equilibrium, and it is the next spiritual exercise.

11

How to Be Sincere and Graceful

SPIRITUAL EXERCISE 2

SOMETIMES THE SATIRICAL NEWSPAPER the *Onion* cuts a little too close to the bone. I'm thinking of a piece titled "Liberal Relieved He Never Has to Introspect Again after Assembling All the Correct Opinions." Here it is in full:

MADISON, WI—Taking a moment to reflect on his hard-won personal accomplishment, area liberal Tom Hudson expressed relief Monday that he would never again have to engage in self-examination after finally assembling all the correct opinions. "It definitely wasn't easy, but now that I have all the proper perspectives on the world all perfectly arranged inside of my head, I know I'll never need to question my own thoughts, beliefs, or opinions ever again," said Hudson, proudly recounting his previous efforts at researching all necessary sociopolitical issues, conducting a rigorous self-exploration to determine which of his behaviors were problematic or harmful, and finally achieving the proper balance of beliefs to ensure once and for all that he is an indisputably good person. "It's such a huge weight off my shoulders.

I never have to consider my place in society or my impact on the issues ever again now that I know exactly how to present myself as one of the good guys. This feels amazing." Hudson was then immediately and savagely attacked by his fellow liberals, who insist that his current views are nowhere near progressive enough.[1]

Know Thyself

Why is this imaginary yet entirely plausible liberal so unlikable? Let me count the ways. His moral sleaziness, for starters, and how he holds his opinions to come across as a "good guy." His smugness is equally annoying. Then there's his closure and finality, as if moral life was about locking in the right opinions once and for all. But it's his lack of self-knowledge that most galls me. His facade of correct opinions will crumble under the slightest pressure or temptation precisely because he holds them for all the wrong reasons.

No one named Tom Hudson ever lived in ancient Greece. Yet he is exactly the kind of man whom Socrates would have reduced to rubble. Socrates was, of course, notorious for doing so to much more eminent figures. One tactic was the so-called elenchus, where he would pose a question to his interlocutor ("what is courage?" for example), have them state their opinion, and then, through further questioning, lead them to affirm the opposite of their original view and reveal that they never knew what they were talking about. These efforts were not always appreciated, to put it mildly. What really got Socrates killed, though, was a different tactic, this time exposing inconsistency not *within* an opinion but rather *between* an opinion and way of living. "To a certain extent," writes Pierre Hadot, "we can say that what interests Socrates is not to define the theoretical and objective contents of morality—that is, what we ought to do—but to know if we really, concretely *want* to do what we consider just and good—in other words, how we must act."[2] So when Socrates declares that "an unexamined life is not worth living," his target is not so much people who don't know X (courage, justice, temperance, or what have you).[3] It is people who don't know *themselves*, and whose principles, judgments, desires, and behaviors do not align.

Which brings us back to Tom. His combination of coherence (at the level of professed opinion) and incoherence (at the level of how he will actually live) is cartoonish. He is, on the one hand, a poster boy for what the ancient Greeks called *akrasia*, the failure to do the right thing out of a weakness of will. On the other hand, he represents a more pernicious problem. If and when Tom pauses to reflect about what he ought to do, he will "know" perfectly well, intellectually speaking, what liberal beliefs require of him. But what about his less-than-conscious experiences and interactions? Most of everyday life takes place on this sub- or semiconscious plane. Will his fine opinions have percolated down to it? Almost certainly not. The problem, then, is not moral weakness and the fork in the road of akrasia. It is moral cluelessness, and that no such fork will present itself to conscious attention in the first place. Liberal opinions and beliefs, and everyday habits and routines, will be ships in the night.

It was to deal with this second kind of problem that John Rawls designed a spiritual exercise to promote self-knowledge and moral coherence at all levels—from the loftiest of principles to the humblest of habits. He called it reflective equilibrium and claimed it was Socratic.[4]

What Is Reflective Equilibrium?

Reflective equilibrium is far from a household term. So what does it mean? In a two-sentence definition, it is a method of personal reflection designed to bring the different components of our moral life (including principles, emotions, perceptions, beliefs, habits, and desires) into alignment (or equilibrium) with one another. The idea is to use those components to reflect on, revise, and ultimately support and justify one another, and through the process, become a more consistent and coherent person.

Stated starkly like this, however, reflective equilibrium seems as abstract as the term itself. To bring out its human core, let's pursue Rawls's observation that it is Socratic in nature.

The first respect in which reflective equilibrium is Socratic is its point of departure: a frank acknowledgment that most of us most of the time live in states of confusion. Socrates took his interlocutors as he found them, and as a first step to guiding them to self-intelligibility, demonstrated (or rather had them demonstrate to themselves) how inconsistent and contradictory they were, even in their most considered opinions.

Although Rawls lacks Socrates's brio, he proceeds in the same manner: "Not only do our considered judgments often differ from those of other persons, but our own judgments are sometimes in conflict with one another. The implications of the judgments we render on one question may be inconsistent or incongruent with those we render on other questions. This point deserves emphasis. Many of our most serious conflicts are conflicts within ourselves. Those who suppose their judgments are always consistent are unreflective or dogmatic; not uncommonly they are ideologues and zealots."[5]

Enter Tom Hudson. At an earlier stage of life, he may have admitted to feelings of uncertainty and confusion. But he resolved the situation by taking his muddled convictions, shoving them deep into a mental drawer, and replacing them en masse with a set of views that cohere nicely on paper. Were it not for his inauthenticity and opportunism, he would be a model ideologue or zealot.

Reflective equilibrium also aims at consistency and self-coherence. But it goes about it differently than Tom—working from within a person's state of confusion rather than simply clearing it away. To understand how exactly, we need to clarify a term introduced a moment ago by Rawls, "considered judgments." A judgment is *considered* when made under favorable circumstances, and without, for example, feeling rushed, uninformed, or pressured by external factors. It is a judgment we feel reasonably confident about. And crucially for Rawls, considered judgments can be made at all levels of generality and range from abstract (such as "our country is built for everyone") to midlevel (for instance, "this workplace policy seems like a step in the right direction") to particular ("it wasn't OK how our boss spoke to you today," for example). All of our judgments, whether about abstract principles or concrete situations, have "initial credibility," and "are capable of having for us, as reasonable and rational, a certain intrinsic reasonableness."[6]

Considered judgments are the raw material for reflective equilibrium to work on. They are what we *reflect* on to bring into *equilibrium*. And here we can draw out the second Socratic feature of reflective equilibrium: its quotidian quality. Socrates was famous for having made philosophy an earthly, sometimes downright earthy, pursuit. In his hands, it dealt essentially with everyday life and matters of the deepest yet also most ordinary human concern. Some, like Cicero, were admirers: "[He] was the first to call philosophy down from the heavens and set her in the cities of men and bring her also into their homes and compel her to ask questions about life and morality and things good and evil."[7] Others, like Callicles, were exasperated: "Good God! You never shut up about cobblers and fullers and cooks and doctors!"[8] Love or hate it, no topic was beneath philosophical interest for Socrates.

What is the connection to reflective equilibrium? When Rawls refers to our considered judgments, it is easy to get the impression that he's being highly cognitivist and talking only about ideas inside our head. But if we interpret him more generously, and especially if we read him alongside the philosophy of emotions, social epistemology, and social theory, it becomes clear that what counts as a considered judgment is vast. Emotions are evaluative judgments.[9] When we feel compassion, for example, we've determined that the suffering in question is serious and undeserved. Perceptions too incorporate all kinds of fine distinctions and evaluations—a glance, intake of breath, or shudder can depend on an array of microevaluations.[10] And habits, routines, and pastimes manifestly involve judgments about what we value and how we want to spend our time.[11] All of this is fodder for reflective equilibrium. The judgments baked into our emotions, perceptions, and habits can all become "considered" if we take a moment to step back and assess that, yes, they do represent what we think and who we are.

Broadened this way, reflective equilibrium can truly lift the hood up on who we are. Everything is up for examination, from the principles we affirm to the judgments we stand by, emotions we warrant, perceptions we validate, and habits we practice. Our entire psyche and sensorium stands, if not on trial, then at least for inspection. One of the best opening paragraphs of a book I've ever read is worth mentioning. It is by Jonathan Lear, who in his commentary on Sigmund Freud, observes that at the end of the day, psychoanalysis has but one single rule. It demands only and exorbitantly for a patient to say to the analyst "whatever it is that comes into his or her mind, without censorship or inhibition."[12] That's the whole of psychoanalysis, its one rule and goal: to get us to speak (and feel and think) fluently. Reflective equilibrium shares the same radicality. If we elicit our considered judgments at all levels of generality, and if we strive to introduce a measure of consistency between them, then we too will become fluent. The components of our moral life will align, and the judgments that we make on one day and at one level of generality will be lucid, and speak with, to, and of the rest of us.

That is the hope, at any rate. How we get there is the third Socratic element of reflective equilibrium: dialogue and personal interrogation.

How to Do Reflective Equilibrium

A year ago, my then twelve-year-old daughter (and my wife, who put her up to it) played a joke on me that still stings. We were about to go surfing and almost out the door when she stopped to say, "Actually Daddy, I don't want to go." "What? Why?" I replied. "You love surfing." Her response: "Yeah, but I'd rather stay home and do reflective equilibrium with you."

Touché. Had I been quicker, I should have said, "Don't worry, we can do both at the same time." Because, as per its third Socratic quality, reflective equilibrium only requires a conversation, whether between two or more people, or just as meaningfully, with oneself as a matter of internal deliberation.

Suppose, though, that I cruelly called her bluff and put away the surfboards. What would we have talked about? In theory, just about anything. Reflective equilibrium involves what philosophers call a "coherentist" theory of truth. That means we consider our beliefs justified not when some final truth is

attained but instead when we reach a point of consistency between them.[13] Deliberation stops, in other words, when our
considered judgments have settled within a point of view (call
it a "theory," or even a "story," if you like) and have been suitably
modified so as to be harmonious.

Opinions on virtually any topic are thus amenable to reflective equilibrium. My daughter and I could, for example, have
engaged in reflective equilibrium about how to raise our puppy
and balance our desire for a dog that doesn't beg at the table
with my delight in giving her scraps while cooking, or our love
of wrestling with her and ensuring she doesn't jump on strang-
ers. The only requirement is, first, to seek greater consistency
among our considered judgments at all levels of generality, and
second, to use those same judgments rather than some external
standard (of truth, beauty, goodness, or whatever else) to revise
and eventually justify one another.

To cultivate a specifically liberal way of life, however, a particular conversation needs to be had. Call it the conversation of
justice. It starts, as does all reflective equilibrium, by eliciting
our considered judgments. As we did with the original position,
let's try this spiritual exercise together, here and now.

Begin by listing a series of high-level general convictions as
to what you regard as manifestly unjust. For instance, tyranny
is unjust, slavery is unjust, sexual and racial discrimination are
unjust, exploitation is unjust, vast inequality of opportunity is
unjust, religious persecution is unjust, and whatever else you
would add. Next, to have a range of considered judgments at
different levels of generality, recall a specific (and preferably
recent, so that it's still fresh) incident when you felt that you or
someone you personally know were treated unfairly. Now ask
yourself: (1) Why was it unfair? (2) How did you feel in the
moment, and do you stand by that reaction? (3) Did you talk

to someone about it, and why or why not? (4) What could have prevented it? (5) What could remedy it? (6) Could you ever imagine yourself doing this unfair thing to someone else?

If you've done all of this, you should have an ample supply of considered judgments at hand—some extracted from abstract principles, and others from sentiments, perceptions, and routines. Consider this data about yourself. We now proceed to the next step of the spiritual exercise. It takes the form of another question: What would you say makes these judgments hang together in a more or less coherent picture rather than as so many isolated bits and pieces? Or more precisely, and to use Rawls's term, which conception of justice (that is, which set of principles and values that underlie the fundamental institutions of our society) implicitly informs and guides the considered judgments you're making?

This question can seem intimidating and even overwhelming. Many people won't know the conception of justice they subscribe to, and even less the alternatives that may better account for their considered judgments. That is why, says Rawls, a third party needs to be brought into the conversation of reflective equilibrium. We need the expertise of a political philosopher.

Coming from two political philosophers (Rawls and me), this may sound a bit rich. But hear us out. In his lectures and books, Rawls makes a plea for the importance of political philosophy.[14] A key service it provides is to help orient citizens in the ideas and values of their own political culture. Now whether you think political philosophy as currently taught in universities plays this role, who could deny the need for it? Our world is filled with chatter about rights, responsibility, justice, fairness, equity, legitimacy, identity, recognition, violence, merit, and the like. In my book, moreover, I've claimed that such talk permeates our private, personal, and professional lives as well.

In such a context, a little philosophical assistance can go a long way by laying out different political conceptions to get our bearings and organize our considered judgments. "The idea is that it belongs to reason and reflection (both theoretical and practical) to orient us in the (conceptual) space, say, of all possible ends, individual and associational, political and social," states Rawls. "Political philosophy, as a work of reason, does this by specifying principles to identify reasonable and rational ends of those various kinds, and by showing how those ends can cohere within a well-articulated conception of a just and reasonable society. Such a conception may offer a unified framework within which proposed answers to divisive questions can be made consistent and insights gained from different kinds of cases can be brought to bear on one another and extended to other cases."[15]

Understood along these lines, political philosophy is a big tent. Together with the historical canon and contemporary professional philosophers, public intellectuals and commentators are included—Rawls, Hannah Arendt, and Martha Nussbaum are in, naturally, but so too are Ezra Klein and John Oliver, Rachel Maddow and Joe Rogan, Naomi Klein and Yuval Levin, and Waleed Ali and Ross Douthat. Even someone who has not so much as read a page of "official" political philosophy may well engage with many of its fundamental ideas and frameworks on a weekly, if not daily, basis, such as when browsing the internet over their morning coffee, playing a podcast on the way to work, or listening to radio during dinner prep.

Do we need to enter into direct dialogue with such figures? Not exactly. We instead use ideas and frameworks we encounter with them to undertake a special and thorough kind of deliberation (again, either with someone else or on our own). Rawls calls it "wide reflective equilibrium" and describes it in an important, if difficult, passage:

> [We] regard as wide reflective equilibrium ... that reflective equilibrium reached when someone has carefully considered alternative conceptions of justice and the force of various arguments for them. More exactly this person has considered the leading conceptions of political justice found in our philosophical tradition (including views critical of the concept of justice itself (some think [Karl] Marx's view is an example), and has weighed the force of the different philosophical and other reasons for them. In this case, we suppose this person's general convictions, first principles, and particular judgments are in line; but now the reflective equilibrium is wide, given the wide-ranging reflection and possibly many changes of view that have preceded it.[16]

Let me put this more plainly. Prior to introducing "wide" reflective equilibrium, Rawls presents a "narrow" version that is both simpler and lazier. With narrow reflective equilibrium, the goal is to identify the conception of justice that most obviously matches your existing considered judgments. You don't canvas alternative conceptions, nor deeply explore the reasons for supporting the one you select. You merely look for the option that, on its face at least, calls for the fewest possible revisions to your convictions and judgments. It is the equivalent of the echo chambers we inhabit online and in real life—a "liberal" switching on MSNBC, a "conservative" tuning into Fox News, or like-minded friends talking it out over dinner. You'll be served and enjoy a familiar dish.

In wide reflective equilibrium, by contrast, you stop to survey the menu. A first glance reveals many different political conceptions, along with their main ingredient: aristocratic (excellence), communist (equality), fascist (commitment), liberal (fairness), libertarian (freedom), neoliberal (efficiency), monarchist (honor), theocratic (piety), utilitarian (happiness), and more. A closer look shows that the history of political philosophy consists almost entirely of mixing these options up. Now it is up to you to investigate which most faithfully expresses your considered judgments.

Here's the rub, however: none will be a perfect fit. First, if you are at all like me, you're a mess of inconsistent judgments that won't map onto a single conception. Second, as we just noted, political conceptions that are purely one thing (for example, a *strictly* liberal or *strictly* aristocratic conception) are archetypes and heuristics. Any system found in the pages of philosophy, not to mention real-world constitutions and regimes, will be mixtures of principles and insights drawn from different conceptions, making any one-to-one reflection between it and yourself highly unlikely.

These caveats noted, and with all of these options on the table, wide reflective equilibrium begins in earnest. And who knows where it will take you? The possibilities are numerous and unpredictable. Most straightforwardly, you can tweak one of your considered judgments to better match the demands of a particular political conception. But that can have knock-on effects and swiftly modify other considered judgments up and down the line. Revising, say, an opinion about progressive taxation might lead to gut-level changes concerning how you feel about desert and privilege, which will then cascade onto how you perceive those of higher and lower social economic status, and ultimately how you regard your own talents and worth. Then, who knows, things can snowball further. Perhaps you reappraise the political conception that, on first impression, seemed the best fit. Another may now appear to be a better match, thereby launching the process of reflective equilibrium anew. Yet however the process goes, bit by bit, piece by piece, your considered judgments will shift and calibrate. Almost as if you were assembling a piece of IKEA furniture, you start by getting things into rough shape, and then go round and round tightening the screws and firming it up. And again just like IKEA furniture (or at least how it feels when assembling it), the process never comes to an end. Inconsistencies will remain, and new ones will be introduced—in part because we are frail and fickle, but mostly because we are temporal creatures fated to grow, change, and learn. The work of reflective equilibrium is never done.

The next section will identify the benefits (that is, the existential perks) of reflective equilibrium. But the first pertains specifically to wide reflective equilibrium: *authenticity*. Remember Tom Hudson? The problem with him is that you never know (and worse, he himself will never know) whether the opinions he professes are really his. Does he believe in liberalism, or is it all a show for social approbation? Reflective equilibrium can help quell that all too human flaw. Why? Because the political conception you affirm is not foisted on you from the outside but instead chosen by you to express your considered judgments at all levels of generality.

Indeed, reflective equilibrium does more than express those judgments; it consolidates and fine-tunes them, making them more your own. It helps you to become you. "Political philosophy," writes Rawls, "cannot coerce our considered convictions any more than the principles of logic can. If we feel coerced, it may be because, when we reflect on the matter at hand, values, principles, and standards are so formulated and arranged that they are freely recognized as ones we do, or should, accept. . . . Our feeling coerced is perhaps our being surprised at the consequences of those principles and standards, at the implications of our free recognition."[17]

With this, our Socratic loop comes to a close. Of the many descriptions Socrates gave to his brand of philosophy (gadfly, torpedo fish, and servant of the gods), midwife is the most famous. He pokes and prods his interlocutors with questions to discover ideas and truths, "a multitude of beautiful things," they already had within themselves.[18] They too experience the gentle coercion Rawls describes—the hold an idea can have over you once you recognize it as your own. The difference is that while Athenians had a Socrates, we must make do with a spiritual exercise. Yet given Socrates and Rawls's shared hope that their fellow citizens would eventually learn to question themselves, perhaps reflective equilibrium is not so poor a substitute.

Self-Coherence

On its own, there is nothing intrinsically liberal about reflective equilibrium, even the wide version Rawls recommends. Should a budding fascist wish to become more authentic and fortify their considered judgments, reflective equilibrium can lend a hand. In fact, a favorite book of mine examines how ordinary Russians under Stalinism voluntarily, passionately, and introspectively sought to remake themselves in line with the illiberal ideals of the regime, undertaking something akin to reflective equilibrium.[19]

In this respect, reflective equilibrium differs from our other two spiritual exercises. The original position and public reason have substantive liberal content, and cultivate qualities that are if not unique to, then at least characteristic of, a liberal way of life. Reflective equilibrium, by contrast, is formal. It does not necessarily liberalize anything, and the existential perks it affords are not distinctive to liberalism. Still, an existential perk is an existential perk, and the spiritual exercise of reflective equilibrium contributes several to a liberal way of life.

The most obvious is *self-coherence*. It seems intuitively desirable. Yet why exactly? Well, any comprehensive doctrine worthy of the name will have goods and lived felicities available only to its devotees. A Christian (or Muslim, Stoic, or so on) will have thoughts and feelings that outsiders only know the name of. Liberal that I am, agapic love remains a mystery. But such things cannot be bought cheaply. To experience any great good of any comprehensive doctrine, you must live it consistently. Or to speak more pointedly, we liberals cannot enjoy the perks of our own doctrine unless we integrate its values and commitments into our considered judgments at all levels of generality. We don't just automatically get to be impartial, autonomous, fun, generous, and grateful. Reflective equilibrium is to any comprehensive doctrine what the ingredient of salt is to cooking. It brings out its distinctive flavors.

The next perk is closely related to self-coherence: *avoidance of hypocrisy*. Think again of Tom Hudson. Being him must be exhausting. At all times he must front his liberal credentials, and if not actively hide the rest of himself, then at least shield it from too much (external or internal) scrutiny. Rawls even shows a degree of sympathy for people like him. The poseur who embarks on a systematic course of deception and hypocrisy "will have to reckon with the psychological cost of taking precautions and maintaining his pose, and with the loss of spontaneity and naturalness that results."[20] Tom may or may not feel that deception is wrong, but he must be aware that its transaction costs are killer. His gait will be halting, always pausing to check and calculate. Slick as he is, fluency eludes him.

Hypocrisy does not afflict liberals only. We are prone to it, though. Because our morality is hegemonic, real kudos attach to pretense and fakery. That makes reflective equilibrium particularly valuable. "Reflective equilibrium," says a historian of philosophy, is "a state of affairs in which all the pieces of the philosophical puzzle fit together well."[21] While perfectly true, the sense of this statement shifts depending on what reflective equilibrium is used to do. Understood as a method of philosophical justification, the pieces of the puzzle are the beliefs contained in our considered judgments at all levels of generality. But understood as a spiritual exercise, the puzzle is us, and the pieces to fit together are all the levels of generality (that is, the different components of moral life, including principles, emotions, perceptions, and habits) from which we extract considered judgments. We seek a unity of not only ideas and beliefs but also character and everyday life. Rawls was after that too. "Justice as fairness," he writes in a whopper of a sentence, "is a theory of our moral sentiments as manifested by our considered judgments in reflective equilibrium."[22] The person who achieves such an equilibrium will be less susceptible to hypocrisy than not. They will have brought their ideas, feelings, principles, and desires into alignment. Fluency and candor, grace and self-command, will be theirs.

This is easier said than done, of course. The issue is less that such exalted living seems reserved for heroes and saints. It is that reflective equilibrium is highly scrutinizing and scours our infrarational selves. Its light can be glaring, and we may be surprised and disappointed at the considered judgments it exposes. Yet perhaps this is a perk in disguise. For when the alignment fails, as will often be the case, and we discover that we are out of joint with ourselves, a liberal way of life should *foster humility along with a reluctance to judge and scorn others.*

Such an attitude is seldom associated with liberals. We sooner picture Tom Hudson's "progressive" "friends" who pounce at the end of the piece—a liberal is a wolf to liberals, to adapt the words of another Tom. Still, an observation Rawls makes in a seminar on moral emotions is apt. In overviewing the concept of shame, he pauses for a moment to reflect on Erik Erikson's description of it as "rage against the self." It can take that form, Rawls admits, but on the whole he thinks Erikson is wrong. "Shame," he concludes, "is not a form of self-hate but of concern for self."[23]

Reflective equilibrium can nurture such a spirit of gentleness. This spiritual exercise starts from a place of solicitude for oneself and a desire to live more integrally. It then proceeds to make two discoveries: first, how inconsistent we are in our considered judgments—an insight that can evoke the constructive type of shame Rawls refers to—and second, how singular each of us is in that any equilibrium we reach will be specific to us as individuals and our constellation of considered judgments. Liberals, more than others, should be wary of casting the first stone. Reflective equilibrium trains us to see weakness and difference in ourselves. The least we can do is extend the courtesy to others.

The penultimate perk that reflective equilibrium brings to a liberal way of life is *to unify the self*. On its face, this seems like just another term for self-coherence. But Rawls has an emphatic vision of how and why liberals can lead a unified life, and even in key sections of *A Theory of Justice*, more so than any other rival way of life.

Rawls's argument is complex and contentious. His line of reasoning is as follows. First, morally speaking, all human beings are free and equal persons. Second, liberalism, and specifically Rawls's version of justice as fairness, institutionalizes our free and equal moral nature in principles of justice that regulate the fundamental institutions of society. Third, when you and

I act from these liberal principles of justice, we express, in the real world and our dealings with other people, our nature as free and equal beings. Fourth, should we view ourselves as free and equal persons, and to the extent that we desire and in fact live up to that self-conception, then our lives become unified. What we see as our personal good will be reconciled with the demands of justice, morality, and reason. As Paul Weithman states, "The only way creatures like us can live as unified selves, at least under modern conditions, is to regulate our pursuit of the good by principles of liberal democratic justice. The alternative to being regulated by the reasonable part of ourselves was, Rawls seemed to suggest, to live lives that lacked rational unity."[24] And so we arrive at the conclusion: a liberal way of life is uniquely unified. We alone combine, in our lived existence, the right and good, the reasonable and rational, and the just and desirable. We alone are whole, and not riven by tensions between our personal and public moral commitments, or divisions between what we privately desire and what we publicly profess. We are liberal all the way down.

This is a lot of argument to swallow, and depending on your temperament, worryingly romantic. That's why I buried the lede. If this notion of unity is appealing, however, then reflective equilibrium is the spiritual exercise for you. Expressing our nature and unifying the self is not an all-or-nothing proposition, as if a switch in an on or off position. "How far we succeed in expressing our nature depends upon how consistently we act from our sense of justice as finally regulative." It is a question of degree, and we can succeed more or less in the endeavor. Yet, continues Rawls, "what we cannot do is express our nature by following a plan that views the sense of justice as but one desire to be weighed against others. For this sentiment reveals what the person is, and to compromise it is not to achieve for the self free reign but to give way to the contingencies and accidents of the world."[25] The danger that Rawls names is all too easy to fall into: confining our desire to be a free and generous liberal person to a single idea, desire, and identity among others, as if it were just one of many hats to wear. If the self contains multitudes in this sense, it will be scattered. It will be the self of liberaldom, not the liberal self.

The goal of reflective equilibrium is not to boost the power of a particular idea or moral commitment, so that when the time comes it trumps all temptations and passes the test of akrasia. Its real purpose is to use a particular idea or moral commitment—a liberal political conception of justice, in the case of wide reflective equilibrium—to calibrate our considered judgments at all levels of generality so that such temptations are only lightly felt to begin with. An ounce of prevention is worth a pound of cure.

You'll remember I started the chapter with Tom Hudson and his particular moral failing: when cruising around everyday life on autopilot, he won't even notice moral dilemmas and crossroads. So oblivious is he to his liberalism, he will be positively Zen-like. Reflective equilibrium strives for a similar state of being, but through the integration, rather than the separation, of liberalism and the everyday. Like many great liberals, Rawls frequently naturalizes theological concepts.[26] In part, that is because liberalism (and all other secular ideologies and conceptions of justice) evolve out of prior religious and politico-religious doctrines.[27] But it is also to reclaim ideas that religion unduly stakes a monopoly over. *Grace*, our final glorious perk, is the word we're looking for here, and the note on which *A Theory of Justice* ends. Liberals may sever its connection to transcendence. Yet why abstain from the word when it marks the highest reward for our way of life? Grace is when the two meanings of liberal—liberty and generosity, freedom and fairness—come together in all different facets of life. In so doing, we become more graceful to the extent that we fulfill the requirements of justice with pleasure and relative ease.

12

How to Keep Calm, Cool, and to Delight in Others

SPIRITUAL EXERCISE 3

I'VE WATCHED *Borat! Cultural Learnings of America for Make Benefit Glorious Nation of Kazakhstan* (2006) more times than I care to admit. With each viewing, I come away convinced that it is a movie (or documentary, mockumentary, or whatever it is) more about US tolerance than intolerance.

Borat does truly outrageous things. He masturbates in public, brawls nude in a packed conference center, presents his feces at a dinner party, kidnaps Pamela Anderson, and the list goes on. Yet more often than not the people he encounters are gracious. There is the car salesman who tries to reason with Borat that no actual artifact called a "pussy magnet" comes with the truck he wants to buy. There is the concierge who explains to an unpacking Borat that the elevator is not his hotel room. Then there is Mike Psenicska, Borat's driving instructor. The scene begins with Borat giving his customary kiss on both cheeks to the men he meets. "I'm not used to that," says a surprised Mike, "but that's fine." Next is this exchange when Borat sees a female driver during his lesson:

BORAT: Look there is a woman in a car! Can we follow her and maybe make a sexy time with her?

MIKE: No, no, no, no, no.

BORAT: Not yet, huh? Why not?

MIKE: Because a woman has a right to choose who she has sex with.

BORAT: What?!

MIKE: How about that? Isn't that amazing?

BORAT: You joke?

MIKE: There must be consent. How about that? That's good, huh?

BORAT: It's not good for me.

MIKE: No, it is good.[1]

Mike may not have known it, but he is speaking the language of public reason, our third spiritual exercise. Unlike the original position and reflective equilibrium, it directly concerns how we interact and engage with other people. The crux of the exercise is to appeal to reasons that respect the understanding of fellow citizens in liberal democracies. And there are great goods and benefits—existential perks—that come from it: cheerfulness, a sense of connection with others, amity, and even an ability to delight in who they are. Mike, for one, is a natural, and his scene finishes as good-naturedly as it began, with Borat asking, "I like you. Do you like me?" "I do like you," says Mike. "You are my friend?" "You're a nice young man, and I am your friend." "You will be my boyfriend?" "Well [laughs], I won't be your boy-friend." "Why not? Do you not like me? "I can be. It depends. Boyfriend? Yeah, I can."

On Dialogue

As with all of our spiritual exercises, it helps to look back to ancient philosophy as the birthplace of tradition. The ancients did not exactly have a conception of public reason. They did, however, have a rich understanding of dialogue, of which public reason is a species. Thanks to Plato, Xenophon, and Cicero, dialogue is a renowned genre of ancient philosophy. It is also, perhaps, its most fundamental spiritual exercise. For to become a better interlocutor, you need to become a better, wiser person (a "philosopher," in the ancient sense). Pierre Hadot tells us what dialogue requires, and what, with practice, it also trains and delivers:

> Being a better dialectician meant not only being skillful at invention or at denouncing tricks in reasoning. Before anything else, it meant knowing how to dialogue, together with all the demands that this entails: recognizing the presence and the rights of one's interlocutor, basing one's replies on what the interlocutor admits he knows, and therefore agreeing with him at each stage of the discussion. Above all, it meant submitting oneself to the demands and norms of reason and the search for truth; finally, it meant recognizing the absolute value of the Good. It therefore meant leaving behind one's individual point of view, in order to rise to a universal viewpoint; and it meant trying to see things within the perspective of the All and the deity, thereby transforming one's vision of the world and one's own inner attitude.[2]

Every YouTube video on how to be a better conversationalist offers the same advice: be present in the moment, be curious, don't pontificate, listen to the other person, and ask questions that build from their point of view. No influencer or content creator, however, has ever dropped this ancient-inspired pearl of wisdom: "Language develops only upon the death of individuals."[3] But that's all we really need to know. Language in general requires that we exit our individuality (or more technically, our ipseity) by translating singular thoughts and ineffable feelings into the common coin of words. Dialogue makes a virtue of this necessity. Good conversation happens when we transcend our individuality and rise to a shared standpoint as represented by what we have in common with our interlocutor. As we all know from experience, it is difficult to achieve and sustain.

On Political Dialogue

Good political conversation is especially elusive. Incivility so often seems the norm rather than the exception. In part, rising polarization is to blame along with the tendency to view people of different political persuasions with suspicion and even loathing.[4] Social media and infotainment add fuel to the fire with their business models of rage and divisiveness.

But historically and philosophically speaking, incivility is a problem with longer and deeper origins. It is tied to our status as equal citizens. Think of it this way: although political power is not always or even usually coercive, at times it must be. The state and its legions of officials tax, regulate, confiscate, punish, imprison, and sometimes put to death. Who does that power belong to? The answer depends on the regime type, of course. In a democratic society, political power belongs to the people. And in a *liberal* democratic society, political power belongs not to "the people" in general but instead to each and every one of its members. We are all, in principle, coholders of our society's legal, constitutional, and political power.

Political power in liberal democracies accordingly needs to be justified to its citizens in a special way. "Liberals," states legal philosopher Jeremy Waldron, "demand that the social order should in principle be capable of explaining itself at the tribunal of each person's understanding."[5] Obviously, "because I said so!" is not an acceptable justification of political power in any humane regime. But in liberal democracy, neither is "because this is what we believe in!"—where *this* stands for a religious, moral, or philosophical conception of the good life or common good.[6] Modern societies are pluralist, and speaking in this manner fails to respect the equal standing of citizens. It is uncivil: not just rude and peremptory, but literally uncitizenly in that it abrogates the political bond between equals. What liberal democracy requires, then, is a way for citizens to speak to one another about political issues—and a way for public officials and politicians to speak to citizens about political issues—where the reasons and terms of discussion can be shared by all reasonable members of the political community, no matter who they are or what they believe in.[7]

That way is public reason. It is argument addressed to fellow citizens using reasons (and ideas, ideals, principles, and values) that all could reasonably accept. As in any good conversation—only this time about public and political matters, and in our standing as equal citizens—we listen to and address one another in terms that are internal to each person's understanding. Public reason is thus more than valid reasoning (though it is that too). It consists of speaking to citizens *as* citizens, and framing issues and positions, even those that benefit particular groups, with reasons we sincerely believe they could also accept. Only then is political power justified and legitimate in a liberal democratic society. Only then is civic conversation made civil.

In a moment, I'll consider the issue of whether the ideal of public reason is realistic. With the creep of religious discourse back into political life, not to mention partisan reasoning that applies only the thinnest veneer of public reason, we may have doubts. But first, a more basic question: What is the content of public reason? What are these wonderful reasons that all reasonable citizens, no matter their conception of the good, can be expected to share?

The short answer is the liberal political conception of justice along with its freestanding concepts, principles, and arguments. This formulation, however, is too jargony. Better to look at examples of public reason that John Rawls provides in the context of the United States and work backward from there.

> A feature of public reasoning [is] that it proceeds entirely within a political conception of justice. Examples of political values include those mentioned in the preamble to the United States Constitution: a more perfect union, justice, domestic tranquility, the common defense, the general welfare, and the blessings of liberty for ourselves and our posterity. These [blessings of liberty] include under them other values: so, for example, under justice we also have equal basic liberties, equality of opportunity, ideals concerning the distribution of income and taxation, and much else.[8]

Rawls died a few years before *Borat* was made. I suspect he wouldn't have enjoyed it. But he would have approved of Mike. When Borat hollers obscenities out the window, what does Mike do? He doesn't tell him to shut up (a command). He doesn't tell him he's an embarrassment and a jerk (aesthetic and moral reproaches). He doesn't use religious condemnations of sin or lechery. No, he uses reasons of a different kind: public, political notions of rights and consent. I have no idea why he spoke that way. Maybe it was how he automatically framed the issue for himself. Maybe, bless him, he hoped that these terms might reach Borat. Regardless, he appealed to values enshrined in the fundamental political institutions of his society. Mike disagreed with Borat and rebuked him, but he spoke in terms that respected him as an equal.

Mike did something else too. Rights and consent, along with the ideas Rawls lists from the US Constitution, are examples of political values. But why? What makes them *political*? To reply that they're in the Constitution is a merely empirical answer (and tautological to boot). Or to say, with Rawls, that they belong to a political conception of justice is correct but doesn't reach the heart of the matter. Phrased that way, political values sound remote, as if they didn't touch us personally.

Yet they do, very much. A value is political, properly speaking, when it is of special interest as well as significance for citizens to achieve and maintain their status as free and equal citizens of a liberal democratic society. Or more pointedly: for free and equal democratic citizens to *remain* free and equal democratic citizens, certain kinds of values need to be upheld.[9] Freedom in liberal democracy calls for, among many things, individual rights, domestic tranquility, and tolerance. Equality in liberal democracy calls for, among many things, fairness and a distribution of resources so that everyone can make effective use of their freedoms. These values are political not because they are "in" our public institution. That mistakes the effect for the cause. Rather, public institutions in liberal democracies exist to protect and promote values that keep us free and equal. And when we reason with one another using the only kind of values that citizens can reasonably be expected to share—*political* values enshrined in *public* institutions—we express and embody a role-specific moral duty of citizenship. We give and take civility, trust, and respect. It doesn't get more personal than that.

This is where Mike shines. His conversation with Borat may just be a moment on film—a drop in the bucket of civic conversation. Yet its everydayness is its beauty. Mike is giving a driving lesson, but we can just as easily picture him at the dog park or grocery shopping. Watching the scene, you don't get the feeling of someone biting his tongue. The impression is of equanimity (of chill, I want to say) from someone who inhabits his status of an equal among equals comfortably and confidently. Stephen Macedo writes, "Political legitimacy—and our own peace of mind, morally speaking—depends on our ability to discern basic principles of political morality that we believe on reflection could be justified to all reasonable people."[10] Mike has peace of mind in spades. And when he chuckles at, bats back, or delights in the weirdness that is Borat, it is from an assumption that the two can find common ground. To our list of everyday liberal heroes, we can add one more: Mike. "Very nice!" as Borat would say.

The Use and Abuse of Public Reason

Public reason is not a magic formula for civic agreement. It is a medium of discussion for how liberal democratic communities can be built *around*, not *despite*, disagreement over fundamental political issues.

Disagreements can remain vast. Take the far-right US news site *Breitbart*, which I visit weekly to take the pulse. On its face, it is loudly and proudly antiliberal. And yes, its comment section is filled with conspiracy theories and racist, homophobic, sexist insults that are patently not about helping the United States to become a fair system of cooperation for all of its members. That said, if I had to assign a number, I would estimate that 50 percent of *Breitbart*'s content sits in this category. The other half is made up of public reason arguments for a vision of a liberal society sharply at odds with what it takes to be the woke and socialist establishment. *Breitbart*, for example, is strongly anti-immigration. But the main reason it gives is recognizably liberal (albeit a nationalist interpretation of liberalism): illegal immigrants have not contributed to the United States' economy, safety net, or culture, and thus undermine the fair system of cooperation *its own* citizens have built up. Its attack on political correctness is of the same kind. Breitbartians feel that the things they have always believed have become suddenly verboten. They feel, in other words, culturally dismissed. This too is a public reason argument, vindicating a need for free speech and tolerance against a woke moral majority perceived to be equal parts fragile and vindictive.[11] While I disagree with both views, I certainly get it. They're speaking my language.

My book is not about polarization, but I will say this. Public reason can diminish or intensify partisan passions, and it is hard to tell which is happening at any given moment and why. We've seen how it can turn down the temperature by giving citizens a common point of view that respects their difference (as people with different conceptions of the good) and togetherness (as citizens of the same polity). Public reason, to cite Rawls's beautiful phrase, specifies the political bond in liberal democracy as one of "civic friendship."[12]

This would be lovely, were we always (or even typically) rational and sincere. The reality is murkier, though. In a polarized age, personal identity becomes entangled with political allegiance, such that partisanship often takes on a quasi-existential quality. "I *am* a Democrat" or "I *am* a Republican," a typical person in the United States might declare. And once that happens, it becomes ambiguous as to what political disagreements are about. Common sense dictates that such disputes are about something substantive: an issue, policy, vision, or anything. But current research in political psychology is depressingly adept at showing how this is not necessarily so. According to a scholar of polarization, when personal and political identities align, "we lose perspective on what we really believe and begin to simply defend the positions that our party takes. . . . The more parts of our identities that are linked with our parties, the more the success of our parties becomes more important than any real policy outcomes."[13] We tell ourselves stories about issues and substance when in fact identity and victory drive the plot.

Public reason is easily enlisted in this subterfuge. It can disguise what we are up to—to friends and foes, and crucially for our purposes of leading a free and generous liberal way of life, to ourselves. Public reason can give the impression that we're fighting for the meaning of the Constitution and the fate of our country, rather than for the vindication of a tribe along with the pleasures of righteousness and exclusion.

Liberals are not alone in abusing public reason. Anyone can apply lipstick to ulterior and semiconscious motivations. Yet it is especially tempting for us. For you see, liberals alone are native speakers of public reason.

The Mother Tongue of Liberals

Philosophers have devised many rival accounts of public reason. Nevertheless, they agree on one point: public reason has its time and place, but it is not for all times and all places. It is, in other words, appropriate only in certain contexts.

Where to draw the line is contested. Rawls confines public reason within strict limits. Citizens and officials should use it for public discussion of constitutional essentials (such as basic rights) and fundamental justice (such as the distribution of resources). Charles Larmore, another leading figure, broadens it to all exercises of coercive power. More expansive still is Gerald Gaus, who claims that public reason should cover all social and moral rules that require or prohibit action.[14] But wherever philosophers draw the line for where public reason does and doesn't belong, draw the line they must. Not to do so, they believe, would be to give public reason a scope that is morally problematic, socially artificial, and psychologically weird. Rawls's worry can stand for the general concern:

> Distinct and separate from [the] public political forum is what I call the background culture. This is the culture of civil society. In a democracy, this culture is not, of course, guided by any one central idea or principle, whether political or religious. Its many and diverse agencies and associations with their internal life reside within a framework of law that ensure the familiar liberties of thought and speech, and the right of free association. The idea of public reason does not apply to the background culture with its many forms of nonpublic reason nor to media of any kind.[15]

A passage like this puts liberals (liberals all the way down, that is) in an awkward spot. We naturally support the sentiment: outside political discussions in public forums, no one (neither an official nor citizen) is obliged to speak in the language of public reason. You want a no-holds-barred argument about politics at the dinner table? Go for it. You want to ask someone out on a date? Public reason will not avail you. (The consent app comes in at a later stage.) Yet it is patently false, as an empirical or descriptive claim, to say that the idea of public reason "does not apply to the background culture," if by *apply* we understand "circulate in" and "inform." As one way to put the contention of this book, our background culture is flooded with public reason. Liberal values and virtues are hegemonic in civil society, and for liberals all the way down, in private life too. Yes, of course, we participate in all kinds of associations and relationships that traffic in other reasons. As an academic, my professional ethics include rigor, excellence, and truth, none of which are liberal in origin or nature. And as a basketball fan, when I shout at the TV that Anthony Davis should not be shooting threes, it is not out of liberal solicitude for fairness to his teammates. Like any other liberal all the way down, I am thoroughly, but not exhaustively or exclusively, liberal (just in the same way that a Christian is thoroughly, but not exhaustively or exclusively, Christian). Even so, public reason is my mother tongue. I speak it with family, friends, and colleagues, not stiffly as if one citizen to another in the public forum, but suitably and subconsciously adapted to all walks of life. A person of faith can be conversant in public reason and fluent in a different register. Liberals are not so bilingual.

Why then recommend public reason as a spiritual exercise? The original position and reflective equilibrium take hard work. If liberals speak public reason as naturally as we breathe, though, what more can we draw from it? In the next section, I propose to think about public reason a little differently: as a way of listening as well as speaking, and as a way of seeing others in the best light as well as trying to persuade them. "A person's religion," Rawls observes, "is often no better or worse than they are as persons."[16] The same holds for their liberalism. In the wrong hands, public reason can fuel sanctimony and recrimination. Practiced with generosity, it can help us to unlearn the ugliest affects and affectations of our polarized culture.

The Happy Perks of a Liberal Way of Life

Of all the existential perks of a liberal way of life, the ones enhanced by public reason are the most conducive to happiness. The impartiality and autonomy of the original position? The self-coherence and humility of reflective equilibrium? Admirable qualities. Still, they are not exactly joyful. Cheerfulness and delight in others? Now we're talking.

You may be skeptical that public reason can cultivate such qualities. If so, consider a thought experiment. Suppose you are someone who rejects the ideal of public reason—not just doubts its feasibility and potential naiveness, but outright denies that political power must be justifiable to all of its members. Further suppose that you're in the political majority of a medium-sized country, and ready and willing to justify constitutional amendments, distribution of basic resources, high court decisions, and police and military violence on the basis of a religious, moral, or philosophical doctrine that millions of your fellow citizens do not share. Now imagine that you must tell one of these citizens, to their face, what you believe. What would you have to say?

Many things.[17] First, cutting to the chase, you'd lead with, "I don't care if my position can't be justified to you." Second, you'd note, "I realize it affects many things that profoundly shape your life." Third, you'd assert, "I can't be bothered to frame it in a way that's acceptable to you." And then fourth, add, "Such a way doesn't exist, probably," followed by, fifth, "I'm no hypocrite. If you come into power I expect the same treatment from you." Then sixth, you'd maintain, "I'm going to do everything I (legally) can to ensure that never happens." Seventh, you'd state, "I don't trust you, and you don't trust me." Finally, you'd proclaim, "We're not really equals."

If that is honestly you, it's best to put the book down. But if you've made it this far, I suspect it's not. At some level, you accept the ideal of public reason: public power should be justifiable to all citizens. Furthermore, assuming the old adage that ought implies can, you also believe this ideal is practicable, however imperfectly realized in our societies. We can speak to one another, and justify our beliefs and conduct, in such a way that strengthens public understanding and trust. Social media and cable news try to tell us that our societies are zero-sum games of mutual opacity and will to power. Yet the better angel of our nature doesn't buy it.

"Fine," you might retort. "But I didn't say I didn't believe in public reason. I doubted that it's all that happy or cheerful!" The thought experiment, though, is meant to suggest that you reject its bleak worldview *because* the public reason you espouse is happy and cheerful—because it depends on a reasonable faith in our society and fellow citizens. You already hold this ideal. And to an extent, you already experience its cheerful affects. What is left to do, as with all of our spiritual exercises, is to more deeply cultivate the kind of person our liberal world has already made us.

How? The key is to practice public reason as a way of listening, not only of speaking. Listening and speaking go hand in hand, and as liberals, we only responsibly speak public reason if we listen well and generously with it.

One of Rawls's final texts will guide us. Near the end of his life, he wrote a touching confession meant only for his friends and family, "On My Religion" (1997). Only nine pages long, he describes his loss of faith in the Second World War, and his later views on religion and theology. Surprisingly, a third of the piece is taken up with a book forgotten to all but specialists of early modern philosophy: Jean Bodin's *Colloquium of the Seven Secrets of the Sublime* (1588).[18]

The *Colloquium* is written as a dialogue, and its setup seems as if from a "walks into a bar" joke. A Calvinist, Jew, Lutheran, Muslim, naturalist, and skeptic are hosted for a week by a Catholic at his palazzo in Venice. For the first few days, they try to refute each other's religious opinions. But once they admit no headway can be made, they change tack, and "encourage one another to describe their religious views so that all may learn what others think and be able to understand what their beliefs are in their best light."[19]

God's perfection, not public reason, is the lingua franca of the *Colloquium*. Only the atheist is excluded; it was the one view Bodin couldn't abide, and none were invited to the party. Everyone else can share and listen. Each presents his worldview as a (metaphysical, moral, aesthetic, political, and psychological) actualization of the shared conviction that God is good and great. And each, crucially, listens to the other worldviews in the same spirit. They give and take the best of themselves as well as each other through the reasons they have in common.

Bodin is not mentioned in Rawls's writings on public reason. Yet his influence is undeniable. In Rawls's final work on public reason, written the same year as "On My Religion," he suggests that citizens of faith should be able to introduce their beliefs into the public forum, provided they can then justify the relevance of those beliefs in terms of shared political values. This concession has many benefits. It helps to include citizens of faith and strengthens the democratic ideal. Importantly, it also allows reasonable citizens, no matter what they believe, to see and admire the worldview of all other reasonable citizens. As Rawls puts it, "[The] benefits of the mutual knowledge of citizens' *recognizing one another's reasonable comprehensive doctrines* bring out a positive ground for introducing such doctrines, which is not merely a defensive ground, as if their intrusion into public discussion were inevitable in any case."[20]

Bodin's interlocutors share a religious discourse. We don't. Yet functionally speaking, public reason does the same work. And what liberals can do better, much better, is listen with the ears of public reason to hear the reasonableness of other ways of being in the world. This doesn't mean naively imputing goodwill to everyone all the time. Bad actors exist, and Rawls is certainly correct when he states, "a society may also contain unreasonable and irrational, and even mad, comprehensive doctrines."[21] For the sake of the civic fabric, however, and our own peace of mind, generalized suspicion should not be our default point of view. So the next time you hear an unfamiliar point of view, make a conscious effort to translate it (in your head and for yourself, not out loud or for the other person) into political values that you and your interlocutor can be presumed to share. This is the spiritual exercise of public reason. Depending on your reaction to the view being expressed, one of three existential perks will follow.

The best-case scenario is *delight in others* of the kind exemplified by Bodin, Rawls, and Mike Psenicska. Imagine that you had never heard of Lot, the Judgment of Solomon, or the Good Samaritan (to gather a trio of parables from the Bible). On first impression, what might seem like strange and fantastic products of the human imagination can, with public reason, be heard as compelling attempts to lead a good life in a world of others. In these examples, a liberal can recognize messages of hospitality and compassion, impartiality and judiciousness, and moral concern and social provision—not only in the parables, but in the people who profess them. Public reason is de-exotifying in the best way. The point is not to assimilate everyone to our way of life, such that *their* moral goodness is benchmarked against *our* liberalism. There are more things in heaven and earth, dear liberals, than are dreamt of in our philosophy. But public reason can build a bridge—from us to them, and them to us—so that we may admire in one another what we are most proud of.

What about when the other person's worldview seems not so much morally good or bad but instead bizarre and something you just don't get? This happens all the time—as, for example, strange and unfamiliar cosmologies. Thankfully, the next perk of public reason and a liberal way of life is a *live-and-let-live attitude of tolerance.* Tolerance is a hallmark of liberalism, and Rawls gives a concise explanation as to why: "In public reason comprehensive doctrines of truth or right [are] replaced by the idea of the politically reasonable addressed to citizens as citizens. Central to the idea of public reason is that it neither criticizes nor attacks any comprehensive doctrine, religious or nonreligious, except insofar as that doctrine is incompatible with the essentials of public reason and a democratic polity."[22]

Liberals are often accused of being relativists. Morally and politically speaking, this is badly false: fairness and reciprocity are nonnegotiable. But with respect to the epistemic truth of other comprehensive doctrines, it is a half-truth. We are not so much relativists or even agnostics as indifferentists. If, as Rawls argues, what liberals care about is fairness and reciprocity, then the metaphysical truth of a worldview is irrelevant and unconcerning. In fact, the issue wouldn't even come up, for liberals do not judge on this score. Or we ought not to, I should say. Here in Australia, for instance, I'm frequently disappointed when journalists take gratuitous shots at Christian belief—dismissing an entire theology, to cite a phrase I've seen many times in print, as a cry for a "Magic Sky Daddy." Who are we to judge? More to the point, why are we to judge? It is petty, mean-spirited, and completely unnecessary, which makes release from such judgy snarkiness not the least perk of public reason.

Final scenario: you understand the view presented, yet it strikes you as stupid and/or wrong (irrational and/or unreasonable, Rawls would say). Herein lies the slippery slope to polarization. How easy it is to slide from dismissing a view to dismissing a person, and then finally, an entire social group. So easy, indeed, that the process typically happens in reverse. In polarized environments, we size others up as friend or foe, and embrace or dismiss the view accordingly. A controversial political thinker of the twentieth century, Carl Schmitt, defines the political enemy as someone we regard as profoundly other—"existentially something different and alien."[23] This is as good a description of polarization as any. The danger such othering poses to our political order is self-evident. Social stability is hard to maintain when social groups regard one another as alien tribes. But it poses a special moral (and indeed psychic) threat to liberals. With our commitment to reciprocity, civility and public friendliness are intrinsic to a liberal way of life. Our morality can justify no other way of treating fellow citizens. Yet liberals are far from helpless victims in the polarizing cycle of dismissal and contempt. We so often exacerbate it by claiming a monopoly on correct opinion. Bad for our society and bad for us, we fuel a culture that betrays who we claim and aspire to be.

Earlier, I observed that public reason de-exotifies those whom we admire. It also de-others those we don't. When you listen with public reason, the goal is to frame a discussion using terms and reasons that fairly describe what both parties think. The goal, in other words, is not to eliminate disagreement but instead to arrive at a nonprejudicial description of it. When I read *Breitbart*, for example, I am liable to charge into emotional reaction. But on my good days, I try to hear its views and grievances, no matter how strongly I disagree, as partaking of the same public reason as I do. And sometimes something clicks: the view expressed is merely different from mine, not foreign or alien. Now I'm not urging anyone to make nice with their local white supremacist or insurrectionist. Nor in the main do I suggest you go out of your way to engage in real-life conversations with people you disagree with. Rather, I ask that you consider the benefits of not walking around with a default mentality that people who think differently are fools or worse. Public reason checks that tendency, and helps liberals *keep civil and cool*—a perk that is as much for our own benefit as everyone else's.

Three scenarios, three perks: agreement and delight, bewilderment and tolerance, and disagreement and civility. The next existential perk—*cheerfulness*—sums it up. The author of a recent study on this emotion ends his book with the following: "[Cheerfulness] is not the 'hope' of the messianic, or the 'optimism' of the cheap politician. It makes more modest promises—to get you through the next few hours, to connect you to a neighbor. You can't build a politics on it. But you probably can't rebuild a world without it."[24] Those are fine words for me to conclude with as well.

Public reason is about neighborliness—civic friendship, to recall Rawls's term. Liberals already speak it in public and private. I have proposed to listen with it as well. And my final word on the topic is to ask you to reflect on how often and ordinarily our fellow citizens do so too. The result may surprise you. "The conception of justice by which [citizens of liberal democracies] live," writes a political philosopher, is "a conception we endorse, not for different reasons we may each discover, and not simply for reasons we happen to share, but instead for reasons that count for us because we affirm them together. This spirit of reciprocity is the foundation of a democratic society."[25]

The philosopher who wrote these lines, as is the norm in the field, presumes an ideal society, full of goodwill and just institutions. This can feel like a bubble—a "this is fine" meme when in the background social, political, and real environmental fires rage on. Still, it is a strange thing to inhabit this world of ours. We look one way and see catastrophe projected 24/7 onto our screens and feeds. Yet we look another way and observe something extraordinary or even magical: a civilization, which took and takes civilizational labor to create and maintain, and professes a system of social cooperation on a footing of mutual respect between its members. To ignore its many failings is irresponsible. So too is it to ignore its singular achievement. Public reason can bring this wonder of community and connection into focus for us, even if only for moments at a time. It is cheering to behold, and even more so to be a part of it.

A Final Perk

To finish up with liberal spiritual exercises, it is only fitting to give Rawls the last word. It comes from one of the rare interviews he gave. To mark his retirement in 1991, he sat down with students to discuss a range of topics on his life, work, reception, and teaching. But in a draft copy of the interview, included in his personal papers at Harvard University, he added a weird and wonderful section that does not appear in the published version (and that it would seem he wrote only for himself). After answering the questions from the students, Rawls noted down a few "Questions They Didn't Ask Me," and proceeded to play the role of interviewer and interviewee. Here is the addendum in full:

There were lots of questions they didn't ask me in [the *Harvard Review of Philosophy* (HRP)] interview. Some of those they could have asked I'll answer here.

HRP (as imagined): You never talk about religion in your classes, although sometimes the discussion borders on it. Why is that? Do you think religion of no importance? Or that it has no role in our life?

JR: On the role of religion, let me put it this way. Let's ask the question: Does life need to be redeemed? And if so, why; and what can redeem it? I would say yes: life does need to be redeemed. By life I mean the ordinary round of being born, growing up, falling in love and marrying and having children; seeing that they grow up, go to school, and have children themselves; of supporting ourselves and carrying on day after day; of growing older and having grandchildren and eventually dying. All that and much else needs to be redeemed.

HRP: Fine, but what's this business about being redeemed? It doesn't say anything to me.

JR: Well, what I mean is that what I call the ordinary round of life—growing up, falling in love, having children and the rest—can seem not enough by itself. That ordinary round must be graced by something to be worthwhile. That's what I mean by redeemed. The question is what is needed to redeem it?[26]

In this book, I have skirted the issue of whether liberalism is a religion. I've called it a way of life and existential option, and proposed spiritual exercises to accompany it. My reason for avoiding the word *religion* is that it carries too much freight. It can be used polemically to attack liberals as either dogmatic or soulless. It can also lead to analytic tangles in trying to spell out what counts as religion. But Rawls in his addendum suggests a way forward. He ties religion to a function. When a need to redeem everyday life is felt, and where there is an organized attempt to provide for it, there is religion.

Redeemed by what? It depends on what you believe in. A theist will have one response, and an atheist or agnostic another. As we know, Rawls was once in the former camp but lost his faith. Even so, he never abandoned the conviction that ordinary life needs to be elevated ("redeemed" or "graced") by something beyond it. He found it in the liberal tradition and devoted his work to showing how a life based on liberal ideals can be not only happy but also worthy of happiness. A liberal way of life, Rawls wants to tell us, can be good in all senses of the word.

Liberalism has no metaphysics to speak of. The soul? The great beyond? The purpose of it all? "Pfffftt," goes the liberal. Yet we've never given up on the core of religion: to seek meaning in life through something beyond us. Our beyond is found not on another plane of existence but instead in something worldly just beyond our grasp—an ideal of becoming a free and generous person in a fair and just society.

Redemption is not found only in liberalism. Heaven forbid. Yet it is there too. And the final perk of a liberal way of life is that it has the moral depth and spiritual range *to redeem everyday life*. Rawls spent his life wrestling with a question: How is it possible for an institutional order to be just? But what if he did so to broach something more fundamental: How is it possible for a human life—yours, mine, or any—to be worthwhile?

Conclusion

REQUIEM FOR A LIBERAL
WAY OF LIFE?

IN HIS LATE MASTERPIECE *The Ancien Régime and the French
Revolution* (1856), Alexis de Tocqueville pinpoints the moment
when the old order of things started to collapse. It wasn't on
August 8, 1788, when the king summoned the estates general of
his kingdom. Nor was it the storming of the Bastille a year
later. It occurred long before, and while the exact calendar
date is lost to history, was far more significant than those nois-
ier events. It was the day when one (smaller) landowner looked
sideways at another (larger) landowner.

"I ask you to imagine the French peasant of the eighteenth
century, or even the peasant you know today, for he remains
forever the same," says Tocqueville in setting up the scene. The
encounter he then narrates is a masterpiece of perspective—of
the old order viewed by the new and the former boss (seigneur)
by his now-emancipated equal.

[See this peasant] so passionately in love with the land that
he uses all his savings to purchase more, no matter what the

price. [Yet] to acquire this new land he must first pay a fee, not to the government but to other nearby landowners, who have as little influence over public affairs and are almost as powerless as he. When he at last gets the land he wants, he plants his heart in it along with his seed. This little corner of the earth that he can call his own fills him with pride and independence. Yet now the same neighbors arrive to take him away from his field and force him to work somewhere else for no pay. . . . And when he returns home and wants to put the remainder of his grain to his own use—grain that he planted with his own hands and watched grow with his own eyes—he cannot do so unless he sends it to be milled in mills and baked in ovens owned by these same men. Part of the income of his small farm goes to paying them rent, and that rent is perpetual and irredeemable. No matter what he does, he encounters these vexatious neighbors along his path, interfering with his pleasure, impeding his work, eating his produce.[1]

This scene boils down to one furious question: "Who the fuck do you think you are?!" And once asked by enough people with enough passion, the old regime is doomed. The aristocrat who once commanded respect is scorned as a parasite. Inequalities that were seen to serve a common good are condemned as irrational and punitive. Most significantly, the social fabric frayed into mutual hatreds—"a cascade of contempt" in the words of a contemporary.[2] The moment all of this happens is when the regime becomes *ancien*, a word that in French means both previous and old.

Have we reached a similar tipping point today? Many smart observers seem to think so. Governance in many liberal democracies is mired in dysfunction, inequality continues its relentless march, environmental catastrophe is the new normal, mass migration destabilizes international politics, and ideological polarization generates alternative epistemic realities.[3] With respect to my own argument, to say that liberalism is on its way out would mean that a critical mass of citizens in liberal democracies no longer believe in it as a fair system of cooperation. And frankly, that might seem like an accurate reading of the landscape. The Far Left speaks as if it had lost faith that liberalism, in anything resembling its present form, can be rehabilitated. Captured by capitalism (and for some critics, racism and patriarchy too), utopian possibilities no longer seem to inhere in it. The Far Right launches a frontal attack, denying that society should be understood in terms of fair cooperation in the first place. Populist and authoritarian rhetoric is defined by a politics of suspicion, and its main message is that liberal elites are busy giving *our* stuff to *them* while taking away from *me* and *mine*. When you see the world like that, pretending that so-called liberal societies are even trying to be fair systems of cooperation is like bringing a picnic basket to a global and intergenerational knife fight.

But let's take a page from Tocqueville. His approach is to always look at the mores of a society—*moeurs* in French, a word that spans the values, customs, embodied practices, and ways of living proper to a society. A glance, expectation, courtesy, or flash of anger is where the regime and its future (or lack thereof) lies. The hero of my own book has been John Rawls, and he provided much of its content, from the opening definition of liberalism as a fair system of cooperation to spiritual exercises that cultivate liberty and liberality. My method, however, has been downright Tocquevillian. By identifying liberalism as the water of our times, and investigating how it saturates the public and background culture, I have claimed that it has percolated down to the bedrock of mores—which is to say, that in idea and emotion, ambition and deed, so many of us are liberals through and through. Hence the question I posed at the outset: Where do you get your values from? All along, this book has been preaching to a choir that doesn't realize that it's a choir.

And here's the thing about mores: they have a duration all of their own. Anchored as they are in one's self-conception and routines, they can be stubborn and resilient. Where, then, do we find ourselves? Yes, the future of liberalism can look bleak. For the privileged behind their computer screens, dire newspaper headlines and the roiling anger of Twitter do not augur well. And for less fortunate citizens, depredation and humiliation seem like features rather than bugs of the system. But to take up Tocqueville's point of view and judge the present by its mores, next time you're out shopping, try an experiment: cut someone off in line and see what happens. Or if that seems too risky, ask yourself the following set of questions: How would you feel if someone more powerful told you to keep quiet? How about if they told a stranger the same? How much schlock on Netflix (comedy, action, romance, or drama—it doesn't matter) do you consume about people finding their true path against all odds? How often do you worry about deep metaphysical questions like the design of the cosmos or endurance of the soul? How would you react if you learned your kid is a bully at school? When you get a parking ticket (and can afford it), do you think to yourself, "Oh well, it's going to pay for something"? Are you OK, honestly, if lower-income housing were to be built in your neighborhood? If your collected answers to the above questions are, roughly speaking, "angry," "still angry," "too much," "not much," "with alarm and shame," "I guess," and "yes," it should tell you something about yourself. Liberalism has a hold on you.

While writing this book, I frequently joked that I had to hurry, lest liberalism be over and done with. Truth is, I'm not so sure. When has liberalism not been in crisis? "Pick any decade since the 1930s," observes a historian, "and you will find an anxious liberal checking liberalism's vital signs or pronouncing the patient dead."[4] To this I'd add that the voices most loudly proclaiming the demise of liberalism today never liked it much to begin with.

What I am confident about, however, is that liberaldom is unstable. It combines moralism from the podium of correct opinion with hypocrisy and inequity on the ground. That is a recipe for resentment, a cascade of contempt for our day. Who knows, maybe the doomsayers are correct? Maybe the current order will come crashing down suddenly and spectacularly, thanks to God knows what proximate cause (the war in Ukraine? COVID-27? Rampant inflation? A Tucker Carlson presidency?). My sense, though, is that liberaldom will limp along for decades, bleeding support daily while the tectonic plates of mores continue to shift against the idea of society as a fair system of cooperation. The last fifty years of the ancien regime were ones where no one, no matter where they stood in the social hierarchy, believed in it. Don't mistake as optimism, then, my uncertainty as to whether the end is nigh. Mine is a *longue durée* view of history based in the belief that while liberaldom has staying power, it will eventually end in one of two ways: liberalism or illiberalism.

Throughout this book, I have presented what philosophers call an "intrinsic" rather than "instrumental" argument for the value of a liberal way of life. I have claimed that it is a good way to live, period, regardless of its beneficial effects on our societies. Yet those effects exist, and an instrumental case for the good of a liberal way of life is one to make. Indeed, it must be made, for liberaldom will be the death of us. Be liberal for yourself then, by all means, but do it also to set a lived example of how much life this regime still has and show how far from exhaustion it is. This is what the present moment requires: for liberals to not just promote their values but live up to them too. That alone will kindle faith in all reasonable citizens (liberal all the way down or not) in our world and help liberaldom to inch toward liberalism rather than slump into illiberalism. The stakes for us liberals couldn't be more personal. Liberalism is the source of my soul. The wager of this book is that the same is probably true of you.

ACKNOWLEDGMENTS

IN THIS BOOK, I make much of the fact that one meaning of the word *liberal* is generous. With that in mind, whatever their political persuasion, I thank many liberal souls: Keith Ansell-Pearson, Peter Anstay, Thomas Besch, Tristan Bradshaw, Karen Carter, Noah Corbett, Michael Freeden, Vafa Ghazavi, Martin Hagglünd, Emily Hulme, Duncan Ivison, Jack Jacobs, John Keane, Samuel Khoo, Melissa Lane, Sandra Laugier, Leonard Lawlor, Beatrice Lefebvre, Georges and Joanne Lefebvre, Elizabeth Li, Juliette Marchant, Wolfgang Merkel, Cindy Milstein, Samuel Moyn, Susan Neiman, Haig Patapan, Paul Patton, Philip Pettit, Michael Schur, Mark Scott, Matthew Sharpe, Samuel Shpall, Peter Singer, Tim Smartt, Michael Spence, Marc Stears, Anna Stilz, Mitchell Stirzaker, Matthew Sussman, Lars Tønder, Nishan Varatharajan, Dimitris Vardoulakis, Miguel Vatter, Hent de Vries, Jessica Whyte, Lucy Williams, and Yanyun Yang. I am especially indebted to Luara Ferracioli, Stephen Macedo, Brendon O'Connor, Helena Rosenblatt, Rob Tempio, and as ever and always, Melanie White for reading the entire manuscript and improving it in so many ways.

This book was written in two places at the same time: physically in Sydney, Australia, and virtually at Princeton University's Center for Human Values, where in 2021–22, I held a (remote, due to COVID-19) Laurance S. Rockefeller Visiting Fellowship. I am grateful to the University of Sydney and Princeton

University for the time, research support, and intellectual communities that made this book possible.

A version of chapter 3 was published as "Liberalism and the Good Life" in the *Journal of Social and Political Philosophy* 1, no. 2 (2022): 152–68, and sections of "The Spiritual Exercises of John Rawls," *Political Theory* 50, no. 3 (2022): 405–27, and "Liberalism and the Self," in *The Research Handbook on Liberalism*, ed. Duncan Ivison (Cheltenham, UK: Edward Elgar, 2024) appear in this book. I thank the publishers for permission to reprint.

NOTES

Chapter One: The Water We Swim In

1. David Foster Wallace, *This Is Water: Some Thoughts, Delivered on a Significant Occasion, about Living a Compassionate Life* (Boston: Little, Brown and Company, 2009), 1–2.

2. "Liberalism," *Oxford English Dictionary* (Oxford: Oxford University Press, 2023).

3. Patrick Deneen, *Why Liberalism Failed* (New Haven, CT: Yale University Press, 2018), 37. For a view on the omnipresence of liberalism from a left-leaning critic, see Raymond Geuss, *Not Thinking like a Liberal* (Cambridge, MA: Harvard University Press, 2022).

4. William Barr, "Attorney General William Barr on Religious Liberty," YouTube, 2019, https://www.youtube.com/watch?v=IM87WMsrCWM.

5. Personal favorites include Jon Baskin, *Ordinary Unhappiness: The Therapeutic Fiction of David Foster Wallace* (Stanford, CA: Stanford University Press, 2019); Sarah Bakewell, *How to Live: A Life of Montaigne in One Question and Twenty Attempts at an Answer* (New York: Vintage Books, 2011); Sarah Bakewell, *At the Existentialist Café: Freedom, Being, and Apricot Cocktails* (New York: Vintage Books, 2016); Stanley Cavell, *Cities of Words: Pedagogical Letters on a Register of the Moral Life* (Cambridge, MA: Harvard University Press, 2005); Ryan Patrick Hanley, *Our Great Purpose: Adam Smith on Living a Better Life* (Princeton, NJ: Princeton University Press, 2019); Martin Hägglund, *This Life: Secular Faith and Spiritual Freedom* (London: Penguin Books, 2019); William B. Irvine, *A Guide to the Good Life: The Ancient Art of Stoic Joy* (Oxford: Oxford University Press, 2009); Susan Neiman, *Moral Clarity: A Guide for Grown-Up Idealists* (New York: Vintage Books, 2009); Susan Neiman, *Why Grow Up? Subversive Thoughts for an Infantile Age* (London: Penguin Books, 2016); Benjamin Storey and Jenna Silber Storey, *Why We Are Restless: On the Modern Quest for Contentment* (Princeton, NJ: Princeton University Press, 2021). The pioneering author of this genre is Pierre Hadot, whom I will discuss shortly.

6. Alexandre Lefebvre, *Human Rights as a Way of Life: On Bergson's Political Philosophy* (Stanford, CA: Stanford University Press, 2013); Alexandre Lefebvre, *Human Rights and the Care of the Self* (Durham, NC: Duke University Press, 2018).

Chapter Two: What Is Liberalism?

1. Gerald Gaus, "Liberalism," in *The Stanford Encyclopedia of Philosophy*, ed. Edward N. Zalta and Uri Nodelman (Stanford, CA: Stanford University, 2018).

2. For liberalism as individual rights, see Ronald Dworkin, *Taking Rights Seriously* (Cambridge, MA: Harvard University Press, 1978). For liberalism as personal freedom, see Isaiah Berlin, "Two Concepts of Liberty," in *Liberty*, ed. Henry Hardy (Oxford: Oxford University Press, 2002), 166–217. For liberalism as freedom from fear, see Judith N. Shklar, "The Liberalism of Fear," in *Political Thought and Political Thinkers*, ed. Stanley Hoffman (Chicago: University of Chicago Press, 1998), 3–20. For liberalism as mutual justification, see Rainer Forst, *The Right to Justification: Elements of a Constructivist Theory of Justice* (New York: Columbia University Press, 2011). Critics of liberalism can also take a stipulative approach, with a negative property identified as the core of liberalism and an intellectual villain attached to it. See, for example, critiques of liberalism as colonial and neocolonial, and bound to the thought of such figures as Locke, Mill, and Alexis de Tocqueville, in Uday Singh Mehta, *Liberalism and Empire: A Study in Nineteenth-Century British Liberal Thought* (Chicago: University of Chicago Press, 1999); Jennifer Pitts, *A Turn to Empire: The Rise of Imperial Liberalism in Britain and France* (Princeton, NJ: Princeton University Press, 2006); Domenico Losurdo, *Liberalism: A Counter-History* (Brooklyn: Verso, 2014); Elisabeth Anker, *Ugly Freedoms* (Durham, NC: Duke University Press, 2021); Pankaj Mishra, *Bland Fanatics: Liberals, Race, and Empire* (New York: Farrar, Straus and Giroux, 2020).

3. Michael Freeden, *Liberal Languages: Ideological Imaginations and Twentieth-Century Progressive Thought* (Princeton, NJ: Princeton University Press, 2009), 20. The contextualist approach derives its name from the claim that an idea can only be understood in the context that gave rise to it (that is, from within the unique group of meanings to which it once belonged). See Duncan Bell, "What Is Liberalism?," *Political Theory* 42, no. 6 (2014): 682–715.

4. See Katrina Forrester, *In the Shadow of Justice: Postwar Liberalism and the Remaking of Political Philosophy* (Princeton, NJ: Princeton University Press, 2019); Anthony Simon Laden, "The House That Jack Built: Thirty Years of Reading Rawls," *Ethics* 113, no. 2 (2003): 367–90.

5. Jason Brennan, "The Five Major Types of Dissertations in Political Philosophy and Political Theory," *Bleeding Heart Libertarians* (blog), 2016, https://bleedingheart libertarians.com/2016/08/the-five-major-types-of-dissertations-in-political -philosophy-and-political-theory/.

6. I've taken this definition of the moralist from Lucien Jaume, *Tocqueville: The Aristocratic Sources of Liberty* (Princeton, NJ: Princeton University Press, 2013), 127, 145–92.

7. John Rawls, *A Theory of Justice*, rev. ed. (Cambridge, MA: Harvard University Press, 1999), 514.

8. See Stephen Macedo, *Liberal Virtues: Citizenship, Virtue, and Community in Liberal Constitutionalism* (Oxford: Oxford University Press, 1990); Paul Weithman, *Why Political Liberalism? On John Rawls's Political Turn* (Oxford: Oxford University Press, 2013); Andrius Gališanka, *John Rawls: The Path to a Theory of Justice* (Cambridge, MA: Harvard University Press, 2019); Sharon Krause, *Civil Passions: Moral Sentiment and Democratic Deliberation* (Princeton, NJ: Princeton University Press, 2008); Eric Nelson, *The Theology of Liberalism: Political Philosophy and the Justice of God* (Cambridge, MA: Harvard University Press, 2019); Mark E. Button, *Contract, Culture, and Citizenship: Transformative Liberalism from Hobbes to Rawls* (University Park: Penn State University Press, 2008); Erin M. Cline, *Confucius, Rawls, and the Sense of Justice* (New York: Fordham University Press, 2012); P. Mackenzie Bok, "To the Mountaintop Again: The Early Rawls and Post-Protestant Ethics in Postwar America," *Modern Intellectual History* 14, no. 1 (2017): 153–85.

9. For a biographical sketch of Rawls's life, see Thomas Pogge, *John Rawls: His Life and Theory of Justice* (Oxford: Oxford University Press, 2007), 3–27. For a touching account of Rawls as a teacher and mentor, see Christine Korsgaard, "Thinking in Good Company," in *Proceedings and Addresses of the American Philosophical Association* 96 (November 2022), https://nrs.harvard.edu/URN-3:HUL.INSTREPOS: 37373852.

10. Ian Malcolm, "A Theory of Justice, 1971," *Harvard University Press* (blog), 2013, https://harvardpress.typepad.com/hup_publicity/2013/04/john-rawls-a-theory-of -justice-1971.html. The friend is Burton Dreben. See Samuel Freeman, *Rawls* (Abingdon, UK: Routledge, 2007), 28.

11. John Rawls, "John Rawls: For the Record," *Harvard Review of Philosophy* 1, no. 1 (Spring 1991): 43.

12. Rawls, *A Theory of Justice*, 4. As he states in his final book, *Justice as Fairness: A Restatement* (Cambridge, MA: Harvard University Press, 2001), "The most fundamental idea in [my] conception of justice is the idea of society as a fair system of social cooperation over time from one generation to the next" (4).

13. Many Rawls scholars describe their first encounter with his work in terms of recognition, a déjà vu experience of coming back to a work they already know. "I was a third-year law student in the mid-1970s when I first read *A Theory of Justice*," says Freeman (*Rawls*, xvi). "Like many people, I felt the book gave philosophical expression to my most deeply held moral convictions. I decided then (foolishly perhaps at the time since I had a one-year-old daughter) to give up a legal career and study

political and moral philosophy." See also Weithman, *Why Political Liberalism?*, 13–16.

14. Leif Wenar, "Panel: Rawls and the Project of Modern Political Thought," You-Tube, 2019, https://www.youtube.com/watch?v=aTTJRdJb0ro. The question of whether society *is* or *ought to be* a "fair system of cooperation" is a central concern of this book. Consider the phrase from two lines above: "[Everyone knows that] the job of the police is to protect them." As a predictive statement—that everyone in a liberal democratic society expects that the police *will* protect them—it is obviously and even offensively false. Black Lives Matter, to name a prominent social movement, is premised on the belief that the police and criminal justice system in the United States discriminates against people of color. Yet as a normative statement, it is power-fully affirmed. It is wrong for police and the justice system to discriminate against Black people *because of* the conviction (enshrined everywhere in the public institu-tions and political culture of liberal democracies) that society *ought to be* (and not in some distant future but instead must immediately be, because that is what a liberal democratic society *is*) a fair system of cooperation for all of its members. From this perspective, much (though not all, as there are radical elements of the movement, such as its abolitionist fringe) of Black Lives Matter is a liberal movement fighting for a fair liberal society (or rather, for a liberal society properly so called, if indeed fairness is its foundational idea). I've raised this issue now to head off any impression that Rawls or I simply assert, as if a truism, that our current societies are fair systems of cooperation. We are offering a radical critique of who we are, both personally and politically.

15. This method is explicit in Rawls's middle and later writings. See John Rawls, "Kantian Constructivism in Moral Theory," in *Collected Papers*, ed. Samuel Freeman (Cambridge, MA: Harvard University Press, 1999), 304–10; John Rawls, *Political Liberalism*, exp. ed. (New York: Columbia University Press, 2005), 8–11, 15–22. Inter-preters, however, have also located it in *A Theory of Justice*. See Weithman, *Why Political Liberalism?*, 11–12, 107–9; Gališanka, *John Rawls*, 1–16. Interestingly, Allan Bloom's review of *A Theory of Justice* highlights its importance (albeit to knock it down): "[Rawls starts] from what we are now and ends there, since there is nothing beyond us. At best Rawls will help us to be more consistent, if that is an advantage." Allan Bloom, "Justice: John Rawls vs. the Tradition of Political Philosophy," *American Political Science Review* 69, no. 2 (June 1975): 649.

16. Rawls is not alone in claiming that fairness, social provision, and collective interdependence are at the heart of liberalism. In the early twentieth century, John Dewey, Leonard Hobhouse, and John Atkinson Hobson said the same. See Freeden, *Liberal Languages*, 45–58, 94–128, 258–59. Rawls is original, however, in anchoring that claim in the self-understanding that citizens of liberal democracy acquire by virtue of inhabiting a liberal democratic public political culture.

17. Billy Eichner, "Billy on the Street: Lightning Round (Name a Woman!)," You-Tube, 2013, https://www.youtube.com/watch?v=bzDlS6JPUtE.

18. This hypothetical is tricky in the context of the United States as the term *liberal* is so often used polemically. For those in the United States who understand them-selves, rightly or wrong, as opponents of something called liberalism, the request to "name a liberal" might well elicit immediate and heated responses, such as "Hillary Clinton!" "Alexandria Ocasio-Cortez!" or "George Soros!"

19. Kazuo Ishiguro, "Nobel Lecture," Nobel Foundation, 2017, https://www.nobelprize.org/uploads/2018/06/ishiguro-lecture_en-1.pdf.

20. Pierre Hadot, *What Is Ancient Philosophy?* (Cambridge, MA: Harvard University Press, 2004), 1–6.

21. Pierre Hadot, "Spiritual Exercises," in *Philosophy as a Way of Life*, ed. Arnold I. Davidson (Malden, MA: Blackwell Publishing, 1995), 81–125; Hadot, *What Is Ancient Philosophy?*, 172–266; Pierre Hadot, *The Present Alone Is Our Happiness: Conversations with Jeannie Carlier and Arnold Davidson* (Stanford, CA: Stanford University Press, 2008), 87–97, 121–44.

22. Rawls, *Justice as Fairness*, 19.

23. See Adam Gopnik, *A Thousand Small Sanities: The Moral Adventure of Liberal-ism* (New York: Basic Books, 2019).

24. Nussbaum has taken to great lengths Rawls's insights on the connection be-tween political stability and the emotional well-being and maturity of its citizens. See especially Martha C. Nussbaum, *Political Emotions: Why Love Matters for Justice* (Cambridge, MA: Harvard University Press, 2015).

25. Hadot, "Spiritual Exercises," 104.

Chapter Three: Liberalism and the Good Life

1. Michael Schur, "The Secret Origin of Parks and Recreation," YouTube, 2019, https://www.youtube.com/watch?v=vMs-Ko0CnLw.

2. Michael Schur, "Parks and Recreation 10th Anniversary Reunion at PaleyFest LA," YouTube, 2019, https://www.youtube.com/watch?v=NbGwFACf4mQ.

3. *Parks and Recreation*, season 2, episode 3, "Beauty Pageant," directed by Jason Woliner, written by Katie Dippold, aired on October 1, 2009, on NBC.

4. The first revisionist work on classical liberalism is Ludwig von Mises's *Liberal-ism: The Classical Tradition* (1927). Its thesis (that twentieth-century liberalism went off the rails and a classical tradition needed to be recovered) was further developed by the Mont Pelerin Society, whose founding members included Mises, Friedrich Hayek, Karl Popper, and Milton Friedman. In an interview given in 1992, Friedman said that there was "no doubt" that the original purpose of the society was "to pro-mote a classical, liberal philosophy, that is, a free economy, a free society, socially,

civilly and in human rights." Cited in Jessica Whyte, *The Morals of the Market: Human Rights and the Rise of Neoliberalism* (Brooklyn: Verso, 2019), 18.

5. Helena Rosenblatt, *The Lost History of Liberalism* (Princeton, NJ: Princeton University Press, 2018), 128.

6. Another term to describe Leslie's amor mundi is Martin Hägglund's *secular faith*, which consists of devoting care and love to projects and places that you know can fail and break down. Martin Hägglund, *This Life: Secular Faith and Spiritual Freedom* (London: Penguin Books, 2019), 39–171. A negative image of Leslie can be found in another formidable character from a US political workplace television comedy that aired at the same time: Selina Meyer in *Veep* (2012–17). The polar opposite of *Parks and Recreation*, *Veep* is a dark take on what can only ironically be called "public service." What amor mundi is to Leslie, amour propre is to Selina. Tellingly, in neither show do politicians and citizens have party identifications, and the words *Republican* and *Democrat* are never used. The shows instead portray two different worlds captured by two different moods. In *Parks and Recreation*, citizens from across the political spectrum come together to practice amor mundi—whether in the form of the long-running, good faith argument between Leslie and her libertarian coworker Ron Swanson, or in the many cameos by politicians from both sides of the aisle (including Cory Booker, Orrin Hatch, John McCain, and Madeleine Albright). In *Veep*, not a single politician or staffer (save for two supporting characters), no matter their professed beliefs, is driven by anything other than self-interest, narcissism, or the desire to humiliate others. Watching these shows side by side, it is hard to resist the conclusion that they were respectively created by those who believe in liberal democracy and those who do not.

7. *Parks and Recreation*, season 6, episode 2, "London, Part 2," directed by Dean Holland, written by Michael Schur, aired on September 26, 2013, on NBC.

8. Barack Obama, *A Promised Land* (London: Penguin Books, 2020), 153–54.

9. This quip is attributed to Irving Kristol, but its origin is difficult to pinpoint. See C. Bradley Thompson, *Neoconservatism: An Obituary for an Idea* (Abingdon, UK: Routledge, 2010), 275. I first heard it when I was a teenager, and it is the first thing I remember learning about liberalism. Kristol's actual words, however, are that "a *neoconservative* is a liberal who's been mugged by reality." Because I didn't know what a neoconservative was back in the mid-1990s, I falsely remembered it as simply "conservative."

10. Edmund Fawcett identifies a belief in human progress as one of the four "guiding ideas" of liberalism. Edmund Fawcett, *Liberalism: The Life of an Idea* (Princeton, NJ: Princeton University Press, 2015), xii–xiv, 10–11, 20, 67–79.

11. Judith N. Shklar, *Ordinary Vices* (Cambridge, MA: Harvard University Press, 1985), 197. For a comprehensive reconstruction of the liberal tradition as based on the Shklar-inspired themes of the prevention of fear and hatred of cruelty, see Alan

Kahan, *Freedom from Fear: An Incomplete History of Liberalism* (Princeton, NJ: Princeton University Press, 2023).

12. Shklar, *Ordinary Vices*, 193. For another outstanding book on liberalism that puts misanthropy front and center while rejecting the myth that liberals are unthinking optimists, see Amanda Anderson, *Bleak Liberalism* (Chicago: University of Chicago Press, 2016). Given Shklar's and Anderson's shared focus on a uniquely liberal sensibility, it is no coincidence that they both make central use of literary authors: Molière and Nathaniel Hawthorne for Shklar, and Charles Dickens, E. M. Forster, and Doris Lessing for Anderson.

13. Several historians have argued this point, but none so systematically as Annelien de Dijn in *Freedom: An Unruly History* (Cambridge, MA: Harvard University Press, 2020). She claims that a liberal conception of freedom is counterrevolutionary in the sense that its ideals (freedom in civil life and small government) were a backlash against the democratic revolutions of the late eighteenth century. Today we live in a golden age of histories of liberalism. For accounts that stress the tension between early liberalism and democracy, see Rosenblatt, *The Lost History of Liberalism*; Gregory Conti, *Parliament and the Mirror of Nature: Representation, Deliberation, and Democracy in Victorian Britain* (Cambridge: Cambridge University Press, 2020); William Selinger, *Parliamentarism: From Burke to Weber* (Cambridge: Cambridge University Press, 2019); Duncan Bell, *Reordering the World: Essays on Liberalism and Empire* (Princeton, NJ: Princeton University Press, 2016); Edward Luce, *The Retreat of Western Liberalism* (Boston: Little, Brown and Company, 2017); Fawcett, *Liberalism*; Samuel Moyn, *Liberalism against Itself: Cold War Liberal Political Thought and the Making of Our Times* (New Haven, CT: Yale University Press, 2023). One reason why historians insist that the origin of liberalism lies in the nineteenth century is to challenge philosophers who propose distant antecedents from the ancient world, Christianity, and the Reformation. See Leo Strauss, *Liberalism Ancient and Modern* (Chicago: University of Chicago Press, 1995); Larry Siedentop, *Inventing the Individual: The Origins of Western Liberalism* (Cambridge, MA: Harvard University Press, 2014); Pierre Manent, *An Intellectual History of Liberalism* (Princeton, NJ: Princeton University Press, 1987). Finally, I note that the tension between liberalism and democracy is today developed by critics of democracy (such as Jason Brennan, *Against Democracy* [Princeton, NJ: Princeton University Press, 2016]) and liberalism (such Alain de Benoist, *The Problem of Democracy* [Budapest: Arktos, 2011]) alike.

14. Rosenblatt, *The Lost History of Liberalism*, 19.

15. Adam Gopnik's *A Thousand Small Sanities: The Moral Adventure of Liberalism* (New York: Basic Books, 2019) has the kind of title (or more accurately, subtitle) I have in mind.

16. Alexis de Tocqueville, *Democracy in America* (Chicago: University of Chicago Press, 2000), 7.

17. See Leo Damrosch, *Tocqueville's Discovery of America* (New York: Farrar, Straus and Giroux, 2011).

18. Gustave de Beaumont and Alexis de Tocqueville, *On the Penitentiary System in the United States and Its Application to France: The Complete Text* (London: Palgrave Macmillan, 2018).

19. See James Schleifer, *The Chicago Companion to Tocqueville's Democracy in America* (Chicago: University of Chicago Press, 2012), 41–45.

20. Tocqueville was also a scathing critic of several features of US society, particularly race relations. See Ralph Lerner, *The Thinking Revolutionary: Principle and Practice in the New Republic* (Ithaca, NY: Cornell University Press, 1987), 174–91.

21. Tocqueville, *Democracy in America*, 663.

22. Tocqueville, *Democracy in America*, 482–503.

23. Lucien Jaume, *Tocqueville: The Aristocratic Sources of Liberty* (Princeton, NJ: Princeton University Press, 2013), 137–42, 154–69.

24. Tocqueville, *Letters from America* (New Haven, CT: Yale University Press, 2010), 28–32. See Benjamin Storey and Jenna Storey, *Why We Are Restless: On the Modern Quest for Contentment* (Princeton, NJ: Princeton University Press, 2021), 140–52.

25. Tocqueville, *Democracy in America*, 409.

26. John Stuart Mill, *On Liberty* (New Haven, CT: Yale University Press, 2003), 126.

27. Patrick Deneen's *Why Liberalism Failed* (New Haven, CT: Yale University Press, 2018) identifies individualism, materialism, and conformity as features of liberalism rather than democracy, and often relies on Tocqueville to make his case. This is an idiosyncratic interpretation. Throughout *Democracy in America*, Tocqueville identifies democracy, not liberalism, as responsible for the individualism, materialism, and conformity of the modern world. To quote an 1836 letter from Tocqueville to his childhood friend Eugène Stöffels, "I cannot believe that people don't see me clearly as a new kind of liberal." Cited in Jaume, *Tocqueville*, 299.

28. For an expanded discussion, see Alexandre Lefebvre, *Human Rights and the Care of the Self* (Durham, NC: Duke University Press, 2018), 61–84.

29. See Damrosch, *Tocqueville's Discovery of America*, 98–107.

30. Robert Gannett, "Tocqueville and Local Government," *Review of Politics* 67, no. 4 (Autumn 2005): 721–36.

31. Tocqueville, *Democracy in America*, 64–65; emphasis added. For a contemporary localist conception of liberal democratic citizenship, see Stephen Macedo, "Populism, Localism, and Democratic Citizens," *Philosophy and Social Criticism* 47, no. 4 (2021): 447–76.

32. Tocqueville, *Democracy in America*, 675.

33. A fascinating way station between Tocqueville's *Democracy in America* and our times is Will Herberg, *Protestant, Catholic, Jew* (Chicago: University of Chicago Press, 1955). Herberg writes about a still deeply religious United States, with

97 percent of its citizens professing a belief in God. Yet he claims that their real operative faith is the "American way of life," something that "synthesizes all that commends itself to the American as the right, good, and the true in actual life. It embraces such seemingly incongruous elements as sanitary plumbing and freedom of opportunity, Coca-Cola and an intense faith in education—all felt as moral questions relating to the proper way of life" (75). Although still enmeshed with religion, liberalism in the 1950s is about to step out on its own as a self-sufficient way of life.

Chapter Four: What Liberals Don't Get about Liberalism

1. John Chapman, "Rawls's Theory of Justice," *American Political Science Review* 69, no. 2 (June 1975): 588.

2. Katrina Forrester, *In the Shadow of Justice: Postwar Liberalism and the Remaking of Political Philosophy* (Princeton, NJ: Princeton University Press, 2019), x.

3. Rawls surveys the criticisms and conversations that led him to write *Political Liberalism* (New York: Columbia University Press, 2005) in its introduction (xxx–xxxiii). I note that political liberalism has two founders: Rawls and Charles Larmore, whose "Political Liberalism" (*Political Theory* 18, no. 3 [August 1990]: 339–60) precedes Rawls's *Political Liberalism* by three years.

4. Rawls, *Political Liberalism*, xvi.

5. Aristotle, *The Politics* (Chicago: University of Chicago Press, 2013), VII.8 1328a26–27.

6. Rawls, *Political Liberalism*, 40–43.

7. John Rawls, *Lectures on the History of Political Philosophy* (Cambridge, MA: Harvard University Press, 2007), 87. See also John Rawls, *A Theory of Justice*, rev. ed. (Cambridge, MA: Harvard University Press, 1999), 211, 304–5.

8. Rawls, *A Theory of Justice*, 398.

9. *Bird Box*, directed by Susanne Bier (Netflix, 2018), film, 124 min.

10. Geoffrey Nunberg, *The Ascent of the A-Word: Assholism, the First Sixty Years* (New York: Perseus Books, 2013); Aaron James, *Assholes: A Theory* (New York: Doubleday, 2012); John McWhorter, *Nine Nasty Words: English in the Gutter* (New York: Avery, 2021), 87–108; Melissa Mohr, *Holy Sh*t: A Brief History of Swearing* (Oxford: Oxford University Press, 2016), 94–96.

11. McWhorter, *Nine Nasty Words*, 104.

12. Rawls, *A Theory of Justice*, 287. See also Rawls, *A Theory of Justice*, 27–30, 228–29.

13. For a discussion of similar themes of ethical ideals, self-definition, and effective motivation, see Sharon Krause, *Liberalism with Honor* (Cambridge, MA: Harvard University Press, 2002).

14. See Forrester, *In the Shadow of Justice*; special issues of the *Journal of the History of Ideas* 78 (2017) and *Modern Intellectual History* 18 (2021). A parallel project by

intellectual and political historians investigates Rawls's intellectual development, starting from his undergraduate thesis on sin and faith, to the long road of research and maturation that led to *A Theory of Justice*. See Andrius Gališanka, *John Rawls: The Path to a Theory of Justice* (Cambridge, MA: Harvard University Press, 2019); Eric Nelson, *The Theology of Liberalism: Political Philosophy and the Justice of God* (Cambridge, MA: Harvard University Press, 2019); P. Mackenzie Bok, "To the Mountaintop Again: The Early Rawls and Post-Protestant Ethics in Postwar America," *Modern Intellectual History* 14, no. 1 (2017): 153–85; Eric Gregory, "Before the Original Position: The Neo-Orthodox Theology of the Young John Rawls," *Journal of Religious Ethics* 35, no. 2 (2007): 179–206; David Reidy, "Rawls's Religion and Justice as Fairness," *History of Political Thought* 31, no. 2 (Summer 2010): 309–43.

15. Forrester, *In the Shadow of Justice*, xi

16. Forrester, *In the Shadow of Justice*, xxii.

17. As a specialist of early twentieth-century philosopher Henri Bergson, I would be remiss not to note that he is the thinker to have most fully explored the importance and mechanics of problems and problem creation. Henri Bergson, *The Creative Mind: An Introduction to Metaphysics* (Mineola, NY: Dover Publications, 2007), 30–91.

18. Rawls, *Political Liberalism*, 4.

19. See Jonathan Quong, *Liberalism without Perfection* (Oxford: Oxford University Press, 2010); Martha C. Nussbaum, "Perfectionism Liberalism and Political Liberalism," *Philosophy and Public Affairs* 39, no. 1 (Winter 2011): 3–45.

20. Sample works from this vast literature include Robert Audi, *Religious Commitment and Secular Reason* (New York: Cambridge University Press, 2000); Charles R. Beitz, *The Idea of Human Rights* (Oxford: Oxford University Press, 2009); Elizabeth Brake, *Minimizing Marriage: Marriage, Morality, and the Law* (Oxford: Oxford University Press, 2011); Harry Brighouse and Adam Swift, *Family Values: The Ethics of Parent-Child Relationships* (Princeton, NJ: Princeton University Press, 2014); Clare Chambers, *Against Marriage: An Egalitarian Defence of the Marriage-Free State* (Oxford: Oxford University Press, 2017); Norman Daniels, *Just Health: Meeting Health Needs Fairly* (Cambridge: Cambridge University Press, 2007); Luara Ferracioli, *Liberal Self-Determination in a World of Migration* (New York: Oxford University Press, 2022); Luara Ferracioli, *Parenting and the Goods of Childhood* (Oxford: Oxford University Press, 2023); James Fleming, *Securing Constitutional Democracy: The Case of Autonomy* (Chicago: University of Chicago Press, 2006); James Fleming and Linda McClain, *Ordered Liberty: Rights, Responsibilities, and Virtues* (Cambridge, MA: Harvard University Press, 2013); Christie Hartley and Lori Watson, *Equal Citizenship and Public Reason: A Feminist Political Liberalism* (New York: Oxford University Press, 2018); Charles Larmore, *What Is Political Philosophy?* (Princeton, NJ: Princeton University Press, 2020); Stephen Macedo, *Just Married: Same-Sex Couples, Monogamy, and the Future of Marriage* (Princeton, NJ: Princeton University Press, 2015); Stephen Macedo, *Diversity and*

Distrust: Civic Education in a Multicultural Democracy (Cambridge, MA: Harvard University Press, 2000); Martha C. Nussbaum, *Frontiers of Justice: Disability, Nationality, and Species Membership* (Cambridge, MA: Harvard University Press, 2006); Martin O'Neill and Thad Williamson, eds., *Property-Owning Democracy: Rawls and Beyond* (Malden, MA: Blackwell Publishing, 2012); Thomas Pogge, *World Poverty and Human Rights* (Cambridge, UK: Polity Press, 2008); Quong, *Liberalism without Perfection*; Gina Schouten, *Liberalism, Neutrality, and the Gendered Division of Labor* (Oxford: Oxford University Press, 2019); Paul Weithman, *Rawls, Political Liberalism, and Reasonable Faith* (Cambridge: Cambridge University Press, 2016).

21. Rawls, *Political Liberalism*, 11–12. See also Rawls, *Political Liberalism*, 11–15, 174–75, 223, 376, 452–53.

22. Rawls, *Political Liberalism*, 12; emphasis added. See also Rawls, *Political Liberalism*, 144–45.

23. Rawls, *Political Liberalism*, 140.

24. Rawls, *Political Liberalism*, xix; emphasis added.

25. Rawls, *Political Liberalism*, 12.

26. Rawls, *Political Liberalism*, 246. See also Rawls, *Political Liberalism*, 158–72, 389. For the term *liberal* as a modifier (for example, a liberal democrat, liberal nationalist, or liberal Buddhist), see Michael Walzer, *The Struggle for a Decent Politics: On "Liberal" as an Adjective* (New Haven, CT: Yale University Press, 2023).

27. On the power of liberalism to reshape comprehensive doctrines, see Macedo, *Diversity and Distrust*, 28–39; Stephen Macedo, "Liberalism beyond Toleration: Religious Exemptions, Civility and the Ideological Other," *Philosophy and Social Criticism* 45, no. 4 (2019): 370–89. Macedo pays special attention to Locke's *Letter Concerning Toleration* (1689) and the remaking of Christianity on the basis of his liberal commitments (as they had developed by the time of the *Letter*). Charity, meekness, and tolerance, says Locke, are the chief virtues of a Christian. This was certainly news for seventeenth-century readers.

28. Rawls, *Political Liberalism*, 13.

29. Rawls, *Political Liberalism*, 169. See also Rawls, *Political Liberalism*, xlv, 37, 78, 98, 145, 159, 199–200, 400.

30. John Stuart Mill, *Autobiography*, in *The Collected Works of John Stuart Mill, Volume 1* (Toronto: University of Toronto Press, 2006), 259. This quotation is how Mill summarizes the "single truth" of *On Liberty*.

31. Truth be told, the comprehensive liberal of political liberalism is a LEGO figure in disguise, insofar as they have a prior comprehensive doctrine that can be detached (or at least semidetached) from a liberal political conception.

32. Joseph Raz, *The Morality of Freedom* (Oxford: Oxford University Press, 1986). Other moral and political philosophers who develop liberal political theories from prior moral and metaphysical commitments include Stanley Cavell (from Ralph

Waldo Emerson and Ludwig Wittgenstein; see Stanley Cavell, *Cities of Words: Peda-gogical Letters on a Register of the Moral Life* [Cambridge, MA: Harvard University Press, 2005]), William Connolly (from Benedict de Spinoza and Gilles Deleuze; see William E. Connolly, *Pluralism* [Durham, NC: Duke University Press, 2005]), and Martin Hägglund (from Karl Marx and Martin Heidegger; see Martin Hägglund, *This Life: Secular Faith and Spiritual Freedom* [London: Penguin Books, 2019]).

33. Whether I am correct that the mainstream background culture of con-temporary liberal democracies is awash with liberal values is a claim that can only be demonstrated empirically (as the next chapter undertakes). If I am, however, it raises a worrying problem for political liberalism. Rawls believes that reasonable pluralism about the good will be ongoing in a liberal society; in fact, it might be a hallmark of such a society that the freedoms it affords generate continuing reason-able disagreement about such matters. See Rawls, *Political Liberalism*, 4, 54–57, 134–44. See also Larmore, *What Is Political Philosophy?*, 1–67; Quong, *Liberalism without Perfection*, 138–45. But what if Rawls (and political liberals) are wrong on this count? What if we shouldn't necessarily expect reasonable pluralism about the good to flourish given that most of us can be expected to absorb a comprehensive liberal doctrine by virtue of growing up under liberal institutions and culture? This indeed is what religious conservatives fear most: their views will die out in the cur-rent culture. If that fear becomes widespread, then Rawls's argument for stability in *Political Liberalism* suffers a potentially fatal setback. Adherents of various compre-hensive doctrines will conclude that there is no continuing place for them in a lib-eral society. Worse, from their point of view it would be rational to opt out and oppose liberalism—comprehensive *or* political—bide their time, and perhaps even when opportunity strikes, use the power and purse of the state to advance their conception of the good (if, that is, they become convinced they cannot hope to win the cultural war without resorting to state power). See Patrick J. Deneen, "Abandon-ing Defensive Crouch Conservatism: Toward a Conservatism That Is Not Liberal-ism," *Postliberal Order* (blog), November 17, 2021, https://postliberalorder.substack .com/p/abandoning-defensive-crouch-conservatism; Sohrab Ahmari, "Against David French-ism," *First Things*, May 29, 2019, https://www.firstthings.com/web -exclusives/2019/05/against-david-french-ism. Political liberalism, then, is argu-ably a ghost story in two respects. The first, the topic of this chapter, is that it gives an outmoded account of comprehensive liberalism. The second, the topic of this note, is that it gives an outmoded account of stability. Yet both failings stem from one and the same source: an inability or unwillingness to acknowledge the takeover by liberalism over the past thirty years of the background culture of contemporary liberal democracies.

34. Judith N. Shklar, "Letter to John Rawls, November 10th, 1986," Papers of John Rawls, Harvard University Archives, box 41, folder 15.

Chapter Five: Six Ways Liberalism Shapes Us (and Vice Versa)

1. Amy McQuire and Max Chalmers, "Curriculum Reviewer Barry Spurr Mocks 'Abos, Mussies, Women, Chinky-Poos,'" *New Matilda*, October 16, 2014, https://newmatilda.com/2014/10/16/curriculum-reviewer-barry-spurr-mocks-abos-mussies-women-chinky-poos/. Spurr was not officially fired by the University of Sydney but instead resigned in the face of furious and ongoing protests.

2. This paragraph on exemplarity, representativeness, and community is indebted to Stanley Cavell, particularly how he envisages claims to knowledge and self-knowledge as claims to community in *The Claim of Reason: Wittgenstein, Skepticism, Morality, and Tragedy* (New York: Oxford University Press, 1999), 3–36, 168–90. See also Andrew Norris, *Becoming Who We Are: Politics and Practical Philosophy in the Work of Stanley Cavell* (New York: Oxford University Press, 2017), 95–140.

3. Melissa Mohr, *Holy Sh*t: A Brief History of Swearing* (Oxford: Oxford University Press, 2013), 3.

4. Mohr, *Holy Sh*t*, 16–54, 88–129.

5. George Carlin, "Seven Words You Can't Say on TV," YouTube, 2014, https://www.youtube.com/watch?v=kyBH5oNQOS0. As a personal aside, the worst movie I've ever seen is *The Aristocrats* (2005), which features famous comics telling versions of the same dirty joke. It is so boring and cringey precisely because the obscenities from Carlin's list no longer shock or titillate.

6. Mohr, *Holy Sh*t*, 254.

7. Steven Pinker, "What the F***? Why We Curse," *New Republic*, October 8, 2007, https://newrepublic.com/article/63921/what-the-f.

8. Hannah Gadsby, *Nanette*, directed by Madeleine Parry and Jon Olb (Netflix, 2018), live comedy performance, 69 min.

9. John McWhorter, *Nine Nasty Words: English in the Gutter* (New York: Avery, 2021), 186.

10. John Rawls, *A Theory of Justice*, rev. ed. (Cambridge, MA: Harvard University Press, 1999), 386.

11. McWhorter, *Nine Nasty Words*, 4.

12. A year after writing these lines, it happened again, only this time the fist bump was between bin Salman and Joe Biden. To paraphrase Marx, all world historic fist bumps occur twice: first as shocking public avowal of cruelty, and then as business-as-usual cravenness.

13. Judith N. Shklar, *Ordinary Vices* (Cambridge, MA: Harvard University Press, 1985), 237.

14. Meryl Streep, "Meryl Streep's Powerful Speech at the Golden Globes," YouTube, 2017, https://www.youtube.com/watch?v=EV8tsnRFUZw.

15. Shklar, *Ordinary Vices*, 8–9.

16. See Kimberly Engels, ed., *The Good Place and Philosophy: Everything Is Forking Fine* (Malden, MA: Blackwell Publishing, 2020). Schur has written a book of philosophy, *How to Be Perfect: The Correct Answer to Every Moral Question* (London: Quercus, 2022), that expands on themes from *The Good Place*.

17. *The Good Place*, season 1, episode 1, "Everything Is Fine," directed by Drew Goddard, written by Michael Schur, aired on September 19, 2016, on NBC.

18. Ross Douthat, *The Decadent Society: How We Became the Victims of Our Own Success* (New York: Simon and Schuster, 2020), 102.

19. Michael Schur, "A Conversation with Mike Schur: Can Television Make Us Better People?," YouTube, 2019, https://www.youtube.com/watch?v=cWCV uml10EI. I note that the final work of philosophy that appears on *The Good Place* is Judith N. Shklar, "Putting Cruelty First," *Daedalus* 111, no. 3 (Summer 1982): 17–27.

20. Schur, "A Conversation with Mike Schur."

21. Jon Stewart, "Acceptance Speech | 2022 Mark Twain Prize," YouTube, 2022, https://www.youtube.com/watch?v=4QzUu78IXU4. Horror, as a film and TV genre, is another privileged site to trace the impact of liberalism on the background culture. Designed to reflect the anxieties of an age, many of today's most influential horror movies (such as *Get Out* [2017]) and television shows (such as *Black Mirror* [2011–]) center on systemic violence to personal identity and freedom.

22. Dave Chappelle, *Deep in the Heart of Texas: Dave Chappelle Live at the Austin City Limits*, directed by Stan Lathan (Netflix, 2017), live comedy performance, 66 min. Chappelle is Muslim and thus not liberal "all the way down." He is, however, private about his faith, and to my knowledge, never discusses it in his comedy. Note that I will not discuss accusations that Chappelle is transphobic in *The Closer*, directed by Stan Lathan (Netflix, 2021), live comedy performance, 72 min. I believe this controversy is an intraliberal debate about free and harmful speech, and more deeply, a dispute as to what it means to be tolerant.

23. For a historical reconstruction of this idea and ethic, see Charles Taylor, "The Politics of Recognition," in *Multiculturalism*, ed. Amy Gutmann (Princeton, NJ: Princeton University Press, 1994), 25–74.

24. See Daniel Wickberg, *Senses of Humor: Self and Laughter in Modern America* (Ithaca, NY: Cornell University Press, 1998). Wickberg identifies the nineteenth century—which, not coincidentally, is when liberalism was born—as the moment when comedy ceases to be about laughing down at social inferiors but instead poking mutual fun at ourselves. As the earliest of all protoliberals observed, "Our own peculiar condition is that we are as fit to be laughed at as able to laugh." Michel de Montaigne, *The Complete Works* (London: Everyman Library, 2003), I.50.

25. See Alexander Zevin, *Liberalism at Large: The World According to the Economist* (Brooklyn: Verso, 2019); Jessica Whyte, *The Morals of the Market: Human Rights and*

the Rise of Neoliberalism (Brooklyn: Verso, 2019); Samuel Moyn, *Not Enough: Human Rights in an Unequal World* (Cambridge, MA: Harvard University Press, 2019); Quinn Slobodian, *Globalists: The End of Empire and the Birth of Neoliberalism* (Cambridge, MA: Harvard University Press, 2020).

26. See Pippa Norris and Ronald Inglehart, *Cultural Backlash: Trump, Brexit, and Authoritarian Populism* (Cambridge: Cambridge University Press, 2019).

27. Daniel Markovits, *The Meritocracy Trap: How America's Foundational Myth Feeds Inequality, Dismantles the Middle Class, and Devours the Elite* (London: Penguin Books, 2019); Michael J. Sandel, *The Tyranny of Merit: What's Become of the Common Good?* (London: Penguin Books, 2020); William Deresiewicz, *Excellent Sheep: The Miseducation of the American Elite* (New York: Free Press, 2015); Gregory Clark, *The Son Also Rises* (Princeton, NJ: Princeton University Press, 2015); David Brooks, *The Second Mountain: The Quest for a Moral Life* (London: Penguin Books, 2019); Richard Reeves, *Dream Hoarders: How the American Upper Middle Class Is Leaving Everyone Else in the Dust, Why That Is a Problem, and What to Do about It* (Washington, DC: Brookings Institution Press, 2017); Jo Littler, *Against Meritocracy: Culture, Power and Myths of Mobility* (Abingdon, UK: Routledge, 2017). For a recent defense of meritocracy, see Adrian Wooldridge, *The Aristocracy of Talent: How Meritocracy Made the Modern World* (London: Penguin Books, 2021).

28. During his presidency, Barack Obama used the phrase "you can make it if you try" 140 times in his speeches and public statements. See Sandel, *The Tyranny of Merit*, 23.

29. Alexis de Tocqueville, *Democracy in America* (Chicago: University of Chicago Press, 2000), 527.

30. Markovits, *The Meritocracy Trap*, 37. See also Adam Gopnik, *A Thousand Small Sanities: The Moral Adventure of Liberalism* (New York: Basic Books, 2019), 90.

31. Markovits, *The Meritocracy Trap*, 124, 146, 26.

32. Antonio Regalado, "Million-Person Genetic Study Finds Gene Patterns Linked to How Long People Stay in School," *MIT Technology Review*, July 23, 2008, https://www.technologyreview.com/2018/07/23/141349/million-person-genetic -study-finds-gene-patterns-linked-to-how-long-people-stay-in-school/.

33. *Parks and Recreation*, season 5, episode 14, "Leslie and Ben," directed by Craig Zisk, written by Michael Schur and Alan Yang, aired on February 21, 2013, on NBC.

34. John Milton, "The Doctrine and Discipline of Divorce," in *The Complete Poems and Major Prose*, ed. Merritt Y. Hughes (Indianapolis, IN: Hackett, 2003), 707. See Stanley Cavell, *Pursuits of Happiness: The Hollywood Comedy of Remarriage* (Cambridge, MA: Harvard University Press, 1984).

35. Eileen Hunt Botting, *Wollstonecraft, Mill, and Women's Human Rights* (New Haven, CT: Yale University Press, 2016).

36. Markovits, *The Meritocracy Trap*, 116.

37. Jeremy Greenwood, Nezih Guner, Georgi Kocharkov, and Cezar Santos, "Marry Your Like: Assortative Mating and Income Inequality," *American Economic Review* 104, no. 5 (May 2014): 348–53.

38. Pornhub has an analytics section, called "Insights." It does not provide information about how many viewers (as opposed to views) a video has. Still, that does not alter the fact that step-incest pornography is far and away the most popular genre on the internet's tenth most visited website. Insights does tell us that the top twenty countries by traffic to Pornhub are all liberal democracies and account for 79 percent of the total views.

39. In one sense, step-incest videos model a certain kind of achievement: that of the "pickup artist," a manosphere misogynist who talks his way into sex. It is indeed difficult—or better, tricky—to get sex from a person who doesn't initially want to give it to you. And the forerunner antiheroes of step-incest porn are of a kind, including the real estate buyer, taxi driver, massager, and cashed-up hustler, all of whom connive their way into sex. I call these gains ill-gotten, however, because the appeal of step-incest pornography derives from short-circuiting the meritocratic credentials (education, status, and wealth foremost) that, accurately or not, are seen to gatekeep sex and romance. I am not endorsing the view that sex is something "merited." I am trying to account for the mass appeal of a seemingly weird genre of pornography by tying it to the violation of a massively accepted social norm.

40. Sandel, *The Tyranny of Merit*, 26.

41. Amia Srinivasan, *The Right to Sex* (London: Bloomsbury, 2021), 73. On incels, see Tom O'Shea, "Sexual Desire and Structural Injustice," *Journal of Social Philosophy* 52, no. 4 (2020): 587–600; Kate Manne, *Entitled: How Male Privilege Hurts Women* (London: Penguin Books, 2021); Samuel Shpall, "Incels, Warriors, and Masculine Self-Love" (forthcoming).

42. Srinivasan, *The Right to Sex*, 84.

43. Ludwig Wittgenstein, *On Certainty* (New York: Harper, 1972), §141.

Chapter Six: Pretend Liberals in a Pretend Liberal World

1. Søren Kierkegaard, "What Christ Judges of Official Christianity," in *The Moment and Late Writings*, ed. Howard Hong and Edna Hong (Princeton, NJ: Princeton University Press, 2009), 133–34.

2. Søren Kierkegaard, "'Salt'; Because 'Christendom' Is: the Decay of Christianity; 'a Christian World' Is: a Falling Away from Christianity," in *The Moment and Late Writings*, ed. Howard Hong and Edna Hong (Princeton, NJ: Princeton University Press, 2009), 41–45.

3. Søren Kierkegaard, "This Must Be Said; So Let It Be Said," in *The Moment and Late Writings*, ed. Howard Hong and Edna Hong (Princeton, NJ: Princeton

University Press, 2009), 74. See also Bruce Kirmmse, *Kierkegaard in Golden-Age Denmark* (Bloomington: Indiana University Press, 1990), 449–81; Clare Carlisle, *Philosopher of the Heart: The Restless Heart of Søren Kierkegaard* (London: Penguin Books, 2019), 233–45.

4. Søren Kierkegaard, "A Thesis—Just One Single One," in *The Moment and Late Writings*, ed. Howard Hong and Edna Hong (Princeton, NJ: Princeton University Press, 2009), 39.

5. Søren Kierkegaard, *The Moment No 2*, in *The Moment and Late Writings*, ed. Howard Hong and Edna Hong (Princeton, NJ: Princeton University Press, 2009), 107.

6. Søren Kierkegaard, *The Moment No 6*, in *The Moment and Late Writings*, ed. Howard Hong and Edna Hong (Princeton, NJ: Princeton University Press, 2009), 206–13.

7. David Law, "Kierkegaard's Anti-Ecclesiology: The Attack on 'Christendom,' 1854–1855," *International Journal for the Study of the Christian Church* 7, no. 2 (2007): 103.

8. John Rawls, *Justice as Fairness: A Restatement* (Cambridge, MA: Harvard University Press, 2001), 4.

9. For two bestsellers, see Thomas Piketty, *Capital in the Twenty-First Century* (Cambridge, MA: Harvard University Press, 2017); Isabel Wilkerson, *Caste: The Lies That Divide Us* (London: Penguin Books, 2020).

10. Pioneering works of critical and nonideal theory in contemporary liberal political philosophy include Elizabeth Anderson, *Private Government: How Employers Rule Our Lives (and Why We Don't Talk about It)* (Princeton, NJ: Princeton University Press, 2017); Elizabeth Anderson, *The Imperative of Integration* (Princeton, NJ: Princeton University Press, 2010); Charles W. Mills, *The Racial Contract* (Ithaca, NY: Cornell University Press, 1999); Charles W. Mills, *Black Rights/White Wrongs: The Critique of Racial Liberalism* (New York: Oxford University Press, 2017); Carole Pateman, *The Sexual Contract* (Cambridge, UK: Polity Press, 1988); Thomas Pogge, *World Poverty and Human Rights* (Cambridge, UK: Polity Press, 2008); Tommie Shelby, *Dark Ghettos: Injustice, Dissent, and Reform* (Cambridge, MA: Harvard University Press, 2018); Tommie Shelby, *The Idea of Prison Abolition* (Princeton, NJ: Princeton University Press, 2022); Monique Deveaux, *Poverty, Solidarity, and Poor-Led Social Movements* (New York: Oxford University Press, 2021); Lea Ypi, *Free: Coming of Age at the End of History* (London: Penguin Books, 2021); Susan Moller Okin, *Justice, Gender, and the Family* (New York: Basic Books, 1989); Duncan Ivison, *Postcolonial Liberalism* (Cambridge: Cambridge University Press, 2002); Duncan Ivison, *Can Liberal States Accommodate Indigenous Peoples?* (Cambridge, UK: Polity Press, 2020). Several traditions in social and political theory (Marxist, feminist, postcolonial, Frankfurt school, poststructural, psychoanalytic, and more) are critical, yet because they rarely explicitly affirm liberal principles, it is not always clear whether they are critics of liberaldom or liberalism.

11. Martin Shuster, *New Television: The Aesthetics and Politics of a Genre* (Chicago: University of Chicago Press, 2017), 85–126. The DVD commentaries on *The Wire* with its creator David Simon are powerful pieces of social criticism. See *The Wire*, season 1, episode 1, "The Target," directed by Clark Johnson, written by David Simon and Ed Burns, aired on June 2, 2002, on HBO.

12. Johnny Harris and Binyamin Appelbaum, "Liberal Hypocrisy Is Fueling American Inequality. Here's How," YouTube, 2021, https://www.youtube.com/watch?v=hNDgcjVGHIw.

13. Stephen Macedo, *Liberal Virtues: Citizenship, Virtue, and Community in Liberal Constitutionalism* (Oxford: Oxford University Press, 1990), 278.

14. Samuel Moyn, *Liberalism against Itself: Cold War Liberal Political Thought and the Making of Our Times* (New Haven, CT: Yale University Press, 2023); Katrina Forrester, *In the Shadow of Justice: Postwar Liberalism and the Remaking of Political Philosophy* (Princeton, NJ: Princeton University Press, 2019).

15. Moyn, *Liberalism against Itself*, 19.

16. I want to offer two comments here to allay potential criticisms. First, the liberal way of life promoted in this book incorporates a progressivist personal ethic; fairness and reciprocity are its core. Second, the "meantime," as I put it, can be long indeed. Life must be lived, and while waiting on and working for social progress, jobs need to be worked, kids raised, and friends and pastimes enjoyed. That doesn't mean liberals should resign themselves to liberaldom, much less embrace it. Still, for now and the foreseeable future, we inhabit it.

17. For a compelling set of practical proposals inspired by Rawls, see Daniel Chandler, *Free and Equal: What Would a Fair Society Look Like?* (London: Penguin Books, 2023).

18. David Bentley Hart, introduction to *The New Testament* (New Haven, CT: Yale University Press, 2018), xxiv.

19. For an excellent look at the depth of Rawls's critique of merit and desert, see Eric Nelson, *The Theology of Liberalism: Political Philosophy and the Justice of God* (Cambridge, MA: Harvard University Press, 2019), 49–72.

20. John Rawls, *A Theory of Justice*, 1st ed. (Cambridge, MA: Harvard University Press, 1971), 102.

21. Rawls, *A Theory of Justice*, 266. For the sake of simplicity, I omit a clause from the second principle (a), on "just savings," requiring that a society's resources not be depleted from one generation to the next.

22. For a convincing portrait of Rawls as a "reticent socialist," see William A. Edmundson, *John Rawls: Reticent Socialist* (Cambridge: Cambridge University Press, 2017). Far from being an apologist for welfare state capitalism, Rawls claimed (particularly in his final book, *Justice as Fairness*) that his two principles of justice could only be realized in regimes he calls "property-owning democracy" or "liberal

(democratic) socialism," with Edmundson arguing that only liberal democratic socialism is up to the task.

23. *Queer Eye*, season 6, episode 6, "Community Allied," aired on December 31, 2021, on Netflix. In a similar spirit, see Timothy Stacey, *Saving Liberalism from Itself: The Spirit of Political Participation* (Bristol: Bristol University Press, 2022), 75–158.

24. Rawls, *A Theory of Justice*, 64–65.

25. John Rawls, *Lectures on the History of Moral Philosophy* (Cambridge, MA: Harvard University Press, 2000), 211. In his eulogy for Rawls, Thomas Nagel, a former student, calls him a natural aristocrat. "Everyone who knew Jack was impressed by his purity and his freedom from the distortions of ego, but this was something beyond virtue: I hope it will not be misunderstood if I say that my dominant sense of Jack was that he was a natural aristocrat." Cited in "Remembraces of John Rawls," Papers of John Rawls, Harvard University Archives, box 42, folder 15. On aristocratic qualities of character in the context of liberal democracy, see Richard Avramenko and Ethan Alexander-Davey, *Aristocratic Souls in Democratic Times* (Lanham, MD: Rowman and Littlefield, 2018); Alan S. Kahan, *Aristocratic Liberalism: The Social and Political Thought of Jacob Burckhardt, John Start Mill, and Alexis de Tocqueville* (Oxford: Oxford University Press, 1992).

26. Peter Berkowitz, "John Rawls and the Liberal Faith," *Wilson Quarterly* 26, no. 2 (Spring 2002): 68–69.

27. Rawls, *A Theory of Justice*, 6–10.

28. G. A. Cohen, *If You're an Egalitarian, How Come You're So Rich?* (Cambridge, MA: Harvard University Press, 2001), 3–4. For Ronald Dworkin, see *Sovereign Virtue: The Theory and Practice of Equality* (Cambridge, MA: Harvard University Press, 2002).

Chapter Seven: Spiritual Exercises

1. The origins of this phrase (*o philoi, oudeis philos*) are unclear. It is not found in Aristotle's collected works but is attributed to him by Diogenes Laertius, Michel de Montaigne, Friedrich Nietzsche, and Jacques Derrida, among others.

2. Pierre Hadot, *The Present Alone Is Our Happiness: Conversations with Jeannie Carlier and Arnold Davidson* (Stanford, CA: Stanford University Press, 2008), 5–9.

3. Hadot, *The Present Alone Is Our Happiness*, 59.

4. Wilfrid Sellars, "Philosophy and the Scientific Image of Man," in *Science, Perception and Reality* (Abingdon, UK: Routledge, 1963), 1.

5. Pierre Hadot, "Spiritual Exercises," in *Philosophy as a Way of Life*, ed. Arnold I. Davidson (Malden, MA: Blackwell Publishing, 1995), 81–125.

6. See Hadot's inaugural lecture at the Collège de France, "Forms of Life and Forms of Discourse in Ancient Philosophy," in *Philosophy as a Way of Life*, ed. Arnold I. Davidson (Malden, MA: Blackwell Publishing, 1995), 49–70.

7. It is important not to make Hadot out to be utterly original, as if he alone had an inkling that the ancients understood philosophy differently than us. His predecessors include Werner Jaeger's *Paideia* (1939) and Paul Rabbow's *Seelenführung* (1954), and we could name Alaisdair MacIntyre's *A Short History of Ethics* (1966) and *After Virtue* (1981) as well as Martha C. Nussbaum's *The Therapy of Desire* (1994) as contemporary fellow travelers. That said, Hadot is the most synoptic and determined explorer of philosophy as a way of life in the ancient world along with its promise for modern times.

8. Cited in Pierre Hadot, "My Books and My Research," in *The Selected Writings of Pierre Hadot: Philosophy as Practice*, ed. Matthew Sharpe and Federico Testa (London: Bloomsbury, 2020), 35.

9. Hadot, "Spiritual Exercises," 83.

10. Hadot, "Forms of Life and Forms of Discourse in Ancient Philosophy," 58.

11. Matthew Sharpe and Michael Ure, *Philosophy as a Way of Life: From Antiquity to Modernity* (London: Bloomsbury, 2021); Hent de Vries, *Spiritual Exercises: Concepts and Practices* (forthcoming). Hadot's interpretation of ancient philosophy in terms of a way of life has not been uncontroversial. Classicists have criticized him for reading trendy existential themes from the twentieth century back into antiquity as well as cherry-picking schools from the end of antiquity that best fit his theory. See John Cooper, *Pursuits of Wisdom: Six Ways of Life in Ancient Philosophy from Socrates to Plotinus* (Princeton, NJ: Princeton University Press, 2012), 17, 31, 62, 226–27.

12. Hadot, *The Present Alone Is Our Happiness*, ix.

13. David Fiordalis, ed., *Buddhist Spiritual Practices: Thinking with Pierre Hadot on Buddhism, Philosophy, and the Path* (Berkeley, CA: Mangalam Press, 2018).

14. Cited in Hadot, *The Present Alone Is Our Happiness*, xii.

15. I have in mind Raymond Aron, Isaiah Berlin, Albert Camus, Reinhold Niebuhr, Eleanor Roosevelt, Judith Shklar, and Lionel Trilling. See Joshua Cherniss, *Liberalism in Dark Times: The Liberal Ethos in the Twentieth Century* (Princeton, NJ: Princeton University Press, 2021).

16. See Jessica Whyte, *The Morals of the Market: Human Rights and the Rise of Neoliberalism* (Brooklyn: Verso, 2019); Mark Zwolinski and John Tomasi, *The Individualists: Radicals, Reactionaries, and the Struggle for the Soul of Libertarianism* (Princeton, NJ: Princeton University Press, 2023).

17. A. K. Ramanujan, *The Collected Essays of A. K. Ramanujan* (Oxford: Oxford University Press, 1999), 158, 161.

18. See Samuel Freeman, *Rawls* (Abingdon, UK: Routledge, 2007), xvi.

19. Pierre Hadot, "Conversion," in *The Selected Writings of Pierre Hadot: Philosophy as Practice*, ed. Matthew Sharpe and Federico Testa (London: Bloomsbury, 2020), 93; translation modified.

20. For many readers, the term "spiritual exercises" calls to mind Ignatius of Loyola (1491–1556), the Spanish priest who devised a set of Christian meditations and prayers, carried out over a four-week period, to better understand and serve God. Ignatius's *Exercitia spiritualia* (1548), however, is itself a Christian version of a Greco-Roman tradition that spanned more than a thousand years and was re-created by later Christian theologians.

21. Pierre Hadot, *What Is Ancient Philosophy?* (Cambridge, MA: Harvard University Press, 2004), 179.

22. Marcus Aurelius, *The Meditations of Marcus Aurelius Antoninus* (Oxford: Oxford University Press, 1989), 2.1.

23. For additional spiritual exercises in Stoicism, see Pierre Hadot, *The Inner Citadel: The Meditations of Marcus Aurelius* (Cambridge, MA: Harvard University Press, 1998); William B. Irvine, *A Guide to the Good Life: The Ancient Art of Stoic Joy* (Oxford: Oxford University Press, 2009).

24. Sharpe and Ure, *Philosophy as a Way of Life*, 338–39.

25. Hadot, *What Is Ancient Philosophy?*, 172–233.

26. Hadot, *The Present Alone Is Our Happiness*, 86.

27. Hadot, *The Present Alone Is Our Happiness*, 66–67.

28. James Hankins, *Virtue Politics: Soulcraft and Statecraft in Renaissance Italy* (Cambridge, MA: Harvard University Press, 2019), 31–62; Michel Foucault, *The Government of the Self and the Government of Others, Lectures at the Collège de France, 1982–1983* (New York: Palgrave Macmillan, 2011).

29. Isaiah Berlin, "Two Concepts of Liberty," in *Liberty*, ed. Henry Hardy (Oxford: Oxford University Press, 2002), 178–81.

Chapter Eight: What Does a Liberal Way of Life Look Like?

1. Patrick Deneen, *Why Liberalism Failed* (New Haven, CT: Yale University Press, 2018), 34. Deneen is joined by many conservative (and often fellow Roman Catholic) critics, such as Sohrab Ahmari, William Barr, Ross Douthat, and Adrian Vermeule. For a discussion of non- and post-Christian conservatives, see Matthew Rose, *A World after Liberalism: Philosophers of the Radical Right* (New Haven, CT: Yale University Press, 2022). Even defenders of liberalism concede the old argument (once made by communitarians on the Left and now by conservatives on the Right) that liberalism lacks a "strong common moral horizon around which community can be built." See Francis Fukuyama, *Liberalism and Its Discontents* (New York: Farrar, Straus and Giroux, 2022), 122. For a related argument of how human rights, that paradigmatic international liberal institution and discourse, remain remote from the concerns and moral motivations of ordinary people (that is, nonelites) from around

the world, see Michael Ignatieff, *The Ordinary Virtues: Moral Order in a Divided World* (Cambridge, MA: Harvard University Press, 2017).

2. Many moral and political philosophers could be cited on this score, but none more brilliant and for me frustrating than Charles Taylor. In his masterpiece *A Secular Age* (Cambridge, MA: Harvard University Press, 2007), he does his utmost to read himself into a liberal mindset, bringing his formidable erudition and powers of interpretive charity to understand what kind of satisfactions and felicities it affords. Yet after hundreds of pages of historical and phenomenological reconstruction, he determines that liberalism (or in his terms, the "exclusive humanism" of the "modern moral order") is insufficient to satisfy our spiritual longings. My problem is not that Taylor criticizes a liberal way of life or rejects it from a theistic perspective. Nor that he assumes everyone has a transcendental itch that liberalism cannot scratch. My issue is that he disguises the opening premise of *A Secular Age* as its reasoned conclusion: that anyone who seeks a full and complete life in liberalism is bound to be disappointed.

3. As Rawls says in a paper published shortly after *A Theory of Justice*, "One thinks of the moral theorist as an observer, so to speak, who seeks to set out the structure of other people's moral conceptions and attitudes." John Rawls, "The Independence of Moral Theory," in *Collected Papers*, ed. Samuel Freeman (Cambridge, MA: Harvard University Press, 1999), 288. For the work of another early observer of liberalism in the public and background culture, see Ronald Inglehart, *The Silent Revolution: Changing Values and Political Styles among Western Publics* (Princeton, NJ: Princeton University Press, 1977).

4. John Rawls, "John Rawls: For the Record," *Harvard Review of Philosophy* 1, no. 1 (Spring 1991): 44.

5. This is most explicit in John Rawls, "The Sense of Justice," in *A Theory of Justice*, rev. ed. (Cambridge, MA: Harvard University Press, 1999), chap. 8, §§69–72.

6. Rawls, *A Theory of Justice*, 424.

7. According to Allan Bloom, a more accurate title for *A Theory of Justice* would have been *A First Philosophy for the Last Man*. Allan Bloom, "Review: Justice: John Rawls vs. the Tradition of Political Philosophy," *American Political Science Review* 69, no. 2 (June 1975): 662.

8. John Rawls, *Justice as Fairness: A Restatement* (Cambridge, MA: Harvard University Press, 2001), 77. For a helpful commentary on Rawls and reciprocity, see Samuel Freeman, *Rawls* (Abingdon, UK: Routledge, 2007), 243–83.

9. Leo Damrosch, *Jean-Jacques Rousseau: Restless Genius* (Boston: Houghton Mifflin, 2005), 184–95.

10. Susan Neiman, *Why Grow Up?: Subversive Thoughts for an Infantile Age* (New York: Farrar, Straus and Giroux, 2015), 41–79.

11. Jeffrey Bercuson, *John Rawls and the History of Political Thought: The Rousseauvian and Hegelian Heritage of Justice as Fairness* (Abingdon, UK: Routledge, 2014), 62–88.

12. John Rawls, *Lectures on the History of Political Philosophy* (Cambridge, MA: Harvard University Press, 2007), 208.

13. Teresa Bejan, "Rawls's Teaching and the 'Tradition' of Political Philosophy," *Modern Intellectual History* 18, no. 4 (December 2021): 1064. In the end, none of Rawls's books or articles have epigraphs. But in the blank first pages of his personal copy of *A Theory of Justice* (Papers of John Rawls, Harvard University Archives, box 12, folder 8), he inscribed a tantalizing set of quotes (thirty-three in total) from philosophers (Immanuel Kant and John Stuart Mill naturally, but also Aristotle, George Wilhelm Friedrich Hegel, Thomas Hobbes, Bertrand de Jouvenel, Joseph de Maistre, Karl Marx, Rousseau, Friedrich von Schiller, Henry Sidgwick, and Alexis de Tocqueville), scientists (Francis Harry Compton Crick, Carl Friedrich Gauss, Albert Einstein, and Georg Friedrich Bernhard Riemann), writers (John Keats, Samuel Johnson, and this gem from Gustave Flaubert: "Be regular + orderly in your life like a bourgeois, so that you may be violent + original in your work"—a reference to the difference principle perhaps?), a put-down (Ronald Dworkin on Joseph Raz: "He has an instinct for the capillary"), and a joke (which I used as the epigraph for this book). What to make of all of this is a topic for a fun article that I hope someone writes.

14. Rawls, *A Theory of Justice*, 405–6; emphasis added. The principle is found in Jean-Jacques Rousseau, *Emile—or On Education* (Lebanon, NH: Dartmouth College Press, 2010), 363: "What transforms this instinct into sentiment, attachment into love, aversion into hate, is the intention manifested to harm us or to be useful to us." This principle is seminal for Rawls's moral psychology right from his 1963 essay "The Sense of Justice," in *Collected Papers*, ed. Samuel Freeman (Cambridge, MA: Harvard University Press, 1999), 96–116.

15. Rousseau, *Emile*, 363.

16. Rawls, *A Theory of Justice*, 433. Rawls's later work also relies on Rousseau's psychological principle. See John Rawls, *Political Liberalism*, exp. ed. (New York: Columbia University Press, 2005), 86; Rawls, *Justice as Fairness*, 196.

17. Franz de Waal, *Primates and Philosophers: How Morality Evolved*, ed. Stephen Macedo and Josiah Ober (Princeton, NJ: Princeton University Press, 2006).

18. Rawls, *Justice as Fairness*, 135–79; William A. Edmundson, *John Rawls: Reticent Socialist* (Cambridge: Cambridge University Press, 2017), 1–16, 128–38.

19. Judith N. Shklar, *The Faces of Injustice* (New Haven, CT: Yale University Press, 1990), 83–126.

20. Pierre Hadot, *What Is Ancient Philosophy?* (Cambridge, MA: Harvard University Press, 2004), 3–4, 104, 175–76.

21. Rawls, *A Theory of Justice*, 365.

22. In Rawls's later work, the language of *person* disappears and he speaks exclusively of the *citizen* (or alternatively, if he uses the word person, he quickly qualifies that it is a strictly political conception). See Rawls, *Political Liberalism*, 29–35; Rawls, *Justice as*

Fairness, 18–24. But as I explained in chapter 4, nothing prevents people, should they wish, from affirming liberalism (or Rawls's theory of justice as fairness) as a comprehensive doctrine. See John Rawls, "Justice as Fairness: Political Not Metaphysical," in *Collected Papers*, ed. Samuel Freeman (Cambridge, MA: Harvard University Press, 1999), 411.

23. See Annelien de Dijn, *Freedom: An Unruly History* (Cambridge, MA: Harvard University Press, 2020); Eric MacGilvray, *Liberal Freedom: Pluralism, Polarization, and Politics* (Cambridge: Cambridge University Press, 2022).

24. Rawls, *Political Liberalism*, 71. This is what Rawls calls the "wide" or "educative" power of a liberal political conception, the purpose of which is not just to state what a liberal subject is but also to bring citizens to recognize themselves in it.

25. The pioneering work about the private life of liberalism's public values is Stephen Macedo, *Liberal Virtues: Citizenship, Virtue, and Community in Liberal Constitutionalism* (Oxford: Oxford University Press, 1990), especially 254–85. See also Joshua Cherniss, *Liberalism in Dark Times: The Liberal Ethos in the Twentieth Century* (Princeton, NJ: Princeton University Press, 2021); Galen Watts, *The Spiritual Turn: The Religion of the Heart and the Making of Romantic Liberal Modernity* (Oxford: Oxford University Press, 2022).

26. Cited in Hannah Arendt, *The Origins of Totalitarianism* (New York: Houghton Mifflin Harcourt, 1968), 275; emphasis added.

27. For a short liberal primer on these issues, see SCRIPTS Berlin, "Living Freely, Living Differently, Living Together?," YouTube, June 8, 2022, https://www.youtube .com/watch?v=kod6AcKmmXI.

28. Rawls, *Political Liberalism*, 29–35. See also Rawls, *Justice as Fairness*, 18–24.

29. Rawls, *Political Liberalism*, 30; Rawls, *Justice as Fairness*, 21. For how this aspect of liberal freedom is lived and embodied, see Macedo, *Liberal Virtues*, 203–52. For a communitarian critique of this conception of freedom and identity (or rather, a critique of freedom conceived as a nonidentity with one's conception of the good), see Michael J. Sandel, *Liberalism and the Limits of Justice* (New York: Cambridge University Press, 1982), 179.

30. Rawls, *Political Liberalism*, 32; Rawls, *Justice as Fairness*, 23.

31. Rawls, *Political Liberalism*, 186, 33–34.

32. Tara Westover, *Educated: A Memoir* (London: Penguin Books, 2018), 350, 342.

33. Westover, *Educated*, 350, 342.

34. John Rawls, "Just Jack," in Papers of John Rawls, Harvard University Archives, box 42, folder 12.

35. Thomas Nagel, "Rawls and Liberalism," in *The Cambridge Companion to Rawls*, ed. Samuel Freeman (Cambridge: Cambridge University Press, 2003), 62–66.

36. Rawls, *A Theory of Justice*, 266.

37. John Rawls, *A Theory of Justice*, 1st ed. (Cambridge, MA: Harvard University Press, 1971), 102.

Chapter Nine: Seventeen Reasons to Be Liberal

1. In *The Crooked Timber of Humanity* (Princeton, NJ: Princeton University Press, 2013), Isaiah Berlin argues that the supreme values of different worldviews are often incommensurable and there is no final horizon from which to reconcile them all. "Some among the Great Goods cannot live together. We are doomed to choose, and every choice may entail an irreparable loss" (14).

2. Alexander Dugin, *The Fourth Political Theory* (Budapest: Arktos, 2012).

3. Michel Houellebecq, *Interventions 2* (Paris: Flammarion, 2009), 36.

4. See Rawls's teaching notes in the file "Moral Feelings I, 1958," Papers of John Rawls, Harvard University Archives, box 34, folder 19.

5. John Rawls, *Political Liberalism*, exp. ed. (New York: Columbia University Press, 2005), 50. See also John Rawls, *Lectures on the History of Political Philosophy* (Cambridge, MA: Harvard University Press, 2007), 48–52, 54–72.

6. See Lisa Adkins, Melinda Cooper, and Martijn Konings, *The Asset Economy* (Cambridge, UK: Polity Press, 2020).

7. Michel Foucault, "The Ethics of the Concern for Self as a Practice of Freedom," in *Ethics: Subjectivity and Truth*, ed. Paul Rabinow (New York: New Press, 1998), 285; translation modified.

8. See Pierre Hadot, *The Inner Citadel: The Meditations of Marcus Aurelius* (Cambridge, MA: Harvard University Press, 1998), 183–242.

9. Michel Foucault, *The Hermeneutics of the Subject: Lectures at the Collège de France, 1982–1983* (New York: Palgrave Macmillan, 2005), 192.

10. John Rawls, *A Theory of Justice*, rev. ed. (Cambridge, MA: Harvard University Press, 1999), 464–65. For how certain vices (hubris, a lack of moral discernment, and recalcitrance) are debilitating for the self and polity alike, see Mark E. Button, *Political Vices* (New York: Oxford University Press, 2016).

11. My interpretation of Rawls as a "care of the self" thinker is inspired by Paul Weithman's commentary on part III of *A Theory of Justice* and the goods of maintaining a sense of justice in Paul Weithman, *Why Political Liberalism? On John Rawls's Political Turn* (Oxford: Oxford University Press, 2013), 42–67, 122–47.

12. This paragraph and the next are in proximity to what is known as the "ethical turn" in political theory, which seeks to identify the kind of personal ethic/ethos most conducive to a flourishing democratic polity. While I am sympathetic to the aims and approaches of this literature, this is the closest my book comes to it insofar as it poses the opposite question. I ask not, What ethic/ethos is best for liberal democracy? But rather, What ethic/ethos is produced by liberal democracy (and liberal democracy at its worst and best)? For a relevant discussion, see Alexandre Lefebvre, *Human Rights and the Care of the Self* (Durham, NC: Duke University Press, 2018), 47–60.

13. Rawls, *A Theory of Justice*, 397–405.

14. Marx and Engels refer to the bourgeois, not the liberal. But given their view that liberal democracy is the political apparatus of a capitalist mode of production, substituting liberal for bourgeois in this case isn't too far a stretch. Karl Marx and Friedrich Engels, *The Communist Manifesto* (New York: Oxford University Press, 1985), 34.

Chapter Ten: How to Be Free, Fair, and Fun

1. Rawls overviews the original position in many places: John Rawls, *A Theory of Justice*, rev. ed. (Cambridge, MA: Harvard University Press, 1999), 15–19, 102–68; John Rawls, *Political Liberalism*, exp. ed. (New York: Columbia University Press, 2005), 22–29; John Rawls, *Justice as Fairness: A Restatement* (Cambridge, MA: Harvard University Press, 2001), 14–18. For a summary, see Anthony Simon Laden, "The Original Position," in *The Cambridge Rawls Lexicon*, ed. John Mandle and David A. Reidy (Cambridge: Cambridge University Press, 2015). For a deep dive, see Timothy Hinton, ed., *The Original Position* (Cambridge: Cambridge University Press, 2015).

2. In §31 of *A Theory of Justice* ("The Four-Stage Sequence"), Rawls identifies different stages where the original position can be used by public officials, including constitutional conventions, national and state legislation, and application to cases by judges and administrators. My own focus, however, is on how ordinary people (rather than officials) can adopt the original position in everyday life.

3. Rawls, *A Theory of Justice*, 118–23.

4. Rawls is not always consistent on the procedure. Sometimes he suggests that in the original position, we need to specify the principles of justice all on our own (Rawls, *Justice as Fairness*, 16). In other places, he states that in the original position, we should imagine that we are handed a list (a menu, as it were, from maître d'Rawls) of historical conceptions of justice (for example, utilitarian, perfectionist, aristocratic, or liberal) and select from it (Rawls, *A Theory of Justice*, 102–9).

5. For the many controversies that the original position has raised in philosophy, economics, and social and political theory, see Katrina Forrester, *In the Shadow of Justice: Postwar Liberalism and the Remaking of Political Philosophy* (Princeton, NJ: Princeton University Press, 2019), 35–36, 116–22, 138, 176–80.

6. Critics of Rawls often miss this point. He is not trying to get us to think more like persons *within* the original position (that is, persons already situated behind the veil using rational choice strategies to secure the best terms for themselves). Rather, he is trying to get us to become the kind of person who *wants to adopt* the veil of ignorance when deliberating and acting on matters of fundamental justice. See Alexandre Lefebvre, "The Spiritual Exercises of John Rawls," *Political Theory* 50, no. 3 (2022): 418–20.

7. Rawls, *A Theory of Justice*, 78–81.

8. Louis C. K., *Chewed Up*, Showtime, 2008. See also Ella Myers, *The Gratifications of Whiteness: W.E.B. Du Bois and the Enduring Rewards of Anti-Blackness* (New York: Oxford University Press, 2022).

9. Rawls, *A Theory of Justice*, 514; emphasis added.

10. G. A. Cohen, "Where the Action Is: On the Site of Distributive Justice," *Philosophy and Public Affairs* 26, no. 1 (Winter 1997): 17.

11. Pierre Hadot, *Philosophy as a Way of Life*, ed. Arnold I. Davidson (Malden, MA: Blackwell Publishing, 1995), 97; Pierre Hadot, *The Present Alone Is Our Happiness: Conversations with Jeannie Carlier and Arnold Davidson* (Stanford, CA: Stanford University Press, 2008), 107; Pierre Hadot, *The Inner Citadel: The Meditations of Marcus Aurelius* (Cambridge, MA: Harvard University Press, 1998), 112–25; Pierre Hadot, *What Is Ancient Philosophy?* (Cambridge, MA: Harvard University Press, 2004), 189–211.

12. As Daniel Dombrowski makes clear, with the phrase sub specie aeternitatis, Rawls is not relying on a classical theistic view of a deity who exists outside time and history. He refers instead to a capacity on the part of those who adopt the original position to transcend our limited duration and heed those far beyond our temporal ken—an intergenerational and quasi-agapic justice as fairness. Daniel Dombrowski, *Pre-Liberal Political Philosophy: Rawls and Plato, Aristotle, Augustine, Aquinas* (Leiden, Netherlands: Brill, 2022), 141–60. For a brief yet relevant discussion of the original position, see Ian Hunter, *Rival Enlightenments: Civil and Metaphysical in Early Modern Germany* (Cambridge: Cambridge University Press, 2001), 372–73.

13. Hadot, *The Present Alone Is Our Happiness*, 86.

14. See Suzy Killmister, *Taking the Measure of Autonomy: A Four-Dimensional Theory of Self-Governance* (Abingdon, UK: Routledge 2018), 3–8.

15. Rawls, *A Theory of Justice*, 221–27.

16. Hadot, *Philosophy as a Way of Life*, 277.

17. Eric Nelson, *The Theology of Liberalism: Political Philosophy and the Justice of God* (Cambridge, MA: Harvard University Press, 2019), 52–70; Joshua Cohen and Thomas Nagel, introduction to *A Brief Inquiry to Sin and Faith*, ed. Joshua Cohen and Thomas Nagel (Cambridge, MA: Harvard University Press, 2010), 7, 15–19.

18. John Rawls, *A Brief Inquiry into the Meaning of Sin and Faith*, ed. Thomas Nagel (Cambridge, MA: Harvard University Press, 2009), 240. Rawls's hostility toward pride, and the positive conception of personhood and social justice that springs from it, makes him a rich precursor of recent attempts in liberal political philosophy to develop a relational conception of autonomy, which foregrounds constructive relationships of care and dependency that foster independence and autonomy. See Jennifer Nedelsky, *Law's Relations: A Relational Theory of Self, Autonomy, and Law* (New York: Oxford University Press, 2011).

19. Judith N. Shklar, *Ordinary Vices* (Cambridge, MA: Harvard University Press, 1985), 87. See also Mark E. Button, *Political Vices* (New York: Oxford University Press,

2016), 87–124. In the first edition of *A Theory of Justice*, Rawls reproaches meritocratic society for being "callous" (and presumably, for producing callous citizens) (100).

20. Rawls, *Justice as Fairness*, 55; Rawls, *A Theory of Justice*, 6–7.

21. Richard Rorty, *Take Care of Freedom and Truth Will Take Care of Itself* (Stanford, CA: Stanford University Press, 2005), 80. On liberal irony, see Ian Afflerbach, *Making Liberalism New: American Intellectuals, Modern Literature, and the Rewriting of a Political Tradition* (Baltimore: Johns Hopkins University Press, 2021), 5–6, 24–25, 150–68.

22. John Harsanyi, "Can the Maximin Principle Serve as a Basis for Morality? A Critique of John Rawls's Theory," *American Political Science Review* 69, no. 2 (June 1975): 594–606.

23. Gordon Schochet, cited in Forrester, *In the Shadow of Justice*, 120.

24. Rawls, *Justice as Fairness*, 105.

25. Rawls, *A Theory of Justice*, 222.

26. Ryan Patrick Hanley, *Our Great Purpose: Adam Smith on Living a Better Life* (Princeton, NJ: Princeton University Press, 2019), 8–9, 96–101; Stephen Macedo, *Liberal Virtues: Citizenship, Virtue, and Community in Liberal Constitutionalism* (Oxford: Oxford University Press, 1990), 275–77.

27. Agnes Callard, ed., *On Anger* (Cambridge, MA: MIT Press, 2020); Amia Srinivasan, "The Aptness of Anger," *Journal of Political Philosophy* 26, no. 2 (2018): 123–44.

28. In his seminars on moral psychology, Rawls often focused on righteous indignation as a moral emotion. See multiple folders in Papers of John Rawls, Harvard University Archives, boxes 34 ("Moral Feeling 1") and 35 ("Moral Feelings").

29. Helen Lewis, "The Mythology of Karen," *Atlantic*, August 19, 2020, https://www.theatlantic.com/international/archive/2020/08/karen-meme-coronavirus/615355/.

30. Hadot, *The Inner Citadel*, 172–82.

31. Rawls, *Justice as Fairness*, 3–4; Rawls, *Lectures on the History of Political Philosophy*, 10.

32. David Foster Wallace, *This Is Water: Some Thoughts, Delivered on a Significant Occasion, about Living a Compassionate Life* (Boston: Little, Brown and Company, 2009), 6.

33. Rawls, *Justice as Fairness*, 3; G.W.F. Hegel, *The Philosophy of History* (Mineola, NY: Dover, 1956), 24–25. See also Michael O. Hardimon, *Hegel's Social Philosophy: The Project of Reconciliation* (Cambridge: Cambridge University Press, 1994).

34. G.W.F. Hegel, *Elements of the Philosophy of Right*, ed. Allen W. Wood (Cambridge: Cambridge University Press, 1991), 21. Cited and discussed in Rawls, *Lectures on the History of Moral Philosophy* (Cambridge, MA: Harvard University Press, 2000), 336, 331–36.

35. Paul Weithman, *Why Political Liberalism? On John Rawls's Political Turn* (Oxford: Oxford University Press, 2013), 369.

36. Rawls, *Justice as Fairness*, 4.

Chapter Eleven: How to Be Sincere and Graceful

1. "Liberal Relieved He Never Has to Introspect Again after Assembling All the Correct Opinions," *Onion*, May 13, 2019, https://www.theonion.com/liberal-relieved -he-never-has-to-introspect-again-after-1834720785.

2. Pierre Hadot, *What Is Ancient Philosophy?* (Cambridge, MA: Harvard University Press, 2004), 35.

3. Plato, *The Apology*, in *Plato Complete Works*, ed. John Cooper (Indianapolis, IN: Hackett, 1997), 38a.

4. John Rawls, *A Theory of Justice*, 1st ed. (Cambridge, MA: Harvard University Press, 1971), 49.

5. John Rawls, *Justice as Fairness: A Restatement* (Cambridge, MA: Harvard University Press, 2001), 30. See also Rawls, *A Theory of Justice*, 44.

6. John Rawls, *Political Liberalism*, exp. ed. (New York: Columbia University Press, 2005), 8; Rawls, *Justice as Fairness*, 30.

7. Cicero, *Tusculan Disputations* (Cambridge, MA: Harvard University Press, 2014), 435.

8. Cited in Plato, *The Gorgias*, in *Plato Complete Works*, ed. John Cooper (Indianapolis, IN: Hackett, 1997), 491a; translation slightly modified.

9. Martha C. Nussbaum, *Upheavals of Thought: The Intelligence of Emotions* (Cambridge: Cambridge University Press, 2001).

10. Luiz Pessoa, *The Entangled Brain: How Perception, Cognition, and Emotion Are Woven Together* (Cambridge, MA: MIT Press, 2022).

11. Pierre Bourdieu, *Outline of a Theory of Practice* (Cambridge: Cambridge University Press, 1977).

12. Jonathan Lear, *Freud*, 2nd ed. (Abingdon, UK: Routledge, 2015), xiv.

13. Norman Daniels, *Justice and Justification: Reflective Equilibrium in Theory and Practice* (Cambridge: Cambridge University Press, 1996), 21–46; Samuel Freeman, *Rawls* (Abingdon, UK: Routledge, 2007), 29–42. Rawls borrowed the idea of reflective equilibrium from the philosophy of science and applied it to ethics and politics. See Andrius Gališanka, *John Rawls: The Path to a Theory of Justice* (Cambridge, MA: Harvard University Press, 2019), 137–49.

14. Rawls, *Justice as Fairness*, 1–5; John Rawls, *Lectures on the History of Political Philosophy* (Cambridge, MA: Harvard University Press, 2007), 10–11.

15. Rawls, *Justice as Fairness*, 3.

16. Rawls, *Justice as Fairness*, 31.

17. Rawls, *Political Liberalism*, 45.

18. Plato, *Theaetetus*, in *Plato Complete Works*, ed. John Cooper (Indianapolis, IN: Hackett, 1997), 150d.

19. Jochen Hellbeck, *Revolution on My Mind: Writing a Diary under Stalin* (Cambridge, MA: Harvard University Press, 2006).

20. Rawls, *A Theory of Justice*, 499.

21. Gališanka, *John Rawls*, 147.

22. Rawls, *A Theory of Justice*, 104.

23. John Rawls, "Seminar V. Excellence and Shame (1964)," Papers of John Rawls, Harvard University Archives, box 35, folder 4.

24. Paul Weithman, *Why Political Liberalism? On John Rawls's Political Turn* (Oxford: Oxford University Press, 2013), 13. See also Weithman, *Why Political Liberalism?*, 183–233; Rawls, *A Theory of Justice*, §40 ("The Kantian Interpretation of Justice as Fairness"), §85 ("The Unity of the Self"). To be clear, Weithman's book explains why Rawls grew dissatisfied with his argument for the unity of the self in *A Theory of Justice*, and how in *Political Liberalism*, he recast it as a "political" assertion about our identity as citizens.

25. Rawls, *A Theory of Justice*, 503.

26. Eric Nelson, *The Theology of Liberalism: Political Philosophy and the Justice of God* (Cambridge, MA: Harvard University Press, 2019), 49–72.

27. Charles Taylor, *A Secular Age* (Cambridge, MA: Harvard University Press, 2007), 159–211.

Chapter Twelve: How to Keep Calm, Cool, and to Delight in Others

1. *Borat! Cultural Learnings of America for Make Benefit Glorious Nation of Kazakhstan*, directed by Larry Charles (20th Century Fox, 2006), film, 84 min.

2. Pierre Hadot, *What Is Ancient Philosophy?* (Cambridge, MA: Harvard University Press, 2004), 178. See also Andrea Wilson Nightingale, *Genres in Dialogue: Plato and the Construction of Philosophy* (Cambridge: Cambridge University Press, 2009).

3. Brice Parain, cited in Hadot, *What Is Ancient Philosophy?*, 50.

4. Lilliana Mason, *Uncivil Agreement: How Politics Became Our Identity* (Chicago: University of Chicago Press, 2018); Nathan Kalmoe and Lilliana Mason, *Radical American Partisanship: Mapping Violent Hostility, Its Causes, and the Consequences for Democracy* (Chicago: University of Chicago Press, 2022); Ezra Klein, *Why We're Polarized* (New York: Simon and Schuster, 2020); Robert B. Talisse, *Overdoing Democracy: Why We Must Put Politics in Its Place* (New York: Oxford University Press, 2019).

5. Jeremy Waldron, "Theoretical Foundations of Liberalism," *Philosophical Quarterly* 37, no. 147 (April 1987): 149. In addition to John Rawls, "The Idea of Public

Reason Revisited," in *Collected Papers*, ed. Samuel Freeman (Cambridge, MA: Harvard University Press, 1999), my account of public reason is informed by Samuel Freeman, *Rawls* (Abingdon, UK: Routledge, 2007), 365–415; Mark E. Button, *Contract, Culture, and Citizenship: Transformative Liberalism from Hobbes to Rawls* (University Park: Penn State University Press, 2008), 207–236; Stephen Macedo, "Why Public Reason? Citizens' Reasons and the Constitution of the Public Sphere," SSRN, August 23, 2010, https://papers.ssrn.com/sol3/papers.cfm?abstract_id=1664085; Teresa Bejan, *Mere Civility: Disagreement and the Limits of Toleration* (Cambridge, MA: Harvard University Press, 2017); Paul Weithman, *Rawls, Political Liberalism, and Reasonable Faith* (Cambridge: Cambridge University Press, 2016), 119–49; Amy Gutmann and Dennis Thompson, *Why Deliberative Democracy?* (Princeton, NJ: Princeton University Press, 2004); Jonathan Quong, "Public Reason," *Stanford Encyclopedia of Philosophy*, May 20, 2013, https://plato.stanford.edu/entries/public-reason/.

6. See the "In the Shadow of Political Liberalism" section in chapter 4 of this book.

7. By "reasonable members of the political community," I mean what Rawls does by "reasonable": a readiness to offer fair terms of social cooperation between equals, and a willingness to accept that reasonable and rational persons will have different views on philosophical, moral, and religious matters. John Rawls, *Political Liberalism*, exp. ed. (New York: Columbia University Press, 2005), 488. In this chapter, I am interested in the relation public reason establishes between citizens, not between public officials and citizens. This does not trouble my use of Rawls as he is explicit that public reason specifies "a constitutional democratic government's relation to its citizens *and their relation to one another.*" John Rawls, *The Law of Peoples* (Cambridge, MA: Harvard University Press, 2001), 132; emphasis added.

8. Rawls, "The Idea of Public Reason Revisited," 584. See also Martha C. Nussbaum, introduction to *Rawls's Political Liberalism*, ed. Thom Brooks and Martha C. Nussbaum (New York: Columbia University Press, 2015), 33.

9. Freeman, *Rawls*, 388–90.

10. Stephen Macedo, *Diversity and Distrust: Civic Education in a Multicultural Democracy* (Cambridge, MA: Harvard University Press, 2000), 174.

11. Other typical public reason arguments in *Breitbart* (and other conservative outlets) include neighborhood safety to justify border controls and increased policing, freedom of movement to protest pandemic lockdowns, bodily autonomy to reject vaccination mandates, and freedom of speech to criticize social media crackdowns and cancel culture.

12. Rawls, "The Idea of Public Reason Revisited," 579.

13. Mason, *Uncivil Agreement*, 74.

14. Quong, "Public Reason." The references in this paragraph are to Rawls, "The Idea of Public Reason Revisited," 577; Charles Larmore, *The Morals of Modernity*

(Cambridge: Cambridge University Press, 1996), 137; Gerald Gaus, *The Order of Public Reason: A Theory of Freedom and Morality in a Diverse and Bounded World* (Cambridge: Cambridge University Press, 2011), 2.

15. Rawls, "The Idea of Public Reason Revisited," 576.

16. John Rawls, "On My Religion," in *A Brief Inquiry into the Meaning of Sin and Faith,* ed. Thomas Nagel (Cambridge, MA: Harvard University Press, 2009), 267.

17. See Weithman, *Rawls, Political Liberalism, and Reasonable Faith,* 123–30.

18. Jean Bodin, *Colloquium of the Seven Secrets of the Sublime* (University Park: Penn State University Press, 1975).

19. Rawls, "On My Religion," 266.

20. Rawls, "The Idea of Public Reason Revisited," 593; emphasis added.

21. Rawls, *Political Liberalism,* xvi–xvii.

22. Rawls, "The Idea of Public Reason Revisited," 574. For an argument that a *political* (not metaphysical) conception of truth has an important role to play in public reason, see Joshua Cohen, "Truth and Public Reason," *Philosophy and Public Affairs* 37, no. 1 (Winter 2009): 2–42.

23. Carl Schmitt, *The Concept of the Political* (Chicago: University of Chicago Press, 1996), 27.

24. Timothy Hampton, *Cheerfulness: A Literary and Cultural History* (Brooklyn: Zone Books, 2022), 228.

25. Charles Larmore, "Public Reason," in *The Cambridge Companion to Rawls,* ed. Samuel Freeman (Cambridge: Cambridge University Press, 2003), 368.

26. John Rawls, "Questions on Reflection: Harvard Review of Philosophy Interview," Papers of John Rawls, Harvard University Archives, box 42, folder 12.

Conclusion

1. Alexis de Tocqueville, *The Ancien Régime and the French Revolution,* ed. Jon Elster, trans. Arthur Goldhammer (New York: Cambridge University Press, 2011), 37–38.

2. Comte de Mirabeau, cited in François Furet and Mona Ozouf, *A Critical Dictionary of the French Revolution* (Cambridge, MA: Harvard University Press, 1989), 1026.

3. See Steven Levitsky and Daniel Ziblatt, *How Democracies Die* (London: Penguin Books, 2018); Jason Stanley, *How Fascism Works: The Politics of Us and Them* (New York: Random House, 2020); Timothy Snyder, *The Road to Unfreedom: Russia, Europe, America* (New York: Crown, 2019); Russell Muirhead and Nancy L. Rosenblum, *A Lot of People Are Saying: The New Conspiracism and the Assault on Democracy* (Princeton, NJ: Princeton University Press, 2020); Anne Applebaum, *Twilight of*

Democracy: The Seductive Lure of Authoritarianism (London: Penguin Books, 2020); Naomi Klein, *This Changes Everything: Capitalism vs. the Climate* (New York: Simon and Schuster, 2015); Nathan Kalmoe and Lilliana Mason, *Radical American Partisanship: Mapping Violent Hostility, Its Causes, and the Consequences for Democracy* (Chicago: University of Chicago Press, 2022).

4. Edmund Fawcett, *Liberalism: The Life of an Idea* (Princeton, NJ: Princeton University Press, 2015), 395.

INDEX

Anderson, Amanda, 251n12

Aristotle, 134; on objectivity in science, 143–44; on a shared conception of the good life, 65

Augustine, Saint: and misanthropy, 43; Pierre Hadot on, 136; on a shared conception of the good life, 65

Aurelius, Marcus: Pierre Hadot on, 139; spiritual exercises of, 142

Australia, 34, 90; and Christmas Day, 2016, 1–7; and commitment to a "fair go," 26–27, 155; inequality in, 171; irreligion of, 3, 231–32

autonomy, 79, 271n18. *See also* existential perks of a liberal way of life: and autonomy; freedom

Baron Cohen, Sacha, 100. See also *Borat!*; Psenicska, Mike

Beaumont, Gustave de, on inequality in the United States, 50–51. *See also* Tocqueville, Alexis de

Bergson, Henri, 32; on the nature of problems, 254n17

Berlin, Isaiah, 119, 264n15; and criticism of positive liberty, 145; on value pluralism, 269n1

Biden, Joe, 21, 38, 257n12

Billy on the Street, 27–28. *See also* Eichner, Billy

bin Salman, Mohammed (prince), and public cruelty, 92–93, 257n12

Bird Box (film), 67–69

Black Lives Matter, as a liberal social movement, 248n14

Bloom, Allan, and critique of Rawls, 248n15, 266n7

Bodin, Jean, on pluralism and public reason, 228–30

Borat! (film), and tolerance, 215–16, 220–22. *See also* Baron Cohen, Sacha; Psenicska, Mike

Breitbart, 34; and public reason, 222–23, 232–33, 275n11. *See also* conservatism

capitalism: liberalism's entanglement with, 117–21, 127, 239; Rawls on, 262–63n22; as a threat to living well, 49, 53. *See also* liberaldom

care of the self, liberalism and, 171–75, 269n11. *See also* existential perks of a liberal way of life

Carlin, George, on swear words, 88–89, 257n5

Cavell, Stanley, 32; as comprehensive liberal, 255n32; and speaking for others, 257n2

Chappelle, Dave, 15; and controversy over *The Closer*, 258n22; and the state of comedy today, 101–3. *See also* comedy

McWhorter, John, on swear words,
90–91

meritocracy: and contemporary pornography, 108–12, 260n39; and
liberalism, 32, 103–8, 117, 121. *See also*
liberaldom

Meyer, Selina (*Veep*, TV show), 250n6

Mill, John Stuart, 32, 37, 164; as a
comprehensive liberal, 78–79, 81;
and democracy, 45, 49, 54; and
liberalism of personal freedom, 21, 127,
246n2; on love and friendship, 109

Milton, John, on love and friendship,
109

misanthropy, as founding attitude and
emotion of liberalism, 41–45, 47,
51–55, 251n12. *See also* Shklar, Judith

Mohr, Melissa, on swear words, 88–89

Montaigne, Michel de: on hatred of
cruelty, 95; on laughter, 258n24;
and the liberalism of fear, 21; and
misanthropy, 42

Montesquieu, Charles, 170; and the
liberalism of fear, 21, 92; and misanthropy, 42–46

Moyn, Samuel, on Cold War liberalism, 119

neoliberalism, 20, 104, 119. *See also*
liberaldom

Nietzsche, Friedrich, 43, 116, 189

Nussbaum, Martha, 32, 204; on philosophy as a way of life, 264n7; on
the role of emotions for political
stability, 249n24

Obama, Barack, 38; on clinging to guns
and religion, 41–42, on meritocracy,
259n28

Office, The (TV show), 15, 37

original position, 32, 176, 179, 270n6;
and autonomy, 185–87; when done
in bad faith, 189–90; and final
paragraph of *A Theory of Justice*,
182–84; and how to do, 180–81;
and impartiality, 184–85; and
intergenerational justice, 271n12;
as personally transformative,
184–94; *See also* existential perks
of a liberal way of life; spiritual
exercises

Parks and Recreation (TV show),
36–42, 108, 250n6. *See also* Knope,
Leslie; Schur, Michael

Pascal, Blaise, 53

Paul, Saint, 116, 141

perfectionism, 61, 74, 119, 160, 181.
See also comprehensive liberalism;
political liberalism

Pinker, Steven, on the N-word, 89

Plato, 118, 170, 217

pluralism: of liberal democratic
societies, 71–75; threat liberalism
poses to, 147, 256n33; and tolerance,
103, 155, 192, 228–34. *See also*
political liberalism

polarization, 218, 223–24, 232

political liberalism: on comprehensive
liberalism, 78–80; and failure to see
liberalism as way of life, 63, 77–78,
80–82, 147, 256n33; and LEGO
people, 75–78; as the orthodoxy
of contemporary political philosophy, 61–62, 74–75; and Rawls, 22,
63–64, 69, 128–29; as a response
to the problem of pluralism, 71–75.
See also comprehensive liberalism; liberalism; perfectionism;
Rawls, John.

A NOTE ON THE TYPE

This book has been composed in Arno, an Old-style serif typeface in the classic Venetian tradition, designed by Robert Slimbach at Adobe.